Religion and Politics

American University Studies

Series X
Political Science

Vol. 28

PETER LANG
New York • Bern • Frankfurt am Main • Paris

Religion and Politics

Major Thinkers on the Relation of Church and State

Edited by
Garrett Ward Sheldon

PETER LANG
New York • Bern • Frankfurt am Main • Paris

BV
630.2
.S54
1990

Library of Congress Cataloging-in-Publication Data

Sheldon, Garrett Ward,
  Religion and politics : major thinkers on the relation of church and state / Garrett Ward Sheldon.
    p. cm. — (American university studies. Series X, Political science ; v. 28)
  Includes bibliographical references and index.
  1. Church and state. 2. Church and state—United States. 3. Church and state—History—Sources.
  4. Church and state—United States—History—Sources.
  5. United States—Church history—Sources. I. Title.
  II. Series.
  BV630.2.S54   1990   26'.7'09—dc20   90-36071
  ISBN 0-8204-1333-X   CIP
  ISSN 0740-0470

© Peter Lang Publishing, Inc., New York 1990

All rights reserved.
Reprint or reproduction, even partially, in all forms such as microfilm, xerography, microfiche, microcard, offset strictly prohibited.

Printed by Weihert-Druck GmbH, Darmstadt, West Germany

For the memory of

two early religious teachers:

my mother

Ethel May Garrett

and

my great-grandfather

Charles M. Sheldon

author
of
In His Steps

ACKNOWLEDGEMENTS

The author gratefully acknowledges permission to reprint portions of the following works:

Paolucci, Henry, Ed., *The Political Writings of St. Augustine.* Washington, D. C.: Regnery Gateway, Inc., 1962. Copyright 1962 by Regnery Gateway, Inc. All rights reserved. Reprinted by special permission.

Martin Luther, "The Freedom of a Christian," translated by W. A. Lambert and revised by Harold J. Grimm, copyright 1951, Muhlenberg Press, reprinted by Permission of Augsburg Fortress; "To the Christian Nobility of the German Nation Concerning the Reform of the Christian Estate," translated by Charles M. Jacobs and revised by James Atkinson, copyright 1966 Fortress Press, reprinted by permission of Augsburg Fortress; "Temporal Authority: To What Extent It Should Be Obeyed," translated by J. J. Schindel and revised by Walter I. Brandt, reprinted by permission of Augsburg Fortress.

John McNeil, ed. John Calvin's *On God and Political Duty,* reprinted with permission of Macmillan Publishing Company, copyright 1956, 1985, by Macmillan Publishing Company.

William Temple, *Christianity and tahe Social Order,* reprinted with permission of Shepheard-Walwyn Publishers, Ltd., London.

Dietrich Bonhoeffer, *Ethics,* reprinted with permission of Macmillan Publishing Company, copyright 1955 by SCM Press Ltd.

Harry Davis and Robert C. Good, eds. *Reinhold Niebuhr on Politics,* reprinted with permission of Charles Scribner's Sons, an imprint of Macmillan Publishing Company, copyright 1960, Charles Scribner's Sons.

Gustavo Gutierrez, *A Theology of Liberation,* copyright 1973, 1988, Orbis Books, SCM Press Ltd., London, by permission.

Jerry Falwell, *Listen America!* copyrighted 1980 by Jerry Falwell, used by permission of Doubleday, a division of Banton, Doubleday, Dell Publishing Group, Inc.

CONTENTS

Preface

General Introduction

PART I

Major Thinkers on the Relationship of Church and State

Chapter I	The Two Cities - St. Augustine	9
Chapter II	Divine and Human Law - St. Thomas Aquinas	31
Chapter III	Separation of Church and State - Martin Luther	55
Chapter IV	Church Polity and Christian Politics - John Calvin	93
Chapter V	Liberal Anglicanism - William Temple	103
Chapter VI	Christian Responsibility - Dietrich Bonhoeffer	123
Chapter VII	Christian Realism - Reinhold Niebuhr	143
Chapter VIII	Liberation Theology - Gustavo Gutierrez	171
Chapter IX	The Christian Right - Jerry Falwell	205

PART II

American Documents on Church and State

1.	The Mayflower Compact	231
2.	John Winthrop's "Little Speech"	232
3.	Jefferson's Statute for Religious Freedom	235
4.	The United States Constitution - First Amendment	237
5.	United States Supreme Court Rulings	238

PREFACE

This book came out of a college course that I taught on Religion and Politics, and it is intended for use in similar university and seminar courses. My first serious interest in this subject came as a graduate assistant to a National Endowment for the Humanities summer seminar for College Teachers on Religion and Politics conducted by Wilson Carey McWilliams at Rutgers University. Later, I was permitted to audit courses in the subject at Princeton Theological Seminary, where my wife, Elaine, was enrolled. My subsequent involvement on The Executive Board of the Episcopal Diocese of Southwestern Virginia and frequent encounters with issues of politics and that Church increased my interest in the field. I am grateful to the many friends and colleagues who have shared this interest with me and thus contributed to this book, especially Carey McWilliams, M. J. Aronoff, Lois Livesay, Richard Battistoni, David Rouse, David Jodrey, Joseph M. Scolnick, Jr., E. L. Henson, Peter Yun, Ray Moore, Robert Cox, and many parishioners of All Saints Episcopal Church, and the Rt. Rev. A. Heath Light. Finally, I am again thankful for the thoughtful preparation of this manuscript by Sharon Daniels.

GWS
Wise, Virginia

GENERAL INTRODUCTION

I.

An old adage enjoins us to avoid the topics of Religion and Politics in polite conversation. "Never discuss Religion or Politics," it says. This book violates that adage in three ways: by discussing Religion, Politics and the relationship between Religion and Politics. Furthermore, it does so deliberately, believing that an intelligent understanding of Religion and Politics is essential to a civilized people, and has been throughout the history of Christendom. As a scholar at Rutgers University recently noted: "Religion and Politics have been inextricably interrelated since the dawn of human culture and civilization."[1] In our own time, the subject of Religion and Politics, as the proper relationship between Church and State, has been revived in American politics, making an informed appreciation of the subject important to all American citizens.

II.

Religion and Politics became a prominent issue in America during the 1980's, when various churches and religious groups became actively involved in influencing the American electoral system and government. The "Christian Right," led by fundamentalist Jerry Falwell and his lobbying organization, "The Moral Majority, Inc.," supported conservative candidates and ostensibly moral issues (school prayer, anti-abortion, anti-ERA, pro-defense, etc.). Falwell's prominence at the Republican National Convention in 1984 earned him the title "Archbishop of America" under the Reagan Administration. And the television evangelists' fall from grace in the late 1980's, after several sex and money scandals, has not diminished the political activism of the Christian Right. At the same time, other, more established churches exerted direct influence on the American political system. The U. S. Catholic Bishops issued pastoral letters on nuclear war and on social and economic policy, enjoining what were widely regarded as liberal positions on defense and social welfare. The Roman Catholic Church, through Archbishop of New York John O'Connor, also affected the platforms of prominent Catholic political candidates (notably Mario Cuomo and Geraldine Ferraro) by saying that Catholics of "good conscience" ought not to vote for candidates who do not oppose abortion. Also during the 1980's Presidential

---

[1] Myron J. Aronoff in his Introduction to *Religion and Politics* (New Brunswick, NJ, 1984).

campaigns, the Rev. Jesse Jackson used churches to register Black voters for the Democratic Party, while Jerry Falwell used Fundamentalist churches to register conservative white voters for the Republican Party.

All of this raised the issue of the proper relationship between Religion and Politics, Church and State in America. With both major political Parties, and most major churches, now involved in the debate, this issue promises to be intense and of long duration. The freedom of expression guaranteed by the U. S. Constitution both enhances and inhibits discussion of this matter: freedom of speech allows full discussion of opposing views, but freedom of religion remains inherently nervous about any mixing of Church and State. The best situation for both the unique opportunities and the unique liabilities of Church-State discussions in America may simply be an informed and tolerant atmosphere.

III.

This book attempts to inform the current discussion of Church and State in America by examining several major thinkers' writings on the subject. This approach immediately reveals some interesting results. The first result of looking at writings on Religion and Politics, from St. Augustine to Jerry Falwell, from Early Church debates to U. S. Supreme Court controversies, is the realization that Church-State issues have been a significant subject for discussion and debate for centuries. Even in the most "settled" period of the Christian Middle Ages, the issue of proper relations between Church and State were neither clear nor simple, as St. Thomas Aquinas' writings reveal. This, I hope to show, is in the nature of the subject itself: at least for Christians, the relationship between Church and State, or "The Two Cities," is always one of tension and complexity, with no simple or easy answers.

The second effect of examining historical writings on Religion and Politics is the revealing of a wide diversity of views on Church-State relations by sincere and respected theologians. Whether one ascribes this to historical and cultural relativism or to the richness of the subject itself, it seems to suggest that there is no single correct "Christian" view of Religion and Politics. Sincere Christians throughout the ages and in our own time disagree on specific issues in Church-State relations, and in a free society, this debate can be healthy for both Church and State.

Such diversity notwithstanding, the third effect of examining great writers on Religion and Politics is to find a certain continuity in Christian theologians' views on the generally proper relations between Church and State. While controversy may remain on specifics, we find a general agreement, from St. Augustine to Reinhold Niebuhr, on the correct stance of the Church to both "The City of God" and "The City of Man." The revealing of this shared view of the proper relation of Church and State seems particularly valuable in our own time, when many seem to have forgotten it.

IV.

To some extent, how one sees the relationship between Religion and Politics depends on how one defines Church and State. Ironically, this seemingly obvious proposition was not made explicit until quite recently, by Dietrich Bonhoeffer, though it exists implicitly in all the theologians presented in this volume. Basically, the questions of definition of Church and State are these: (1) is the State simply a criminal justice system, or "the sword," to capture and punish socially unacceptable vice; or does the State have an ethical dimension, nurturing, encouraging and rewarding virtue? And how, if at all, are the two related? And (2) is the Church purely a spiritual entity, nurturing men's souls and preparing them for the afterlife, or does it have a worldly charge, giving it an obligation to engage the world; or is it both, and if so, how are these two roles reconciled? Out of the various definitions of Church and State will come views on their proper relationship. The basic issue here is: if Church and State are not totally distinct and separate in this world, how should they relate? Does the Church attempt to influence the State and vice-versa, and if so, what are appropriate methods of influence? The theologians examined here provide a variety of answers to these questions, as a brief summary of their ideas will reveal.

St. Augustine considered all earthly governments, regardless of their form, as representative of the fallen and imperfect "City of Man." The State provided the "sword" to discipline sinful man through law and education. The Church, for St. Augustine, represented the perfect and eternal "City of God," preserving the Divine otherworldly values of peace, love, hope and charity. Hence, Church and State are separate but related: they occupy different realms and hold different values, but both exist in this world. The Church, for St. Augustine, as the Body of Christ, presents the values of the transcendent City of God to the City of Man, encouraging earthly kingdoms to strive for the perfect justice of the Heavenly Kingdom, even while knowing the inevitable falling-short of that striving. The Church, occupying a higher station than the State, ought to enjoy a privileged position in the world and governments should heed the advice of the Church.

St. Thomas Aquinas defined the State as author and executor of Human Law, whose charge is the punishment of vice and encouragement of virtue. The Church is the interpreter of Divine Law through Natural Law, of which Human Law is an inferior part. Hence, for St. Thomas, the Church properly advises the State on many matters, especially those relating to moral legislation. As with St. Augustine, if a conflict occurs between Church and State, St. Thomas conceives of the Church as rightly occupying the high ground, it representing Divine Law and closer to God in the universal hierarchy.

Martin Luther makes a radical break with traditional Christian theology and Catholic Church polity by leveling the institutional hierarchy through "the priesthood of all believers," and by separating Church and State in this world. By defining the State purely as a "hangman," charged with establishing worldly peace through punishment of crime, and considering the Church as primarily concerned with spiritual matters unrelated to politics, Luther effectively separates the secular authority from the ecclesiastical and places the Church under the governance of the State in this world.

The other leading Reformation theologian, John Calvin, preserves the democratic "priesthood of all believers," but re-establishes a distinct Church institution through the governance of Presbyters, Elders and Deacons. Calvin also reasserts the political role of the Church by both making the Church "political" and the State religious. Christians are obliged to govern their Church deliberately and collectively as a "priesthood of all believers," and governors are to understand themselves as God's ministers (social harmony and justice being unachievable without appreciation of God's justice). The formal separation of Church and State is modified by Calvin in the interdependence of their roles in this world. An interesting lesson of Calvin's is that if the State takes its role of promoting moral conduct seriously (which it can only learn from the Church) it will not have to exercise its role as "hangman" as frequently, as a Godly citizenry will be less inclined to criminality. Thus, Calvin reasserts the legitimacy of the Church involving itself in worldly politics, after Luther's removal of it into a purely spiritual realm.

Dietrich Bonhoeffer, a twentieth-century German theologian and Lutheran pastor, redefined the relationship of the State and the Protestant Church in Germany (in a remarkably Calvinist fashion) and was executed by the Nazi regime for his efforts. Bonhoeffer restored the clerical institution to the Lutheran Church through his concept of "the spiritual office" and restored its political dimension through its charge to represent the Kingdom of God in this world. The State, for Bonhoeffer, assumes an ethical dimension alongside its role as "hangman" and requires the Church, therefore, to advise it on matters of morality. Thus, Church and State, for Bonhoeffer, reside on separate, but equal, planes in this world and are united by each being under the rule of Christ. Church and State functions are separate but overlapping and complementary: the Church advises the State on moral matters but respects its autonomy on purely worldly affairs; the State respects the autonomy of the Church and accepts its rebuke when its "purely worldly matters" impinge on moral concerns. The Church openly and publicly criticizes the State's atrocities according to the standards of the transcendent Kingdom of God. Such open condemnation of the Nazi regime and his insistence on "calling sin by its name" earned Bonhoeffer martyrdom in 1945.

Reinhold Niebuhr's "Christian Realism" reasserted the Augustinian and Calvinist emphasis on human sin and the potential for State power to amplify individual sin. Niebuhr considered the State to have both positive and negative functions (promoting virtue and punishing vice), but because of the potential for abuse of State power (especially in the name of virtue), he recommended a system of Madisonian pluralism in the government. The Church is to represent the ideals of the Kingdom of God in the world, to encourage society to strive for Heavenly perfection while never assuming that it can reach it by human efforts. Thus, Niebuhr encouraged the Church to support policies and movements that reflected Christian values, but not to be subsumed by social movements or political ideologies or to presume that any worldly system or ideology, realized the perfect justice of the transcendent City of God. Niebuhr was especially critical of Enlightenment liberalism and Marxist Socialism, which optimistically believed in Heavenly salvation on earth through human technology and "historical progress."

Gustavo Gutierrez's "Liberation Theology" defines the State in Marxist terms, as the violent apparatus of the ruling economic class. He encourages the Church, especially in Latin America, to abandon the transcendent Kingdom of God and engage directly in "progressive" revolutionary politics. Gutierrez portrays the violent struggle for socialism as an appropriate striving for the Kingdom of God.

Jerry Falwell, as a leading representative of the contemporary "Christian Right," conceives of the State as a conservative capitalist: limited and "free," encouraging business values and free enterprise. He identifies the Church with his own Fundamentalist Independent Baptist Church, amplified through television evangelism. Falwell believes in the separation of Church and State but not Religion and Politics, by which he means the State should pass legislation against sin (abortion, pornography, homosexuality, etc.) and in favor of virtue (school prayer, traditional families, capitalism, etc.). Falwell encourages the Church to engage in politics through public lobbying organizations, such as "The Moral Majority, Inc." This organization's policy positions (strong defense, reduced welfare, etc.) are virtually identical with conservative Republican Party ideology.

Despite this rich diversity of views on Religion and Politics, a basic continuity emerges from the great thinkers examined. First, there is a general agreement that the Church, as the Body of Christ in this world, is *in,* but *not of* the world. St. Augustine's exegesis of the Scripture describing the trial and death of Christ and its implications for the Church's calling in this world perhaps best exemplifies this. Even the "Christian Left" (Liberation Theology) and the "Christian Right" (The Moral Majority), which advance particular political ideologies in the name of religion, would admit, I think, that a transcendent Kingdom of God exists, against which even Capitalism and Communism might fall short. Second, the Church in this position is obliged to both "accept" the Kingdom of Man for what it is (imperfect, incomplete, etc.) and criticize it from the higher standard of the Kingdom of God--ever encouraging on the world--to the perfect peace and justice of God's Kingdom, without ever presuming to achieve it without God. Hence, the Church, as the individual Christian, resides in the inevitable tension between the Two Cities: acknowledging the Fallen, imperfect nature of this world, but knowing also the redemptive mission of Christ and the ultimate victory of God, origin of all power.

In politics, this places the Church, again, "in, but not of" the world: acknowledging the necessity and Divine nature of earthly regimes and movements, but also the limited and imperfect condition of them *all,* when measured against the Church: the obligation to be "in" the political world without being subsumed in worldly movements and ideologies; and the obligation to be "above" the world, preserving the transcendent values of the Kingdom of God, without becoming totally removed from the world. This tenuous position of the Church is difficult to maintain, impossible without the Grace of God. As with individual Christians, it would be easier if the Church were either "in" or "not of" the world--if it could simply accept the Fallen nature of things and not be obligated to strive for God's Kingdom, or if it could strive for perfection with some expectation of achieving it through its own efforts. But God has not placed the Church in such an easy position; it must, with all its human weaknesses, strive to be "in, but not of" this world, as Christ was. Historically, as The Late Archbishop of Canterbury, William Temple, points out, the Church has erred in two ways:

> So the (Medieval) Church as one institution set out to control the State as another institution; and for this it adopted the methods of the State; it waged wars and levied taxes; so it lost the spiritual kind of control which belonged to it, without even successfully usurping the political kind of control which did not. This brought discredit on the whole notion of the authority of religion in commercial and political affairs. In the reaction

(called the Reformation) the Church recovered its spiritual function, but passed under the control of the State; this was admittedly so in Germany and England....this also was an evil, for it unduly limited the sphere of the Church, and to its subjection to an oligarchic state must largely be attributed its disastrous inactivity throughout the Industrial Revolution.[2]

From this classically Christian perspective of the Church's role in politics, to be "in, but not of" the world; to neither control the government, nor be controlled by the government, America's conception of "Freedom of Religion" came into being as possibly the best solution.

V.

Constitutionally guaranteed Freedom of Religion in America has alternately been seen as providing the greatest hope for the true realization of the proper relationship between Church and State and producing the most ineffectual Church in the most unreligious society, obsessed with trivia and absorbed by "secular humanism." As usual, the truth is probably somewhere in between; but it cannot be denied that Freedom of Religion in America provides some unique opportunities and dangers to Church-State relations.

As shown in the last section of this book, America began with the Puritans (who were English Calvinists), as a decidedly religious State. The diversity of religious backgrounds of the immigrants that followed the Puritans, however, made religious freedom and toleration the only practicable approach to Church-State relations. Virginia is a classic example of this: while settled and dominated by the Established Church of England, it had, by the time of Jefferson's Statute for Religious Freedom, a majority of citizens that were not Anglican, having received waves of immigrants from the Presbyterian, Lutheran, Methodist and Baptist churches. Complete separation of Church and State and total religious freedom and toleration was compelled under such circumstances. Still, in spite of this diversity of religious persuasions, America remained, culturally, a deeply religious nation. As Carey McWilliams notes, Scripture has always been the "second voice" in an American culture dominated by secular liberalism.[3] That voice continues to speak,

---

[2] William Temple, *Essays in Christian Politics and Kindred Subjects* (London: 1933), p. 30.

[3] Wilson Carey McWilliams, "The Bible in the American Political Tradition," in *Religion and Politics,* edited by M. J Aronoff (Transaction Press, New Brunswick, NJ, 1984), p. 11.

even through the First Amendment guaranteeing religious liberty.

For the religious clause of the First Amendment of the United States Constitution actually says two things:

> Congress shall make no law respecting an establishment of religion, or prohibiting the free exercise thereof...

The first statement in this Amendment (the "establishment" clause) forbids the State to establish a particular Church, while the second statement (the "free exercise" clause) forbids the State to prohibit religious belief and practice. The result of these two clauses (apart from a highly complex Constitutional Law tradition) is the freeing of the churches, while the outlawing of one official Church. This, it may be argued, finally places the Church in its proper relationship with the State: free from State interference but not burdened with the obligatory (and corrupting) status of a State Church. The Church in this situation of freedom might finally assume its proper role as defined by the great theologians: residing "in" the world by being able to advise and reproach the State (with impunity), but "not of" the world, by virtue of having no official status, remaining true to its transcendent standard of the Kingdom of God. In this favorable view of religious freedom, the American churches should be as effectual in their mission of bringing the City of Man as close to the Heavenly Kingdom as possible, as any Church in history.

Critics of religious freedom suggest that the current state of morality in America proves the crippling effect of pure toleration on the Church's mission in this world. Freedom of religion, without some public support, and in a liberal society, may ultimately render the Church impotent and irrelevant, as secular values of wealth and power consume the entire society, including the Church. Fears of the Church becoming identified with this or that political movement, or generating millions of dollars in income through mass-marketing techniques, may support this concern.

Regardless of the trend (or trends) in America, proper and healthy Church-State relations cannot be harmed by clarity of the issues involved. It is my hope and prayer that this volume will contribute to the clarification of the significant aspects of Religion and Politics, and make it once more an appropriate topic for polite and learned conversation.

CHAPTER I The Two Cities

ST. AUGUSTINE

St. Augustine

INTRODUCTION

St. Augustine (354-430) was a Bishop of the Church in Northern Africa and the first major Christian theologian to write extensively on Religion and Politics. Living to see the Fall of Rome (sacked by Alaric the Goth in 410), St. Augustine developed the first distinctively Christian political philosophy, partly in response to the manifest failure of Classical Greek and Roman political thought. The center of Augustinian political theory is his conception of the "Two Cities": the City of God and the City of Man. For St. Augustine, these Two Cities are "co-mingled" in this world and Christians are residents, to some extent, of each realm.

The City of God, or Kingdom of Heaven, is that transcendent realm ruled directly by the Almighty and characterized by perfect justice, peace and goodness. St. Augustine often refers to this Heavenly City as "Jerusalem," and its presence in this world is identified with the love of God before the love of man and the life of the spirit as opposed to the life of the flesh.

The City of Man encompasses all earthly kingdoms or governments (regardless of their form) which are always characterized by St. Augustine as possessing imperfect justice, peace and virtue. They are necessary, as the "sword," to control man's sinful nature through the discipline of "law and education," and they have a kind of peace and justice of their own, but it is not the perfect goodness of the City of God. These imperfect, transient earthly realms, which St. Augustine often refers to as "Rome" or "Babylon," are dominated by their love of man before the love of God and the life of the flesh over the life of the spirit. The values of the City of Man are wealth, power, prestige and the gratification of human desires, not poverty, humility, meekness and the love of God and neighbors.

In this world, the Two Cities are present together, since Christ revealed the Kingdom of Heaven on earth. This "mingling" of the City of Man and the City of God, for St. Augustine, creates inevitable tensions in society, not unlike the tension between Sin and Grace within each individual Christian. And, as the Church is the holder of the divine principles of the City of God, the tensions between the Two Cities in this world take the form of conflicts between Church and State. The Church, for St. Augustine, is the Body of Christ on earth and it is charged, after Christ, to measure the worldly realms against the ideal of the Heavenly Kingdom. The Church, like Christ, is "in, but not of," this world and it strives to show the world that its values are incomplete and inferior to God's perfect Kingdom. Therefore, Church and State are inevitably related, but separate; the Church for St. Augustine is called to influence the City of Man without being subsumed within it, to stand above the City of Man without being wholly removed from it. The Church, then, is obliged to perform that difficult task of all Christians: to accept the imperfections of the world, while continually striving to bring it closer to the perfect Kingdom of God.

For St. Augustine, this means that the Church intervenes in the affairs of State encouraging the governors to strive for God's peace and justice while acknowledging the sinful nature of man and the inability to ever completely attain the Kingdom of Heaven without the Lord's direct rule. Thus, the Church admonishes both the cynicism that says man can be nothing but a self-interested animal and the pride that claims he can be God and build the Kingdom of Heaven here on earth by his own efforts.

St. Augustine's own life and work as Bishop of Hippo reveals this attitude towards correct Church-State relations. He does not ask that the Church directly rule the earthly kingdoms, or presume that it can usher in the City of God; but the Church does have a duty to advise the worldly governors, to bring this world as close as possible to God's justice. St. Augustine's letters to various magistrates, contained in the following selections, reveal his affinity for advising the secular realm from the position of the sacred. He is not afraid to remind the magistrates that all power comes from God and that the Church represents God on earth; and he is not bashful about suggesting that in a conflict between Church and State, the former occupies a superior position in the hierarchy of authorities, being closer to God. Hence, if the individual Christian receives conflicting orders from his government and the Church, St. Augustine does not hesitate to advise him to follow the Church, even at the cost of martyrdom. By implication, then, the Church has ultimate authority on earth, even in "purely worldly" matters. This view of Church-State relations, applied by the Catholic church in the Middle Ages, follows from this hierarchy of authority presented by St. Augustine and found late in these selections:

GOD
Church
Emperor
Procouncul
Magistrate
Parents

In normal times, St. Augustine expects the State to perform its delegated function of preseving earthly peace and order (controlling and punishing sinful man's worst excesses), but always remaining open to the Church's counsel on even these matters and encouraging the citizenry to support the religious establishment. This the State does not only for its own good and the good of the Church, but for the benefit of the citizens and the love of God. St. Augustine insists that the City of Man will be unable to achieve even its limited justice without rulers who are Godly and open to the Church's counsel. Still, he acknowledges that in a direct contest between Church and State the latter will likely possess greater material power and may even temporarily vanquish the Church; but as with our Lord Jesus, St. Augustine maintains, God will ultimately redeem what the world destroys.

St. Augustine remains almost unique in the breadth of his influence on later Christian thought. Both the Roman Catholic and major Protestant Churches claim him as one of their chief theologians; as is seen in their selections in this book, St. Thomas Aquinas and John Calvin cite St. Augustine in their own political writings as an authoritative source, and both consider themselves within the Augustinian tradition. This almost universal quality of St. Augustine's doctrines, as well as the parameters which his writings on Religion and Politics set for all subsequent writers, justifies the lengthy excerpts from his enormous corpus found in this volume. These selections are drawn from his principal book on the subject, *The City of God,* and from letters, treatises and sermons dealing with Church-State relations. The last selection ("Captivity in Babylon"), is a brilliantly moving exegesis of the Scripture dealing with Christ's trial before Pilate and the implications of that event for the role of Religion in Politics and the Church in this world.

The selections used here are drawn from *The Political Writings of St. Augustine* edited by Henry Paulucci (Chicago: Regnery Gateway, 1962) who uses the following translations:

The City of God, trs. M. Dods, J. J. Smith, and G. Wilson. Edinburgh: 1872.

Expositions on the Book of Psalms, Vols. III-VI, eds. C. Marriot and H. Walford, trs. T. Scratton, H. M. Wilkins, and H. Walford. Oxford: 1849-1857.

Lectures or Tractates on the Gospel According to St. John, Vols. I-II, tr. J. Gibb. Edinburgh: 1873, 1874.

Letters of St. Augustine, Vols. I-II, tr. J. G. Cunningham. Edinburgh: 1872, 1875.

Letters (Fathers of the Church Edition), Vol. III, tr. Sister W. Parsons. New York: 1953. Used with the kind permission of the Catholic University of America Press.

Sermons on Selected Lessons of the New Testament, Vols. I-II, tr. R. G. Macmullen. Oxford: 1844, 1845.

Writings in Connection with the Manichaean Heresy, tr. R. Stothert.

Edinburgh: 1872.

Many passages of the translations used, especially those from Dods' version of *The City of God,* have been considerably revised to bring them into closer accord with the Latin texts as found in the Corpus Scriptorum Ecclesiasticorum Latinorum or Migne's Patrologiae Cursus Completus: Series Latina. Slight modifications, consistent with the meaning of the Latin text have occasionally been introduced to facilitate transitions from one selection to the next.

St. Augustine

Origins of Coercive Government

Fallen Nature and the Two Cities

God, desiring not only that the human race might be able by their similarity of nature to associate with one another, but also that they might be bound together in harmony and peace by the ties of relationship, was pleased to derive all men from one individual. And He created men with such a nature that the members of the race should not have died, had not the first two (of whom one was created out of nothing, and the other out of him) merited this with their disobedience; for by them so great a sin was committed, that by it the human nature was altered for the worse, and was transmitted also to their posterity.

That the whole human race has been condemned in its first origin, this life itself, if life it is to be called, bears witness by the host of cruel ills with which it is filled. Is not this proved by the profound and dreadful ignorance which produces all the errors that enfold the children of Adam, and from which no man can be delivered without toil, pain, and fear? Is it not proved by his love of so many vain and hurtful things, which produces gnawing cares, disquiet, griefs, fears, wild joys, quarrels, law-suits, wars, treasons, angers, hatreds, deceit, flattery, fraud, theft, robbery, perfidy, pride, ambition, envy, murders, parricides, cruelty, ferocity, wickedness, luxury, insolence, impudence, shamelessness, fornications, adulteries, incests, and the numberless uncleannesses and unnatural acts of both sexes, which it is shameful so much as to mention; sacrileges, heresies, blasphemies, perjuries, oppression of the innocent, calumnies, plots, falsehoods, false witnessings, unrighteous judgments, violent deeds, plunderings, and innumerable other crimes that do not easily come to mind, but that never absent themselves from the actuality of human existence? These are indeed the crimes of wicked men, yet they spring from that root of error and misplaced love which is born with every son of Adam.

First, we must see what it is to live after the flesh, and what to live after the spirit. For any one who either does not recollect, or does not sufficiently weigh, the language of sacred Scripture, may, on first hearing what we have said, suppose that the Epicurean philosophers live after the flesh, because they place man's highest good in bodily pleasure; and that those others do so who have been of opinion that in some form or other bodily good is man's supreme good; and that the mass of men do so who, without dogmatizing or philosophizing on the subject, are so prone to lust that they cannot delight in any pleasure save such as they receive from bodily sensations: and he may suppose that the Stoics, who place the supreme good of men in the soul, live after the spirit; for what is man's soul, if not spirit? But in the sense of the divine Scripture both are proved to live after the flesh. For by flesh it means not only the body of a terrestrial and mortal animal, as when it says, "All flesh is not the same flesh, but there is one kind of flesh of men, another flesh of beasts, another of fishes, another of birds," but it uses this word in many other significations. . . .If we are to ascertain what it is to live after the flesh (which is certainly evil, though the nature of flesh is not itself evil), we must carefully examine that passage of the epistle which the Apostle Paul wrote to the Galatians, in which he says, "Now the works of the flesh are manifest, which are these: adultery, fornication, uncleanness, lasciviousness, idolatry, witchcraft, hatred, variance, emulations, wrath, strife, seditions, heresies, envyings, murders, drunkenness, revellings, and such like: of the which I tell you before, as I have also told you in time past, that they which do such things shall not inherit the kingdom of God." This whole passage of the apostolic epistle being considered, so far as it bears on the matter in hand, will be sufficient to answer the question, what it is to live after the flesh.

In enunciating this proposition of ours, then, that because some live according to the flesh and others according to the spirit there have arisen two diverse and conflicting cities, we might equally well have said, "because some live according to man, others according to God." For Paul says very plainly to the Corinthians, "For whereas there is among you envying and strife, are ye not carnal, and walk according to man?" So that to walk according to man and to be carnal are the same; for by *flesh,* that is, by a part of man, man is meant.

But the character of the human will is of moment; . . .for the man who lives according to God, and not according to man, ought to be a lover of good, and therefore a hater of evil. And since no one is evil by nature, but whosoever is evil is evil by vice, he who lives according to God ought to cherish toward evil men a perfect hatred, so that he shall neither hate the man because of his vice, nor love the vice because of the man. For the vice being cursed, all that ought to be loved, and nothing that ought to be hated, will remain.

He who resolves to love God, and to love his neighbor as himself, not according to man but according to God, is on account of this love said to be of a good will; and this is in Scripture more commonly called charity, but it is also, even in the same books, called love. . . The right will is, therefore, well-directed love, and the wrong will is ill-directed love. Love yearning to have what is loved, is desire; and having and enjoying it, is joy; fleeing what is opposed to it, is fear; and feeling what is opposed to it, when it has befallen it, is sadness. Now these motions are evil if the love is evil; good if the love is good.

Two cities have been formed, therefore, by two loves: the earthly by love of self, even to contempt of God; the heavenly by love of God, even to contempt of self. The former glories in itself, the latter in the Lord. For the one seeks glory from men; but the greatest glory of the other is God, the witness of conscience. The one lifts up its head in its own glory; the other says to its God, "Thou art my glory, and the lifter up of mind head." In the one, the princes and the nations it subdues are ruled by the love of ruling; in the other, the princes and the subjects serve one another in love, the latterobeying, while the former take thought for all. The one delights in its own strength, represented in the persons of its rulers; the other says to its God, "I will love Thee, O Lord, my strength." And therefore the wise men of the one city, living according to man, have sought for profit to their own bodies or souls, or both, and those who have known God "glorified Him not as God, neither were thankful, but became vain in their imaginations, and their follish hearts were darkened; professing themselves to be wise"–that is, glorying in their own wisdom, and being possessed by pride–"they became fools, and changed the glory of the incorruptible God into an image made like to corruptible man, and to birds, and four-footed beasts, and creeping things." For they were either leaders or followers of the people in adoring images, "and worshipped and served the creature more than the Creator, who is blessed for ever." But in the other city there is no human wisdom, but only godliness, which offers due worship to the true God, and looks for its reward in the society of the saints, of holy angels as well as holy men, "that God may be all in all." And when these two cities severally achieve what they wish, they live in peace, each after its kind.

Now peace is a good so great, that even in this earthly and mortal life there is no word we hear with such pleasure, nothing we more strongly desire, or enjoy more thoroughly when it comes. So that if we dwell for a little longer on this subject, we shall not, in my opinion, be wearisome to our readers who will bear with us both for the sake of understanding what is the end of this city of which we speak, and for the sake of the sweetness of peace which is dear to all.

Everyone who has observed the conduct of men's affairs and common human nature will agree with me in this: that just as there is no man who does not long for joy, so there is no man who does not long for peace. Even those who want war, want it really only for victory's sake: that is, they want to attain a glorious peace by fighting. For what is victory if not the subjugation of those who resist us? And when this is done, peace follows.

Further, justice is that virtue which gives every one his due. Where, then, is the justice of man, when he deserts the true God and yields himself to impure demons? Is this to give every one his due? Or is he who keeps back a piece of ground from the purchaser, and gives it to a man who has no right to it, unjust, while he who keeps back himself from the God who made him, and serves wicked spirits, is just?

This same book, *De Republica,* advocates the cause of justice against injustice with great force and keenness. The pleading for injustice against justice was first heard, and it was asserted (as we noted earlier) that without injustice a republic could neither increase nor even subsist, for it was laid down as an absolutely unassailable position that it is unjust for some men to rule and some to serve; and yet the imperial city to which the republic belongs cannot rule her provinces without having recourse to this injustice. It was replied in behalf of justice, that this ruling of the provinces is just, because servitude may be advantageous to the provincials, and is so when rightly administered–that is to say, when lawless men are prevented from doing harm. And further, as they became worse and worse so long as they were free, they will improve by subjection. To confirm this reasoning, there is added an eminent example drawn from nature: for "why," it is asked, "does God rule man, the soul the body, the reason the passions and other vicious parts of the soul?" This example leaves no doubt that, to some, servitude is useful; and, indeed, to serve God is useful to all. And it is when the soul serves God that it exercises a right control over the body; and in the soul itself the reason must be subject to God if it is to govern as it ought the passions and other vices. Hence, when a man does not serve God, what justice can we ascribe to him, since in this case his soul cannot exercise a just control over the body, nor his reason over his vices? And if there is no justice in such an individual, certainly there can be none in a community composed of such persons. Here, therefore, there is not that common acknowledgement of right which makes an assemblage of men a people whose affairs we call a republic. And why need I speak of the advantageousness, the common participation in which, according to the definition, makes a people? For although, if you choose to regard the matter attentively, you will see that there is nothing advantageous to those who live godlessly, as every one lives who does not serve God but demons, whose wickedness you may measure by their desire to receive the worship of men though they are most impure spirits, yet what I have said of the common acknowledgement of right is enough to demonstrate that, according to the above definition, there can be no people, and therefore no republic, where there is no justice. For if they assert that in their republic the Romans did not serve unclean spirits, but good and holy gods, must we therefore again reply to this evasion, though already we have said enough, and more than enough, to expose it? He must be an uncommonly stupid, or a shamelessly contentious person, who . . . can yet question whether the Romans served wicked and impure demons. But, not to speak of their character, it is written in the law of the true God, "He that sacrificeth unto any god save unto the Lord only, he shall be utterly destroyed." He, therefore, who uttered so menacing a commandment decreed that no worship should be given either to good or bad gods.

And where there is not that justice whereby the one supreme God rules the obedient city according to His grace, so that it sacrifices to none but Him, and whereby, in all the citizens of this obedient city, the soul consequently rules the body and reason the vices in the rightful order, so that, as the individual just man, so also the community and people of the just, live by faith, which works by love, that love whereby man loves God as He ought to be loved, and his neighbour as himself–there, I says, there is not an assemblage associated by a common acknowledgement of right, and by a community of interests. But if there is not this, there is not a people, if our definition be true, and therefore there is no republic; for where there is no people there can be no republic.

For though the soul may seem to rule the body admirably, and the reason the vices, if the soul and reason do not themselves obey God, as God has commanded them to serve Him, they have no proper authority over the body and the vices. For what kind of mistress of the body and the vices can that mind be which is ignorant of the true God, and which, instead of being subject to His authority, is prostituted to the corrupting influences of the most vicious demons? It is for this reason that the virtues which it seems to itself to possess, and by which it restrains the body and the vices that it may obtain and keep what it desires, are rather vices than virtues so long as there is no reference to God in the matter. For although some suppose that virtues which have a reference only to themselves, and are desired only on their own account, are yet true and genuine virtues, the fact is that even then they are inflated with pride, and are therefore to be reckoned vices rather than virtues.

Thus, in fact, true justice has no existence save in that republic whose founder and ruler is Christ, if at least any choose to call this a republic; and indeed we cannot deny that it is the people's weal. But if perchance this name, which has become familiar in other connections, be considered alien to our common parlance, we may at all events say that in this city is true justice; the city of which Holy Scripture says, "Glorious things are said of thee, O city of God."

All men that earthly things do mind, all men that do choose earthly felicity before God, all men that seek their own things, not the things which are of Jesus Christ, to that one city belong, which is called Babylon mystically, and which hath for king the devil. But all men who mind those things which are above, who on heavenly things do meditate, who with carefulness live in the world that they may not offend God, who are careful not to sin, who if sinning are not ashamed to confess, humble, mild, holy, just, godly, good, all these to that one City do belong, which for King hath Christ. For the former on earth as it were is the greater in age, not by elevation, not by honour. For the former city was first born, the latter city was after born. For that began from Cain, this from Abel. These two Bodies, serving under two kings, to their several cities belonging, are . . . meanwhile mingled, at the end to be severed; against each other mutually in conflict, the one for iniquity, the other for the truth. And sometimes this very temporal mingling bringeth it to pass that certain men belonging to the city Babylon, do order matters belonging to Jerusalem, and again certain men belonging to Jerusalem, do order matters belonging to Babylon.

I think ye have not forgotten, that I brought to your notice, or rather to your recollection, that every one who is trained in the holy Church ought to know of what place we are citizens, and where we are wandering, and that the cause of our wandering is sin, the gift of our return, the remission of our sins, and our justification by the grace of God. Ye have heard and know that there are two cities, for the present outwardly mingled together, yet separated in heart, running together through the course of time until the end; one whose end is everlasting peace, and it is called Jerusalem; the other whose joy is peace in this world, and it is called Babylon. The meanings of these names too ye remember, that Jerusalem means 'vision of peace;' Babylon, 'confusion.' Jerusalem was held captive in Babylon, but not all, for the Angels too are its citizens. But as regards men predestined to the glory of God, to become by adoption joint-heirs with Christ, whom He has redeemed from this very captivity by His own Blood, that this part, I says, of the citizens of Jerusalem are held captive in Babylon on account of sin, but first begin to go forth from thence in spirit by confession of sin and love of righteousness, and then afterwards at the end of the world are to be separated in body also; this we set before you in that Psalm, which we first handled here with you, beloved, which begins thus: *For Thee, O God, a hymn is meet in Sion, and to Thee shall the vow be performed in Jerusalem.* But to-day we have sung, *By the waters of Babylon we sat down and wept, when we remembered Sion.* Observe, that in the former it is said, *For Thee, O God, a hymn is meet in Sion;* but here, *By the waters of Babylon we sat down and wept, when we remembered Sion,* that Sion where a *hymn is meet for God.*

What then are *the waters of Babylon?* and what is our sitting and weeping in remembrance of Sion? For if we be citizens of Sion, we not only chant this, but do it. If we are citizens of Jerusalem, that is Sion, and in this life, in the confusion of this world, in this Babylon, do not dwell as citizens, but are detained as captives, it befits us not only to chant these things, but also to do them, with affectionate regard, with religious longing for our everlasting city. This city too which is called Babylon hath its lovers, who look for peace in this world, and hope for nothing beyond, but fix their whole joy in this, end it in this, and we see them toil exceedingly for their earthly country: but whosoever live faithfully even therein, if they seek not therein pride, and perishable elation, and hateful boasting, but exhibit true faith, such as they can, as long they can, to whom they can, so far as they see earthly things, and understand the nature of their citizenship, God suffereth them not to perish in Babylon; He hath predestinated them to be citizens of Jerusalem. He understandeth their captivity, and sheweth to them another city for which they ought truly to sigh, for which they ought to use every endeavour, to win which they ought to the utmost of their power to urge their fellow-citizens, now their fellow-wanderers. Therefore saith the Lord Jesus Christ, *He that is faithful in that which is least, is faithful also in much;* and again He saith, *If ye have not been faithful in that which is another man's, who will give you that which is your own?*

He, then, who prefers what is right to what is wrong, and what is well-ordered to what is perverted, sees that the peace of unjust men is not worthy to be called peace in comparison with the peace of the just. And yet even what is perverted must of necessity be in harmony with, and in dependence on, and in some part of the order of things, for otherwise it would have no existence at all. Suppose a man hangs with his head downwards, this is certainly a perverted attitude of body and arrangement of its members; for that which nature requires to be above is beneath, and *vice versa.* This perversity disturbs the peace of the body, and is therefore painful. Nevertheless the spirit is at peace with its body, and labours for its preservation, and hence the suffering; but if it is banished from the body by its pains, then, so long as the bodily framework holds together, there is in the remains a kind of peace among the members, and hence the body remains suspended. And inasmuch as the earthly body tends towards the earth, and rests on the bond by which it is suspended, it tends thus to its natural peace, and the voice of its own weight demands a place for it to rest; and though now lifeless and without feeling, it does not fall from the peace that is natural to its place in creation, whether it already has it, or is tending towards it. For if you apply embalming preparations to prevent the bodily frame from mouldering and dissolving, a kind of peace still unites part to part, and keeps the whole body in a suitable place on the earth–in other words, in a place that is at peace with the body. If, on the other hand, the body receive no such care, but be left to the natural course, it is disturbed by exhalations that do not harmonize with one another, and that offend our senses; for it is this which is perceived in putrefaction until it is assimilated to the elements of the world, and particle by particle enters into peace with them. Yet throughout this process the laws of the most high Creator and Governor are strictly observed, for it is by Him the peace of the universe is administered. For although minute animals are produced from the carcase of a larger animal, all these little atoms, by the law of the same Creator, serve the animals they belong to in peace. And although the flesh of dead animals be eaten by others, no matter where it be carried, nor what it be brought into contact with, nor what it be converted and changed into, it still is ruled by the same laws which pervade all things for the conservation of every mortal race, and which bring things that fit one another into harmony.

The peace of the body then consists in the duly proportioned arrangement of its parts. The peace of the irrational soul is the harmonious repose of the appetites, and that of the rational soul the harmony of knowledge and action. The peace of body and soul is the well-ordered obedience of faith to eternal law. Peace between man and man is well-ordered concord. Domestic peace is the well-ordered concort between those of the family who rule and those who obey. Civil peace is a similar concord among the citizens. The peace of the celestial city is the perfectly ordered and harmonious enjoyment of God, and of one another in God. The peace of all things is the tranquillity of order. Order is the distribution which allots things equal and unequal, each to its own place. And hence, though the miserable, in so far as they are such, do certainly not enjoy peace, but are severed from that tranquallity of order in which there is no disturbance, nevertheless, inasmuch as they are deservedly and justly miserable, they are by their very misery connected with order. They are not, indeed, conjoined with the blessed, but they are disjoined from them by the law of order. And though they are disquieted, their circumstances are notwithstanding adjusted to them, and consequently they have some tranquillity of order, and therefore some peace. But they are wretched because, although not wholly miserable, they are not in that place where any mixture of misery is impossible. They would, however, be more wretched if they had not that peace which arises from being in harmony with the natural order of things. When they suffer, their peace is in so far disturbed; but their peace continues in so far as they do not suffer, and in so far as their nature continues to exist. As, then, there may be life without pain, while there cannot be pain without some kind of life, so there may be peace without war, but there cannot be war without some kind of peace, because war supposes the existence of some natures to wage it, and these natures cannot exist without peace of one kind or other . . . .

God, then, the most wise Creator and most just Ordainer of all natures, who placed the human race upon earth as its greatest ornament, imparted to men some good things adapted to this life, to wit, temporal peace, such as we can enjoy in this life from health and safety and human fellowship, and all things needful for the preservation and recovery of this peace, such as the objects which are accommodated to our outward senses, light, night, the air, and waters suitable for us, and everything the body requires to sustain, shelter, heal, or beautify it: and all under this most equitable condition, that every man who made a good use of these advantages suited to the peace of his mortal condition, should receive ampler and better blessings, namely, the peace of immortality, accompanied by glory and honour in an endless life made fit for the enjoyment of God and of one another in God; but that he who used the present blessings badly should both lose them and should not receive the others.

    The whole use, then, of things temporal has a reference to this result of earthly peace in the earthly community, while, in the city of God it is connected with eternal peace. And therefore, if we were irrational animals, we should desire nothing beyond the proper arrangement of the parts of the body and the satisfaction of the appetites–nothing, therefore, but bodily comfort and abundance of pleasures, that the peace of the body might contribute to the peace of the soul. For if bodily peace be wanting, a bar is put to the peace even of the irrational soul, since it cannot obtain the gratification of its appetites. And these two together help out the mutual peace of soul and body, the peace of harmonious life and health. For as animals, by shunning pain, show that they love bodily peace, and, by pursuing pleasure to gratify their appetites, show that they love peace of soul, so their shrinking from death is a sufficient indication of their intense love of that peace which binds soul and body in close alliance. But, as man has a rational soul, he subordinates all this which he has in common with the beasts to the peace of his rational soul, that his intellect may have free play and may regulate his actions, and that he may thus enjoy the well-ordered harmony of knowledge and action which constitutes, as we have said, the peace of the rational soul. And for this purpose he must desire to be neither molested by pain, nor disturbed by desire, nor extinguished by death, that he may arrive at some useful knowledge by which he may regulated his life and manners. But, owing to the liability of the human mind to fall into mistakes, this very pursuit of knowledge may be a snare to him unless he has a divine Master, whom he may obey without misgiving, and who may at the same time give him such help as to preserve his own freedom. And because, so long as he is in this mortal body, he is a stranger to God, he walks by faith, not by sight; and he therefore refers all peace, bodily or spiritual or both, to that peace which mortal man has with the immortal God, so that he exhibits the well-ordered obedience of faith to eternal law. But as this divine Master inculcates two precepts–the love of God and the love of our neighbour–and as in these precepts a man finds three things he has to love–God, himself, and his neighbour–and that he who loves God loves himself thereby, it follows that he must endeavour to get his neighbour to love God, since he is ordered to love his neighbour as himself. He ought to make this endeavour in behalf of his wife, his children, his household, all within his reach, even as he would wish his neighbour to do the same for him if he needed it; and consequently he will be at peace, or in well-ordered concord, with all men, as far as in him lies. And this is the order of this concord, that a man, in the first place, injure no one, and, in the second, do good to every one he can reach. Primarily, therefore, his own household are his care, for the law of nature and of society gives him readier access to them and greater opportunity of serving them. And hence the apostle says, "Now, if any provide not for his own, and specially for those of his own house, he hath denied the faith, and is worse than an infidel." This is the origin of domestic peace, or the well-ordered concord of those in the family who rule and those who obey. For they who care for the rest rule–the husband the wife, the parents the children, the masters the servants; and they who are cared for obey–the women their husbands, the children their parents, the servants their masters. But in the family of the just man who lives by faith and is as yet a pilgrim journeying on to the celestial city, even those who rule serve those whom they seem to command; for they rule not from a love of power, but from a sense of the duty they owe to others–not because they are proud of authority, but because they love mercy.

The earthly city, which does not live by faith, seeks an earthly peace, and the end it proposes, in the well-ordered concord of civic obedience and rule, is the combination of men's wills to attain the things which are helpful to this life. The heavenly city, or rather the part of it which sojourns on earth and lives by faith, makes use of this peace only because it must, until this moral condition which necessitates it shall pass away. Consequently, so long as it lives like a captive and a stranger in the earthly city, though it has already received the promise of redemption, and the gift of the Spirit as the earnest of it, it makes no scruple to obey the laws of the earthly city, whereby the things necessary for the maintenance of this mortal life are administered; and thus, as this life is common to both cities, so there is a harmony between them in regard to what belongs to it. But, as the earthly city has had some philosophers whose doctrine is condemned by the divine teaching, and who, being deceived either by their own conjectures or by demons, supposed that many gods must be invited to take an interest in human affairs, and assigned to each a separate function and a separate department–to one the body, to another the soul; and in the body itself, to one the head, to another the neck, and each of the other members to one of the gods; and in like manner, in the soul, to one god the natural capacity was assigned, to another education, to another anger, to another lust; and so the various affairs of life were assigned–cattle to one, corn to another, wine to another, oil to another, the woods to another, money to another, navigation to another, wars and victories to another, marriages to another, births and fecundity to another, and other things to other gods: and as the celestial city, on the other hand, knew that one God only was to be worshippped, and that to Him alone was due that service which can be given only to a god, it has come to pass that the two cities could not have common laws of religion, and that the heavenly city has been compelled in this matter to dissent, and to become obnoxious to those who think differently, and to stand the brunt of their anger and hatred and persecutions, except in so far as the minds of their enemies have been alarmed by the multitude of the Christians and quelled by the manifest protection of God accorded to them. This heavenly city then, while it sojourns on earth, calls citizens out of all nations, and gathers together a society of pilgrims of all languages, not scrupling about diversities in the manners, laws, and institutions whereby earthly peace is secured and maintained, but recognising that, however various these are, they all tend to one and the same end of earthly peace. It therefore is so far from rescinding the abolishing these diversities, that it even preserves and adapts them, so long only as no hindrance to the worship of the one supreme and true God is thus introduced. Even the heavenly city, therefore, while in its state of pilgrimage, avails itself of the peace of earth, and, so far as it can without injuring faith and godliness, desires and maintains a common agreement among men regarding the acquisition of the necessaries of life.

To Donatus, His Noble and Deservedly Honourable Lord, and Eminently Praise- worthy Son, Augustine sends greeting in the Lord.
I would indeed that the African Church were not placed in such trying circumstances as to need the aid of any earthly power. But since, as the apostle says, "there is no power but of God," it is unquestionable that, when by you the sincere sons of your Catholic Mother help is given to her, our help is in the name of the Lord, "who made heaven and earth." For oh, noble and deservedly honourable lord, and eminently praiseworthy son, who does not perceive that in the midst of so great calamities no small consolation has been bestowed upon us by God, in that you, such a man, and so devoted in the name of Christ, have been raised to the dignity of proconsul, so that power allied with your goodwill may restrain the enemies of the Church from their wicked and sacrilegious attempts? In fact, there is only one thing of which we are much afraid in your administration of justice, viz., lest perchance, seeing that every injury done by impious and ungrateful men against the Christian society is a more serious and heinous crime than if it had been done against others, you should on this ground consider that it ought to be punished with a severity corresponding to the enormity of the crime, and not with the moderation which is suitable to Christian forbearance. We beseech you, in the name of Jesus Christ, not to act in this

manner. For we do not seek to revenge ourselves in this world; nor ought the things which we suffer to reduce us to such distress of mind as to leave no room in our memory for the precepts in regard to this which we have received from Him for those truth and in whose name we suffer; we "love our enemies," and we "pray for them." It is not their death, but their deliverance from error, that we seek to accomplish by the help of the terror of judges and of laws, whereby they may be preserved form falling under the penalty of eternal judgment; we do not wish either to see the exercise of discipline towards them neglected, or, on the other hand, to see them subjected to the severer punishments which they deserve. Do you, therefore, check their sins in such a way, that the sinners may be spared to repent of their sins.

To Marcellinus, My Noble Lord, Justly Distinguished, My Son Very Much Beloved, Augustine sends greetings in the Lord.

In fine, you have been sent hither for the benefit of the Church. I solemnly declare that what I recommend is expedient in the interests of the Catholic Church, or, that I may not seem to pass beyond the boundaries of my own charge, I protest that it is for the good of the Church belonging to the diocese of Hippo. If you do not hearken to me asking this favour as a friend, hearken to me offering this counsel as a bishop although, indeed, it would not be presumption for me to say–since I am addressing a Christian, and especially in such a case as this–that it becomes you to hearken to me as a bishop commanding with authority, my noble and justly distinguished lord and much-loved son.

Augustine, Bishop, Servant of Christ and of His Family, gives greeting in the Lord to his Beloved Son, Macedonius.

Since we know that you are devoted to the public welfare, you must see how plainly the sacred writings show that the happiness of the state has no other source than the happiness of man.

If you recognize that you have received the virtues which you have, and if you return thanks to Him from whom you have received them, directing them to His service even in your secular office; if you rouse the men subject to your authority and lead them to worship God, both by the example of your own devout life and by your zeal for their welfare, whether you rule them by love or by fear if, in working for their greater security, you have no other aim than that they should thus attain to Him who will be their happiness–then yours will be true virtues, then they will be increased by the help of Him whose bounty lavished them on you, and they will be so perfected as to lead you without fail to that truly happy life which is no other than eternal life. In that life, evil will no longer have to be distinguished from good by the virtue of prudence, because there will be no evil there; adversity will not have to be borne with fortitude, because there will be nothing there but what we love; temperance will not be needed to curb our passions, because there will be no enticements to passion there; nor shall we have to practise justice by helping the poor out of our abundance, for there we shall find no poor and no needy. There will be but one virtue there, and it will be the same as the reward of virtue, which the speaker in the sacred writings mentions as the object of his love: 'But it is good for me to stick close to my God.' This will constitute the perfect and eternal wisdom, as it will constitute the truly happy life, because to attain it is to attain the eternal and supreme good, and to stick close to God forever is the sum of our good.

Power to Crucify and Power to Release

What Pilate said to Christ, or what He replied to Pilate, has to be considered and handled in the present discourse. For after the words had been addressed to the Jews, "Take ye him, and judge him according to your law," and the Jews had replied, "It is not lawful for us to put any man to death, Pilate entered again into the judgment hall, and called Jesus, and said unto Him, Art though the King of the Jews? And Jesus answered, Sayest thou this thing of thyself, or did others tell it thee of me?" The Lord indeed knew both what He Himself asked, and what reply the other was to give; but yet He wished it to be spoken, not for the sake of information to Himself, but that what He wished us to know might be recorded in Scripture. "Pilate answered, Am I a Jew? Thine own nation, and the chief priests, have delivered thee unto me: what has thou done? Jesus answered, My kingdom is not of this world. If my kingdom were of this world, then would my servants fight, that I should not be delivered to the Jews: but now is my kingdom not from hence."

"Then saith Pilate unto Him, Speakest thou not unto me? knowest thou not that I have power to crucify thee, and have power to release thee? Jesus answered: Thou wouldest have no power against me, except it were given thee from above: therefore he that delivered me unto thee hath the greater sin." Here, you see, He replied; and yet wherever He replied not, it is not as one who is criminal or cunning, but as a lamb; that is, in simplicity and innocence He opened not His mouth. Accordingly, where He made no answer, He was silent as a sheep where He answered, He taught as the Shepherd. Let us therefore set ourselves to learn what He said, what He taught also by the apostle, that "there is no power but of God;" and that he is a greater sinner who maliciously delivereth up to the power the innocent to the slain, than the power itself, if it slay him through fear of another power that is greater still. Of such a sort, indeed, was the power which God had given to Pilate, that he should also be under the Power of Caesar. Wherefore "thou wouldest have," He says, "no power against me," that is, even the little measure thou really hast, "except" this very measure, whatever its amount, "were given thee from above." But knowing as I do its amount, for it is not so great as to render thee altogether independent, "therefore he that delivered me unto thee hath the greater sin." He, indeed, delivered me to thy power at the bidding of envy, whilst thou art to exercise thy power upon me through the impulse of fear. And yet not even through the impulse of fear ought one man to slay another, especially the innocent; nevertheless to do so by an officious zeal is a much greater evil than under the constraint of fear. And therefore the truth-speaking Teacher saith not, "He that delivered me to thee," he only hath sin, as if the other had none; but He saith, "hath the greater sin," letting him understand that he himself was not exempt from blame. For that of the latter is not reduced to nothing because the other is greater.

"Hence Pilate sought to release Him." What is to be understood by the word here used, "hence," as if he had not been seeking to do so before? Read what precedes, and thou wilt find that he had already for some time been seeking to release Jesus. By the original word, therefore, we are to understand, *on this account,* that is, *for this reason,* that he might not contract sin by slaying an innocent man who had been delivered into his hands, even though his sin would be less than that of the Jews, who delivered Him to him to be put to death. "From thence," therefore, that is, for this reason, that he might not commit such a sin, "he sought" not now for the first time, but from the beginning, "to release Him."

"But the Jews cried out, saying, If thou let this man go, thou art not Caesar's friend: whosoever maketh himself a king, speaketh against Caesar." They thought to inspire Pilate with greater fear by terrifying him about Caesar, in order that he might put Christ to death, than formerly when they said, "We have the law, and by the law he ought to die, because he made himself the Son of God." It was not their law, indeed, that impelled him through fear to the deed of murder, but rather it was his fear of the Son of God that held him back from the crime. But now he could not set Caesar, who was the author of his own power, at nought, in the same way as the law of another nation.

Subject unto the Higher Powers

We know what persecutions the body of Christ, that is, the holy Church, suffered from the kings of the earth. Let us therefore here also recognize the words of the Church: *Princes have persecuted me without a cause; and my heart hath stood in awe of Thee.* For how had the Christians injured the kingdoms of the earth, although their King promised them the kingdom of heaven? How, I ask, had they injured the kingdoms of the earth? Did their King forbid His soldiers to pay and to render due service to the kings of the earth? Saith He not to the Jews who were striving to calumniate Him, *Render unto Caesar the things that are Caesar's, and unto God the things that are God's?* Did he not even in His own Person pay tribute from the mouth of a fish? Did not His forerunner, when the soldiers of this kingdom were seeking what they ought to do for their everlasting salvation, instead of replying, Loose your belts, throw away your arms, desert your king, that ye may wage war for the Lord, answer, *Do violence to no man: neither accuse any falsely: and be content with your wages?* Did not one of His soldiers, His most beloved companion, say to his fellow soldiers, the provincials, so to speak, of Christ, *Let every soul be subject unto the higher powers?* And a little lower he added, *Render to all their dues; tribute to whom tribute is due; custom to whom custom: fear to whom fear: honour to whom honour. Owe no man any thing, but to love one another.* Does he not enjoin the Church to pray for even kings themselves? How then have the Christians offended against them? What due have they not rendered? in what have not Christians obeyed the monarchs of the earth? The kings of the earth therefore have persecuted the Christians without a cause. But heed what he hath subjoined: *And my heart hath stood in awe of Thy word.* They too had their threatening words: I banish, I proscribe, I slay, I torture with claws, I burn with fires, I expose to beasts, I tear the limbs piecemeal: but rather *of Thy word hath my heart stood in awe. Fear not them which kill the body, but are not able to kill the soul: but rather fear Him which is able to destroy both soul and body in hell.* My heart hath stood in awe of these words of Thine; and I have scorned man who persecuteth me, and have overcome the devil that would seduce me.

At present indeed the righteous suffer in some measure, and at present the unrighteous sometimes tyrannize over the righteous. In what ways? Sometimes the unrighteous arrive at worldly honours: when they have arrived at them, and have been made either judges or kings; for God doth this for the discipline of His folk, for the discipline of His people; the honour due to their power must needs be shewn them. For thus hath God ordained His Church, that every power ordained in the world may have honour, and sometimes from those who are better than those in power. For the sake of illustration I take one instance; hence calculate the grades of all powers. The primary and every day relation of authority between man and man is that between master and slave. Almost all houses have a power of this sort. There are masters, there are also slaves; these are different names, but men and men are equal names. And what saith the Apostle, teaching that slaves are subject to their masters? *Servants, be obedient to them that are your masters according to the flesh:* for there is a Master according to the Spirit. He is the true and everlasting Master; but those temporal masters are for a time only. When thou walkest in the way, when thou livest in this life, Christ doth not wish to make thee proud. It hath been thy lot to become a Christian, and to have a man for thy master: thou wast not made a Christian, that thou mightest disdain to be a servant. For when by Christ's command thou servest a man, thou servest not the man, but Him who commanded thee. He saith this also: *Servants, be obedient to them that are your masters according to the flesh, with fear and trembling, in singleness of heart, as unto Christ; not with eye-service, as men-pleasers, but as the servants of Christ, doing the will of God from the heart; with good will.* Behold, he hath not made men free from being servants, but good servants from bad servants. How much do the rich owe to Christ, who orders their house for them! So that if thou hast had an unbelieving servant, suppose Christ convert him, and say not to him, Leave thy master, thou hast now known Him Who is thy true Master: he perhaps is ungodly and unjust, thou art now faithful and righteous: it is unworthy that a righteous and faithful man should serve an unjust and unbelieving master. He spoke not thus unto him, but rather, Serve him: and to confirm the servant, added, Serve as I served; I before thee served the unjust. From whom but His servants did the Lord suffer so much in His Passion? from whom, but evil servants? For if they had been good servants, they would honour their Master. But since they were evil servants, they wronged Him. What did He, on the other hand? He recompensed love for hatred: for He said, *Father, forgive them: for they know not what they do.* If the Lord of heaven and earth, through Whom all things were created, served the unworthy, asked mercy for His furious persecutors, and, as it were, shewed Himself as their Physician at His Advent: (for physicians also, better both in art and health, serve the sick:) how much more ought not a man to disdain, with his whole mind, and his whole good will, with his whole love to serve even a bad master! Behold, a better serveth an inferior, but for a season. Understand what I have said of the master and slave, to be true also of powers and kings, of all the exalted stations of this world. For sometimes they are good powers, and fear God; sometimes they fear not God. Julian was an infidel Emperor, an apostate, a wicked man, an idolater; Christian soldiers served an infidel Emperor; when they came to the cause of Christ, they acknowledged Him only Who was in heaven. If he called upon them at any time to worship idols, to offer incense; they preferred God to him: but whenever he commanded them to deploy into line, to march against this or that nation, they at once obeyed. They distinguished their everlasting from their temporal master; and yet they were, for the sake of their everlasting Master, submissive to their temporal master.

But will it be thus always, that the ungodly have power over the righteous? It will not be so. See what this Psalm saith: *For God will not leave the rod of the ungodly upon the lot of the righteous.* The rod of the ungodly is felt for a season upon the lot of the righteous; but it is not left there, it will not be there for ever. A time will come, when Christ, appearing in his glory, shall gather all nations before Him; and shall separate them one from another, as a shepherd divideth his sheep from the goats: and He shall set the sheep on His right hand, but the goats on the left. And thou wilt see there many slaves among the sheep, and many masters among the goats; and again many masters among the sheep, many slaves among the goats. For all slaves are not good–do not infer this from the consolation we have given to servants–nor are all masters evil, because we have thus repressed the pride of masters. There are good masters who believe, and there are evil: there are good servants who believe, and there are evil. But as long as good servants serve evil masters, let them endure for a season. *For God will not leave the rod of the ungodly upon the lot of the righteous.* Why will he not? *Lest the righteous put forth their hand unto wickedness:* that the righteous may endure for a season the domination of the ungodly, and may understand that this is not for ever, but may prepare themselves to possess their everlasting heritage. What heritage? When all principalities and powers shall be subdued, *that God may be all in all.*

The Apostle himself saith, *Let every soul be subject unto the higher powers, for there is no power but of God, the powers that be are ordained of God. He then who resisteth the power, resisteth the ordinance of God.* But what if it enjoin what thou oughtest not to do? In this case by all means disregard the power through fear of the Power.

Run over now the list of those above thee. First are thy father and mother, if they are educating thee aright; if they are bringing thee up for Christ; they are to be heard in all things, they must be obeyed in every command; let them enjoin nothing against one above themselves, and so let them be obeyed. And who, thou wilt say, is above him who begat me? He who created thee. For man begets, but God creates. How it is that man begets, he does not know; and what he shall beget, he does not know. But He who saw thee that He might make thee, before that he whom He made existed, is surely above thy father. Thy country again should be above thy very parents; so that whereinsoever thy parents enjoin aught against thy country, they are not to be listened to.

Consider these several grades of human powers. If the magistrate enjoin any thing, must it not be done? Yet if his order be in opposition to the Proconsul, thou does not surely despite the power, but choosest to obey a greater power. Nor in this case ought the less to be angry, if the greater be preferred. Again, if the Proconsul himself enjoin any thing, and the Emperor another thing, is there any doubt, that disregarding the former, we ought to obey the latter? So then if the Emperor enjoin one thing, and God another, what judge ye? Pay me tribute, submit thyself to my allegiance. Right, but not in an idol's temple. In an idol's temple He forbids it. Who forbids it? A greater Power. Pardon me then: thou threatenest a prison, He threateneth hell. Here must thou at once take to thee thy *faith as a shield, whereby thou mayest be able to quench all the fiery darts of the enemy.*

CHAPTER II Divine and Human Law

ST. THOMAS AQUINAS

St. Thomas Aquinas

INTRODUCTION

St. Thomas Aquinas (1225-1274) was the leading Medieval philosopher and theologian, known as the "Angelic Doctor." Born of a noble Italian family, St. Thomas (against their objections) entered a Dominican order. He studied at the University of Paris, where he came under the influence of Aristotle's philosophical writings. St. Thomas later became Professor of Theology at Paris and served as a Papal consultant. He was Canonized in 1323.

St. Thomas' political ideas center around the view that the State is part of the universal empire, of which God is the maker and ultimate ruler. A government's authority, therefore, ultimately rests with God, which commends both subjects' obedience to their rulers and rulers obedience to God. The way in which earthly rule is connected to Godly rule is through a series of laws.

Three major kinds of law are described by St. Thomas: (1) Divine Law (God's eternal, perfect order of the universe); (2) Natural Law (through which all natural creatures are governed, and known by man through his reason, so that he might govern himself); and (3) Human or Positive Law (man-made law, through which the Natural Law is applied to particular times and places).

After Aristotle, who identified excellence or superiority with completeness, St. Thomas regards Divine Law superior to Natural Law because it encompasses it. Similarly, Human or Positive Law, being a particular expression of Natural Law, is inferior in being merely a portion of Natural Law.

DIVINE LAW

NATURAL LAW

HUMAN LAW

It is in this manner that St. Thomas develops his hierarchy of Laws which places sacred, Divine Law above secular Human Law. And, since the Church interprets Divine Law, of which the government's Positive Law is merely an inferior part, the Church properly occupies a superior position to the State, even in worldly matters. The State with its Human Law is incomplete apart from Natural and Divine Law, which is understood only by the Church. This view justified the Medieval Church's intervention in earthly kingdoms. Of course, by "Church" St. Thomas means the ordained Roman Catholic clergy, the hierarchy of priests, Bishops, Cardinals and the Pope.

The State, therefore, remains separate but subordinate to the Church. Human Law for St. Thomas, is to make people good through discipline and education; it is to punish vice and encourage virtue. But as it can do neither without knowledge of ultimate truth in religion, the State must rely on the Church for much of the substance of its legislation and serves more as an instrument of carrying out God's plan on earth.

If a conflict appears between Human and Divine Laws, as between State and Church, the Divine and Ecclesiastical would naturally take precedence over the Human and governmental, as it encompasses and is superior to its parts. Hence, the Church supports subjects' obedience to their earthly rulers, so long as those governors do not violate the Almighty Ruler, as interpreted by the Church. If a subject receives conflicting commands from his State and the Church, St. Thomas insists he must follow the Church, which is higher than the State. And the Church will communicate its decisions to the subjects through the ordained, clerical hierarchy, the institutionalized Church. Justice, for St. Thomas Aquinas, resides in the proper ordering of the universal hierarchy, each element knowing its place and obeying its superior.

St. Thomas, after Aristotle, asserts that the form of government (e.g., monarchy, aristocracy, democracy) is of less significance than its justice (i.e., serving the common good and recognizing its place in the universal hierarchy); but, writing in the Middle Ages, he argued that Monarchy seemed to be the most "natural" regime.

The selections given here are from St. Thomas' greatest work, *The Summa Theologica,* and include descriptions of the various kinds of Law, as well as ways in which they interact in Property and Obedience. The original Thomist form of exposition, involving propositions, objections and replies, is not retained here; for the sake of brevity, only St. Thomas' replies are presented here.[1]

---

[1] These selections from *The Summa Theologica* are taken from *The Political Ideas of St. Thomas Aquinas,* edited by Dino Bigongiar, (New York: Hafner Press, 1981).

THE SUMMA THEOLOGICA

[First Part of the Second Part]

QUESTION 90

OF THE ESSENCE OF LAW

We have now to consider the extrinsic principles of acts. Now the extrinsic principle inclining to evil is the devil, of whose temptations we have spoken in the first Part (Q. 114). But the extrinsic principle moving to good is God, Who both instructs us by means of His law and assists us by His grace; wherefore in the first place we must speak of law; in the second place, of grace.

Concerning law, we must consider (1) law itself in general, (2) its parts. Concerning law in general three points offer themselves for our consideration: (1) its essence; (2) the different kinds of law; (3) the effects of law.

Under the first head there are four points of inquiry: (1) whether law is something pertaining to reason? (2) concerning the end of law; (3) its cause; (4) the promulgation of law.

It belongs to the law to command and to forbid. But it belongs to reason to command, as stated above. Therefore law is something pertaining to reason.

I answer that, Law is a rule and measure of acts whereby man is induced to act or is restrained from acting; for *lex* (law) is derived from *ligare* (to bind), because it binds one to act. Now the rule and measure of human acts is the reason, which is the first principle of human acts, as is evident from what has been stated above, since it belongs to the reason to direct to the end, which is the first principle in all matters of action, according to the Philosopher. Now that which is the principle in any genus is the rule and measure of that genus: for instance, unity in the genus of numbers, and the first movement in the genus of movements. Consequently it follows that law is something pertaining to reason.

Reply Obj. 1. Since law is a kind of rule and measure, it may be in something in two ways. First, as in that which measures and rules; and since this is proper to reason, it follows that, in this way, law is in the reason alone.–Secondly, as in that which is measured and ruled. In this way law is in all those things that are inclined to something by reason of some law, so that any inclination arising from a law may be called a law, not essentially but by participation as it were. And thus the inclination of the members to concupiscence is called "the law of the members."

Reply Obj. 2. Just as, in external action, we may consider the work and the work done–for instance, the work of building and the house built, so in the acts of reason we may consider the act itself of reason, i.e., to understand and to reason, and something produced by this act. With regard to the speculative reason, this is first of all the definition; secondly, the proposition; thirdly, the syllogism or argument. And since also the practical reason makes use of a syllogism in respect of the work to be done, as stated above and as the Philosopher teaches, hence we find in the practical reason something that holds the same position in regard to operations as, in the speculative intellect, the proposition holds in regard to conclusions. Suchlike universal propositions of the practical intellect that are directed to actions hae the nature of law. And these propositions are sometimes under our actual consideration, while sometimes they are retained in the reason by means of a habit.

Reply Obj. 3. Reason has its power of moving from the will, as stated above, for it is due to the fact that one wills the end that the reason issues its commands as regards things ordained to the end. But in order that the volition of what is commanded may have the nature of law, it needs to be in accord with some rule of reason. And in this sense is to be understood the saying that the will of the sovereign has the force of law; otherwise the sovereign's will would savor of lawlessness rather than of law.

I answer that, As stated above (A. 1), the law belongs to that which is a principle of human acts, because it is their rule and measure. Now as reason is a principle of human acts, so in reason itself there is something which is the principle in respect of all the rest; wherefore to this principle chiefly and mainly law must needs be referred.--Now the first principle in practical matters, which are the object of the practical reason, is the last end; and the last end of human life is bliss or happiness, as stated above. Consequently the law must needs regard principally the relationship to happiness. Moreover, since every part is ordained to the whole, as imperfect to perfect; and since one man is a part of the perfect community, the law must needs regard properly the relationship to unversal happiness. Wherefore the Philosopher, in the above definition of legal matters, mentions both happiness and the body politic, for he says that we call those legal matters *just,*"which are adapted to produce and preserve happiness and its parts for the body politic," since the state is a perfect community, as he says in *Politics i. 1.*

[Now, in every genus that thing which reaches the highest degree is the principle (cause) of the rest (in that genus), and these others are graded with respect to it. So fire, which possesses heat in the highest degree, is the cause of heat in mixed bodies], and these are said to be hot in so far as they have a share of fire. Consequently, since the law is chiefly ordained to the common good, any other precept in regard to some individual work must needs be devoid of the nature of a law, save in so far as it regards the common good. Therefore every law is ordained to the common good.

Reply Obj. 1. A command denotes an application of a law to matters regulated by the law. Now the order to the common good, at which the law aims, is applicable to particular ends. And in this way commands are given even concerning particular matters.

Reply Obj. 2. Actions are indeed concerned with particular matters, but those particular matters are referable to the common good, not as to a common genus or species, but as to a common final cause, according as the common good is said to be the common end.

Reply Obj. 3. Just as nothing stands firm with regard to the speculative reason except that which is traced back to the first indemonstrable principles, so nothing stands firm which regard to the practical reason unless it be directed to the last end which is the common good; and whatever stands to reason in this sense has the nature of a law.

WHETHER THE REASON OF ANY MAN IS COMPETENT TO MAKE LAWS?

I answer that, A law, properly speaking, regards first and foremost the order to the common good. Now to order anything to the common good belongs either to the whole people or to someone who is the viceregent of the whole people. And therefore the making of a law belongs either to the whole people or to a public personage who has care of the whole people, since in all other matters the directing of anything to the end concerns him to whom the end belongs.

Reply Obj. 1. As stated above (A. 1 *ad* 1), a law is in a person not only as in one that rules, but also by participation as in one that is ruled. In the latter way each one is a law to himself, in so far as he shares the direction that he receives from one who rules him. Hence the same text goes on, "who show the work of the law written in their hearts."

Reply Obj. 2. A private person cannot lead another to virtue efficaciously, for he can only advise, and if his advice be not taken, it has no coercive power, such as the law should have in order to prove an efficacious inducement to virtue, as the Philospher says. But this coercive power is vested in the whole people or in some public personage to whom it belongs to inflict penalties, as we shall state further on (Q. 92, A. 2 *ad 3*; II-II, Q. 64, A.3). Wherefore the framing of laws belongs to him alone.

Reply Obj. 3. As one man is a part of the household, so a household is a part of the state; and the state is a perfect community, according to *Politics* i. 1. And therefore, as the good of one man is not the last end, but is ordained to the common good, so, too, the good of one household is ordained to the good of a single state, which is a perfect community. Consequently he that governs a family can indeed make certain commands or ordinances, but not such as to have properly the force of law.

WHETHER PROMULGATION IS ESSENTIAL TO A LAW?

On the contrary, It is laid down in the *Decretals,* dist. 4, that "laws are established when they are promulgated."

I answer that, As stated above (A. 1), a law is imposed on others by way of a rule and measure. Now a rule or measure is imposed by being applied to those who are to be ruled and measured by it. Wherefore, in order that a law obtain the binding force which is proper to a law, it must needs be applied to the men who have to be ruled by it. Such application is made by its being notified to them by promulgation. Wherefore promulgation is necessary for the law to obtain its force.

Thus from the four preceding articles the definition of law may be gathered; and it is nothing else than an ordinance of reason for the common good, made by him who has care of the community, and promulgated.

Reply Obj. 1. The natural law is promulgated by the very fact that God instilled it into man's mind so as to be known by him naturally.

Reply Obj. 2. Those who are not present when a law is promulgated are bound to observe the law, in so far as it is notified or can be notified to them by others, after it has been promulgated.

Reply Obj. 3. The promulgation that takes place now extends to future time by reason of the durability of written characters, by which means it is continually promulgated. Hence Isidore says that "*lex* (law) is derived from *legere* (to read) because it is written."

QUESTION 91

OF THE VARIOUS KINDS OF LAW

Augustine says: "That Law which is the Supreme Reason cannot be understood to be otherwise than unchangeable and eternal."

I answer that, As stated above (Q. 90, A. 1 *ad 2*; AA. 3, 4), a law is nothing else but a dictate of practical reason emanating from the ruler who governs a perfect community. Now it is evident, granted that the world is ruled by divine providence, as was stated in the First Part, that the whole community of the universe is governed by divine reason. Wherefore the very Idea of the government of things in God the Ruler of the universe has the nature of a law. And since the divine reason's conception of things is not subject to time but is eternal, according to Proverbs viii. 23, therefore it is that this kind of law must be called eternal.

Reply Obj. 1. Those things that are not in themselves exist with God, inasmuch as they are foreknown and preordained by Him, according to Romans iv. 17, "Who calls those things that are not, as those that are." Accordingly the eternal concept of the divine law bears the character of an eternal law in so far as it is ordained by God to the government of things foreknown by Him.

Reply Obj. 2. Promulgation is made by word of mouth or in writing; and in both ways the eternal law is promulgated, because both the divine word and the writing of the Book of Life are eternal. But the promulgation cannot be from eternity on the part of the creature that hears or reads.

Reply Obj. 3. The law implies order to the end actively, in so far as it directs certain things to the end, but not passively–that is to say, the law itself is not ordained to the end–except accidentally, in a governor whose end is extrinsic to him, and to which end his law must needs be ordained. But the end of the divine government is God Himself, and His law is not distinct from Himself. Wherefore the eternal law is not ordained to another end.

WHETHER THERE IS IN US A NATURAL LAW?

On the contrary, A gloss on Romans ii. 14: "When the Gentiles, who have not the law, do by nature those things that are of the law," comments as follows: "Although they have no written law, yet they have the natural law, whereby each one knows, and is conscious of, what is good and what is evil."

I answer that, As stated above (Q. 90, A. 1 *ad 1*), law, being a rule and measure, can be in a person in two ways: in one way, as in him that rules and measures; in another way, as in that which is ruled and measured, since a thing is ruled and measured in so far as it partakes of the rule or measure. Wherefore, since all things subject to divine providence are ruled and measured by the eternal law, as was stated above (A. 1), it is evident that all things partake somewhat of the eternal law, in so far as, namely, from its being imprinted on them, they derive their respective inclinations to their proper acts and ends. Now among all others the rational creature is subject to divine providence in the most excellent way, in so far as it partakes of a share of providence, by being provident both for itself and for others. Wherefore it has a share of the eternal reason, whereby it has a natural inclination to its proper act and end: and this participation of the eternal law in the rational creature is called the natural law. Hence the Psalmist after saying: "Offer up the sacrifice of justice," as though someone asked what the works of justice are, adds: "Many say, Who showeth us good things?" in answer to which question he says: "The light of Thy countenance, O Lord, is signed upon us"; thus implying that the light of natural reason, whereby we discern what is good and what is evil, which is the function of the natural law, is nothing else than an imprint on us of the divine light. It is therefore evident that the natural law is nothing else than the rational creature's participation of the eternal law.

Reply Obj. 1. This argument would hold if the natural law were something different from the eternal law, whereas it is nothing but a participation thereof, as stated above.

Reply Obj. 2. Every act of reason and will in us is based on that which is according to nature, as stated above; for every act of reasoning is based on principles that are known naturally, and every act of appetite in respect of the means is derived from the natural appetite in respect of the last end. Accordingly the first direction of our acts to their end must needs be in virtue of the natural law.

Reply Obj. 3. Even irrational animals partake in their own way of the eternal reason, just as the rational creature does. But because the rational creature partakes thereof in an intellectual and rational manner, therefore the participation of the eternal law in the rational creature is properly called a law, since a law is something pertaining to reason, as stated above (Q. 90, A. 1). Irrational creatures, however, do not partake thereof in a rational manner, wherefore there is no participation of the eternal law in them, except by way of similitude.

WHETHER THERE IS A HUMAN LAW?

Augustine distinguishes two kinds of law–the one eternal; the other temporal, which he calls human.

I answer that, As stated above (Q. 90, A. 1, *ad 2*), a law is a dictate of the practical reason. Now it is to be observed that the same procedure takes place in the practical and in the speculative reason, for each proceeds from principles to conclusions, as stated above. Accordingly we conclude that just as, in the speculative reason, from naturally known indemonstrable principles we draw the conclusions of the various sciences, the knowledge of which is not imparted to us by nature, but acquired by the efforts of reason; so, too, it is from the precepts of the natural law, as from general and indemonstrable principles, that the human reason needs to proceed to the more particular determination of certain matters. These particular determinations, devised by human reason, are called human laws, provided the other essential conditions of law be observed, as stated above (Q. 90, AA. 2, 3, 4). Wherefore Cicero says in his *Rhetoric* that "justice has its source in nature; thence certain things came into custom by reason of their utility; afterward these things which emanated from nature and were approved by custom were sanctioned by fear and reverence for the law."

Reply Obj. 1. The human reason cannot have a full participation of the dictate of the divine reason but according to its own mode, and imperfectly. Consequently, as on the part of the speculative reason, by a natural participation of divine wisdom, there is in us the knowledge of certain general principles, but not proper knowledge of each single truth, such as that contained in the divine wisdom; so, too, on the part of the practical reason man has a natural participation of the eternal law, according to certain general principles, but not as regards the particular determinations of individual cases, which are, however, contained in the eternal law. [Hence the necessity that human reason proceed to certain particular sanctions of law.]

Reply Obj. 2. Human reason is not of itself the rule of things, but the principles impressed on it by nature are general rules and measures of all things relating to human conduct, whereof the natural reason is the rule and measure, although it is not the measure of things that are from nature.

Reply Obj. 3. The practical reason is concerned with practical matters, which are singular and contingent, but not with necessary things, with which the speculative reason is concerned. Wherefore human laws cannot have that inerrancy that belongs to the demonstrated conclusions of sciences. Nor is it necessary for every measure to be altogether unerring and certain, but according as it is possible in its own particular genus.

WHETHER THERE WAS ANY NEED FOR A DIVINE LAW?

I answer that, Besides the natural and the human law it was necessary for the directing of human conduct to have a divine law. And this for four reasons. First, because it is by law that man is directed how to perform his proper acts in view of his last end. And indeed, if man were ordained to no other end than that which is proportionate to his natural faculty, there would be no need for man to have any further direction on the part of his reason besides the natural law and human law which is derived from it. But since man is ordained to an end of eternal happiness which is inproportionate to man's natural faculty, as stated above, therefore it was necessary that, besides the natural and the human law, man should be directed to his end by a law given by God.

Secondly, because, on account of the uncertainty of human judgment, especially on contingent and particular matters, different people form different judgments on human acts; whence also different and contrary laws result. In order, therefore, that man may know without any doubt what he ought to do and what he ought to avoid, it was necessary for man to be directed in his proper acts by a law given by God, for it is certain that such a law cannot err.

Thirdly, because man can make laws in those matters of which he is competent to judge. But man is not competent to judge of interior movements that are hidden, but only of exterior acts which appear; and yet for the perfection of virtue it is necessary for man to conduct himself aright in both kinds of acts. Consequently human law could not sufficiently curb and direct interior acts, and it was necessary for this purpose that a divine law should supervene.

Fourthly, because, as Augustine says, human law cannot punish or forbid all evil deeds; since while aiming at doing away with all evils, it would do away with many good things, and would hinder the advance of the common good, which is necessary for human intercourse. In order, therefore, that no evil might remain unforbidden and unpunished, it was necessary for the divine law to supervene, whereby all sins are forbidden.

And these four causes are touched upon in Psalm cxviii. 8, where it is said: "The law of the Lord is unspotted," i.e., allowing no foulness of sin; "converting souls," because it directs not only exterior but also interior acts; "the testimony of the Lord is faithful," because of the certainty of what is true and right; "giving wisdom to little ones," by directing man to an end supernatural and divine.

Reply Obj. 1. By natural law the eternal law is participated in proportionately to the capacity of human nature. But to his supernatural end man needs to be directed in a yet higher way. Hence the additional law given by God, whereby man shares more perfectly in the eternal law.

QUESTION 92

OF THE EFFECTS OF LAW

WHETHER AN EFFECT OF LAW IS TO MAKE MEN GOOD?

The Philosopher says that the 'intention of every lawgiver is to make good citizens."

I answer that, As stated above (Q. 90, A. 1 *ad 2*; AA. 3, 4), a law is nothing else than a dictate of reason in the ruler by [which] his subjects are governed. Now the virtue of any subordinate thing consists in its being well subordinated to that by which it is regulated; thus we see that the virtue of the irascible and concupiscible faculties consist in their being obedient to reason; and accordingly "the virtue of every subject consists in his being well subjected to his ruler," as the Philosopher says. But every law aims at being obeyed by those who are subject to it. Consequently it is evident that the proper effect of law is to lead its subjects to their proper virtue; and since virtue is "that which makes its subject good," it follows that the proper effect of law is to make those to whom it is given good, either simply or in some particular respect. For if the intention of the lawgiver is fixed on true good, which is the common good regulated according to divine justice, it follows that the effect of the law is to make men good simply. If, however, the intention of the lawgiver is fixed on that which is not simply good, but useful or pleasurable to himself, or in opposition to divine justice, then the law does not make men good simply, but in respect to that particular government. In this way good is found even in things that are bad of themselves: thus a man is called a good robber because he works in a way that is adapted to his end.

WHETHER THE NATURAL LAW IS THE SAME IN ALL MEN?

I answer that, As stated above (AA. 2, 3), to the natural law belong those things to which a man is inclined naturally; [and among these it is a special property of man to be inclined to act according to reason. Now reason proceeds from what is common, or general, to what is proper, or special, as stated in *Physics* i. But there is a difference in this regard between the speculative reason and practical reason. The speculative reason is concerned primarily with what is necessary, that is, with those things which cannot be other than they are; and therefore, in the case of speculative reason, both the common principles and the special conclusions are necessarily true. In the case of the practical reason, on the other hand, which is concerned with contingent matters, such as human actions, even though there be some necessary truth in the common principles, yet the more we descend to what is proper and peculiar, the more deviations we find. Therefore in speculative matters the same truth holds among all men both as to principles and as to conclusions, even though all men do not discern this truth in the conclusions but only in those principles which are called axiomatic notions. In active matters, on the other hand, all men do not hold to the same truth or practical rectitude in what is peculiar and proper, but only in what is common. And even among those who hold to the same line of rectitude in proper and peculiar matters, such rectitude is not equally known to all. It is clear, therefore, that as far as common principles are concerned in the case of speculative as well as of practical reason the same truth and the same rectitude exists among all and is equally known to all. In the case, however, of the proper or peculiar conclusions of speculative reason, the same truth obtains among all, even though it is not known equally to all. For it is true among all men that the three angles of a triangle are equal to two right angles, even though not all men know this. But in the case of the proper or peculiar conclusions of the practical reason there is neither the same truth and rectitude among all men, nor, where it does exist, is it equally known to all. Thus it is true and right among all men that action proceed in accordance with reason. From this principle there follows as a proper conclusion that deposits should be restored to the owner. This conclusion is indeed true in the majority of cases. But a case may possibly arise in which such restitution is harmful and consequently contrary to reason; so, for example, if things deposited were claimed so that they might be used against the fatherland. This uncertainty increases the more particular the cases become: as, for example, if it were laid down that the restitution should take place in a certain way, with certain *definite* precautions; for as the limiting particular conditions become more numerous, so do the possibilities decrease that render the principle normally applicable, with the result that neither the restitution nor the failure to do so can be rigorously presented as right.

It follows therefore that natural law in its first common principles is the same among all men, both as to validity and recognition (something is right for all and is so by all recognized). But as to certain proper or derived norms, which are, as it were, conclusions of these common principles, they are valid and are so recognized by all men only in the majority of cases. For in special cases they may prove defective both as to validity because of certain particular impediments (just as things of nature in the sphere of generation and corruption prove to be defective because of impediments) and also as to recognition. And this because some men have a reason that has been distorted by passion, or by evil habits, or by bad natural relations. Such was the case among the ancient Germans, who failed to recognize theft as contrary to justice, as Julius Caesar relates, even though it is an explicit violation of natural law.]

QUESTION 95

OF HUMAN LAW

WHETHER IT WAS USEFUL FOR LAWS TO BE FRAMED BY MEN?

I answer that, As stated above (Q. 63, A. 1; Q. 94, A. 3), man has a natural aptitude for virtue, but the perfection of virtue must be acquired by man by means of some kind of training. Thus we observe that man is helped by industry in his necessities, for instance, in food and clothing. Certain beginnings of these he has from nature, viz., his reason and his hands, but he has not the full complement, as other animals have to whom nature has given sufficiency of clothing and food. Now it is difficult to see how man could suffice for himself in the matter of this training, since the perfection of virtue consists chiefly in withdrawing man from undue pleasures, to which above all man is inclined, and especially the young, who are more capable of being trained. Consequently a man needs to receive this training from another, whereby to arrive at the perfection of virtue. And as to those young people who are inclined to acts of virtue, by their good natural disposition, or by custom, or rather by the gift of God, paternal training suffices, which is by admonitions. But since some are found to be depraved and prone to vice, and not easily amenable to words, it was necessary for such to be restrained from evil by force and fear, in order that, at least, they might desist from evil-doing and leave others in peace, and that they themselves, by being habituated in this way, might be brought to do willingly what hitherto they did from fear, and thus become virtuous. Now this kind of training which compels through fear of punishment is the discipline of laws. Therefore, in order that man might have peace and virtue, it was necessary for laws to be framed, for, as the Philosopher says, "as man is the most noble of animals if he be perfect in virtue, so is he the lowest of all if he be severed from law and righteousness"; because man can use his reason to devise means of satisfying his lusts and evil passions, which other animals are unable to do.

Reply Obj. 1. Men who are well disposed are led willingly to virtue by being admonished better than by coercion, but men who are evilly disposed are not led to virtue unless they are compelled.

Reply Obj. 2. As the Philosopher says, "It is better that all things be regulated by law than left to be decided by judges"; and this for three reasons. First, because it is easier to find a few wise men competent to frame right laws than to find the many who would be necessary to judge aright of each single case. Secondly, because those who make laws consider long beforehand what laws to make, whereas judgment on each single case has to be pronounced as soon as it arises; and it is easier for man to see what is right by taking many instances into consideration than by considering one solitary fact. Thirdly, because lawgivers judge in the abstract and of future events, whereas those who sit in judgment judge of things present, toward which they are affected by love, hatred, or some kind of cupidity; wherefore their judgment is perverted.

Since then the animated justice of the judge is not found in every man, and since it can be deflected, therefore it was necessary, whenever possible, for the law to determine how to judge, and for very few matters to be left to the decision of men.

Reply Obj. 3. Certain individual facts which cannot be covered by the law "have necessarily to be committed to judges," as the Philosopher says in the same passage; for instance, "concerning something that has happened or not happened," and the like.

WHETHER EVERY HUMAN LAW IS DERIVED FROM THE NATURAL LAW?

Cicero says: "Things which emanated from nature and were approved by custom were sanctioned by fear and reverence for the laws."

I answer that, As Augustine says, "that which is not just seems to be no law at all"; wherefore the force of a law depends on the extent of its justice. Now in human affairs a thing is said to be just from being right according to the rule of reason. But the first rule of reason is the law of nature, as is clear from what has been stated above (Q. 91, A. 2 *ad 2*). Consequently, every human law has just so much of the nature of law as it is derived from the law of nature. But if in any point it deflects from the law of nature, it is no longer a law but a perversion of law.

But it must be noted that something may be derived from the natural law in two ways: first, as a conclusion from premises; secondly, by way of determination of certain generalities. The first way is like to that by which, in the sciences, demonstrated conclusions are drawn from the principles, while the second mode is likened to that whereby, in the arts, general forms are particularized as to details: thus the craftsman needs to determine the general form of a house to some particular shape. Some things are therefore derived from the general principles of the natural law by way of conclusions, e.g., that "one must not kill" may be derived as a conclusion from the principle that "one should do harm to no man"; while some are derived therefrom by way of determination, e.g., the law of nature has it that the evildoer should be punished; but that he be punished in this or that way is not directly by natural law but is a derived determination of it.

Accordingly, both modes of derivation are found in the human law. But those things which are derived in the first way are contained in human law, not as emanating therefrom exclusively, but having some force from the natural law also. But those things which are derived in the second way have no other force than that of human law.

QUESTION 96

OF THE POWER OF HUMAN LAW

WHETHER HUMAN LAW SHOULD BE FRAMED FOR THE COMMUNITY RATHER THAN FOR THE INDIVIDUAL?

The Jurist says that "laws should be made to suit the majority of instances; and they are not framed according to what may possibly happen in an individual case."

I answer that, Whatever is for an end should be proportionate to that end. Now the end of law is the common good; because, as Isidore says, "law should be framed, not for any private benefit, but for the common good of all the citizens." Hence human laws should be proportionate to the common good. Now the common good comprises many things. Wherefore law should take account of many things, as to persons, as to [activities], and as to times; because the community of the state is composed of many persons and its good is procured by many actions; nor is it established to endure for only a short time, but to last for all time by the citizens succeeding one another, as Augustine says.

WHETHER IT BELONGS TO HUMAN LAW TO REPRESS ALL VICES?

I answer that, As stated above (Q. 90, AA. 1, 2), law is framed as a rule or measure of human acts. Now a measure should be homogeneous with that which it measures, as stated in *Metaphysics* x. text. 3, 4, since different things are measured by different measures. Wherefore laws imposed on men should also be in keeping with their condition, for, as Isidore says, law should be "possible both according to nature, and according to the customs of the country." Now possibility or faculty of action is due to an interior habit or disposition, since the same thing is not possible to one who has not a virtuous habit as is possible to one who has. Thus the same is not possible to a child as to a full-grown man; for which reason the law for children is not the same as for adults, since many things are permitted to children which in an adult are punished by law or at any rate are open to blame. In like manner many things are permissible to men not perfect in virtue which would be intolerable in a virtuous man.

Now human law is framed for a number of human beings, the majority of whom are not perfect in virtue. Wherefore human laws do not forbid all vices from which the virtuous abstain, but only the more grievous vices from which it is possible for the majority to abstain; and chiefly those that are to the hurt of others, without the prohibition of which human society could not be maintained: thus human law prohibits murder, theft, and suchlike.

WHETHER HUMAN LAW PRESCRIBES ACTS OF ALL THE VIRTUES?

The Philosopher says that the law "prescribes the performance of the acts of a brave man . . . and the acts of the temperate man . . . and the acts of the meek man; and in like manner as regards the other virtues and vices, prescribing the former, forbidding the latter."

I answer that, The species of virtues are distinguished by their objects, as explained above. Now all the objects of virtues can be referred either to the private good of an individual or to the common good of the multitude: thus matters of fortitude may be achieved either for the safety of the state or for upholding the rights of a friend, and in like manner with the other virtues. But law, as stated above (Q. 90, A. 2), is ordained to the common good. Wherefore there is no virtue whose acts cannot be prescribed by the law. Nevertheless human law does not prescribe concerning all the acts of every virtue, but only in regard to those that are ordainable to the common good–either immediately, as when certain things are done directly for the common good, or mediately, as when a lawgiver prescribes certain things pertaining to [proper instruction] whereby the citizens are directed in the upholding of the common good of justice and peace.

QUESTION 66

OF THEFT AND ROBBERY

WHETHER IT IS NATURAL FOR MAN TO POSSESS EXTERNAL THINGS?

I answer that, External things can be considered in two ways. First, as regards their nature, and this is not subject to the power of man, but only to the power of God, Whose mere will all things obey. Secondly, as regards their use, and in this way man has a natural dominion over external things, because, by his reason and will, he is able to use them for his own profit, as they were made on his account, for the imperfect is always for the sake of the perfect, as stated above. It is by this argument that the Philosopher proves that the possession of external things is natural to man. Moreover, this natural dominion of man over other creatures, which is competent to man in respect of his reason, wherein God's image resides, is shown forth in man's creation by the words: "Let Us make man to Our image and likeness, and let him have dominion over the fishes of the sea," etc.

WHETHER IT IS LAWFUL FOR A MAN TO POSSESS A THING AS HIS OWN?

Augustine says: "The 'Apostolici' are those who with extreme arrogance have given themselves that name, because they do not admit into their communion persons who are married or possess anything of their own, such as both monks and clerics who in considerable number are to be found in the Catholic Church." Now the reason why these people are heretics is because, severing themselves from the Church, they think that those who enjoy the use of the above things, which they themselves lack, have no hope of salvation. Therefore it is erroneous to maintain that it is unlawful for a man to possess property.

I answer that, Two things are competent to man in respect of exterior things. One is the power to procure and dispense them, and in this regard it is lawful for man to possess property. Moreover this is necessary to human life for three reasons. First, because every man is more careful to procure what is for himself alone than that which is common to many or to all; since each one would shirk the labor and leave to another that which concerns the community, as happens where there is a great number of servants. Secondly, because human affairs are conducted in more orderly fashion if each man is charged with taking care of some particular thing himself, whereas there would be confusion if everyone had to look after any one thing indeterminately. Thirdly, because a more peaceful state is insured to man if each one is contented with his own. Hence it is to be observed that quarrels arise more frequently where there is no division of the things possessed.

The second thing that is competent to man with regard to external things is their use. In this respect man ought to possess external things, not as his own, but as common, so that, to wit, he is ready to communicate them to others in their need. Hence the Apostle says: "Charge the rich of this world . . . to give easily, to communicate to others," etc.

WHETHER IT IS LAWFUL TO STEAL THROUGH STRESS OF NEED

In cases of need all things are common property, so that there would seem to be no sin in taking another's property, for need has made it common.

I answer that, Things which are of human right cannot derogate from natural right or divine right. Now, according to the natural order established by divine providence, inferior things are ordained for the purpose of succoring man's needs by their means. Wherefore the division and appropriation of things which are based on human law do not preclude the fact that man's needs have to be remedied by means of these very things. Hence whatever certain people have in superabundance is due, by natural law, to the purpose of succoring the poor. For this reason Ambrose says, and his words are embodies in the *Decretals:* "It is the hungry man's bread that you withhold, the naked man's cloak that you store away, the money that you bury in the earth is the price of the poor man's ransom and freedom."

Since, however, there are many who are in need, while it is impossible for all to be succored by means of the same thing, each one is entrusted with the stewardship of his own things, so that out of them he may come to the aid of those who are in need. Nevertheless, if the need be so manifest and urgent that it is evident that the present need must be remedied by whatever means be at hand (for instance when a person is in some imminent danger, and there is no other possible remedy), then it is lawful for a man to succor his own need by means of another's property, by taking it either openly or secretly; nor is this, properly speaking, theft or robbery.

QUESTION 104

OF OBEDIENCE

WHETHER ONE MAN IS BOUND TO OBEY ANOTHER?

It is prescribed: "Obey your prelates and be subject to them."

I answer that, Just as the actions of natural things proceed from natural powers, so do human actions proceed from the human will. In natural things it behooved the higher to move the lower to their actions by the excellence of the natural power bestowed on them by God; and so in human affairs also the higher must move the lower by their will in virtue of a divinely established authority. Now to move by reason and will is to command. Wherefore just as in virtue of the divinely established natural order the lower natural things need to be subject to the movement of the higher, so too in human affairs, in virtue of the order of natural and divine law, inferiors are bound to obey their superiors.

Reply Obj. 1. God left man in the hand of his own counsel, not as though it were lawful to him to do whatever he will, but because, unlike irrational creatures, he is not compelled by natural necessity to do what he ought to do but is left the free choice proceeding from his own counsel. And just as he has to proceed on his own counsel in doing other things, so too has he in the point of obeying his superiors. For Gregory says: "When we humbly give way to another's voice, we overcome ourselves in our own hearts."

Reply Obj. 2. The will of God is the first rule whereby all rational wills are regulated; and to this rule one will approaches more than another, according to a divinely appointed order. Hence the will of the one man who issues a command may be as a second rule to the will of this other man who obeys him.

Reply Obj. 3. A thing may be deemed gratuitous in two ways. In one way on the part of the deed itself, because, to wit, one is not bound to do it; in another way on the part of the doer, because he does it of his own free will. Now a deed is rendered virtuous, praiseworthy, and meritorious chiefly according as it proceeds from the will. Wherefore although obedience be a duty, if one obey with a prompt will one's merit is not for that reason diminished, especially before God, Who sees not only the outward deed but also the inward deed.

WHETHER GOD OUGHT TO BE OBEYED IN ALL THINGS?

It is written: "All things that the Lord hath spoken we will do, and we will be obedient."

I answer that, As stated above (A. 1), he who obeys is moved by the command of the person he obeys, just as natural things are moved by their motive causes. Now just as God is the first mover of all things that are moved naturally, so too is He the first mover of all wills, as shown above. Therefore just as all natural things are subject to the divine motion by a natural necessity, so too all wills, by a kind of necessity of justice, are bound to obey the divine command.

Reply Obj. 1. Our Lord in telling the blind men to conceal the miracle had no intention of binding them with the force of a divine precept, but, as Gregory says, "gave an example to His servants who follow Him, that they might wish to hide their virtue and yet that it should be proclaimed against their will, in order that others might profit by their example."

Reply Obj. 2. Even as God does nothing contrary to nature (since "the nature of a thing is what God does therein," according to a gloss on Romans xi) and yet does certain things contrary to the wonted course of nature, so too God can command nothing contrary to virtue, since virtue and rectitude of human will consist chiefly in conformity with God's will and obedience to His command, although it be contrary to the wonted mode of virtue. Acordingly, then, the command given to Abraham to slay his innocent son was not contrary to justice, since God is the author of life and death. Nor again was it contrary to justice that He commanded the Jews to take things belonging to the Egyptians, because all things are His, and He gives them to whom He will. Nor was it contrary to chastity that Osee was commanded to take an adulteress, because God Himself is the ordainer of human generation, and the right manner of intercourse with woman is that which He appoints. Hence it is evident that the persons aforesaid did not sin, neither by obeying God nor by willing to obey Him.

Reply Obj. 3. Though man is not always bound to will what God wills, yet he is always bound to will what God wills him to will. This comes to man's knowledge chiefly through God's command, wherefore man is bound to obey God's commands in all things.

WHETHER SUBJECTS ARE BOUND TO OBEY THEIR SUPERIORS IN ALL THINGS?

It is written: "We ought to obey God rather than men." Now sometimes the things commanded by a superior are against God. Therefore superiors are not to be obeyed in all things.

I answer that, As stated above (AA. 1, 4), he who obeys is moved at the bidding of the person who commands him by a certain necessity of justice, even as a natural thing is moved through the power of its mover by a natural necessity. That a natural thing be not moved by its mover may happen in two ways. First on account of a hindrance arising from the stronger power of some other mover; thus wood is not burned by fire if a stronger force of water intervene. Secondly, through lack of order in the movable with regard to its mover, since, though it is subject to the latter's action in one respect, yet it is not subject thereto in every respect. Thus a humor is sometimes subject to the action of heat as regards being heated, but not as regards being dried up or consumed. In like manner there are two reasons for which a subject may not be bound to obey his superior in all things. First on account of the command of a higher power. For as a gloss says on Romans xiii. 2, "They that resist the power, resist the ordinance of God. If a commissioner issue an order, are you to comply if it is contrary to the bidding of the proconsul? Again if the proconsul command one thing and the emperor another, will you hesitate to disregard the former and serve the latter? Therefore if the emperor commands one thing and God another, you must disregard the former and obey God." Secondly, a subject is not bound to obey his superior if the latter command him to do something wherein he is not subject to him. For Seneca says: "It is wrong to suppose that slavery falls upon the whole man; for the better part of him is excepted. His body is subjected and assigned to his master, but his soul is his own." Consequently in matters touching the internal movement of the will man is not bound to obey his fellow man, but God alone.

Nevertheless man is bound to obey his fellow man in things that have to be done externally by means of the body; and yet, since by nature all men are equal, he is not bound to obey another man in matters touching the nature of the body, for instance, in those relating to the support of his body or the begetting of his children. Wherefore servants are not bound to obey their masters, nor children their parents, in the question of contracting marriage or of remaining in the state of virginity or the like. But in matters concerning the disposal of actions and human affairs a subject is bound to obey his superior within the sphere of his authority; for instance, a soldier must obey his general in matters relating to war, a servant his master in matters touching the execution of the duties of his service, a son his father in matters relating to the conduct of his life and the care of the household, and so forth.

WHETHER CHRISTIANS ARE BOUND TO OBEY THE SECULAR POWER?

It is written: "Admonish them to be subject to princes and powers"; and: "Be ye subject . . . to every human creature for God's sake, whether it be to the king as excelling or to governors as sent by him."

I answer that, Faith in Christ is the origin and cause of justice, according to Romans iii. 22: "The justice of God by faith of Jesus Christ"; wherefore faith in Christ does not void the order of justice, but strengthens it. Now the order of justice requires that subjects obey their superiors, else the stability of human affairs would cease. Hence faith in Christ does not excuse the faithful from the obligation of obeying secular princes.

Reply Obj. 1. As stated above (A. 5), the subjection whereby one man is bound to another regards the body, not the soul, which retains its liberty. Now, in this state of life we are freed by the grace of Christ from defects of the soul, but not from defects of the body, as the Apostle declares by saying of himself that in his mind he served the law of God, but in his flesh the law of sin. Wherefore those that are made children of God by grace are free from the spiritual bondage of sin, but not from the bodily bondage, whereby they are held bound to earthly masters, as a gloss observes on I Timothy vi. 1, "Whosoever are servants under the yoke," etc.

Reply Obj. 2. The Old law was a figure of the New Testament, and therefore it had to cease on the advent of truth. And the comparison with human law does not stand, because thnereby one man is subject to another. Yet man is bound by divine law to obey his fellow man.

Reply Obj. 3. Man is bound to obey secular princes in so far as this is required by the order of justice. Wherefore if the prince's authority is not just but usurped, or if he commands what is unjust, his subjects are not bound to obey him, except perhaps accidentally, in order to avoid scandal or danger.

CHAPTER III   Separation of Church and State

MARTIN LUTHER

Martin Luther

INTRODUCTION

Martin Luther (1483-1546) was a German Theologian and a leading figure of the Protestant Reformation. Son of a miner, he was ordained a Roman Catholic priest in 1507. He studied and became Professor of Scripture at the recently founded University of Wittenberg. Luther rebelled against the Catholic Church over the practice of selling Indulgences, over which he nailed his famous 95 Theses to the Church door at Wittenberg. After lengthy disputes with the Church authorities over doctrine, Luther was excommunicated in 1521, thereafter living under the protection of Frederick III, a German Prince.

Luther accomplished the most radical change in Christian political theory (up to this time dominated by St. Augustine and St. Thomas Aquinas) by, first, redefining the "Two Cities" or "Two Kingdoms," and then reversing the hierarchy of Church and State, so that secular governments have authority over the Church.

Luther begins this Reformation by tearing down the Catholic hierarchy through his concept of "The priesthood of all believers." In it, all Christians are equally members of a spiritual priesthood, attained through faith nurtured by the Word of God. Hence, Luther's attack on the separate priesthood mediating the faithful's relation to God and his encouragement of the individual's direct communion with God through prayer and reading of Scripture. Luther's translation of the Bible from the Latin to the vernacular German, along with the development of the printing press furthered this last doctrine.

Along with keeping individual believers from the Word of God, Luther accused the Catholic Church hierarchy of interfering with the duties of temporal rulers.

Making a rather strict separation of body and soul, faith and works, Luther proceeds to make a strict separation between Church and State. According to this view, the Church is primarily concerned with men's spiritual lives, cultivating their faith and preparing their souls for the hereafter. The State handles matters of this world, primarily through discipline and punishment of the body, training and controlling man's sinful propensities with "The Sword." The State, for Luther, is a "hangman."

As all men (clergy and laity alike) are equal through the "priesthood of all believers," there is no separate Church institution (representing the City of God and standing against the government institutions) apart from all Christian citizens. And, because all citizens are subject to the jurisdiction of the State, the Church (the priesthood of all believers) is also under the governance of the State. The Church, therefore, as Luther says in one of the following essays, "just like all of us, shall be made subject to the sword."

Because the State governs matters pertaining to this world, the Church does not become involved with politics, as politics have to do with the body and the Church is concerned with the soul. Hence, the Church, for Luther, is not to advise its parishioners on matters of politics, except to obey the State in all matters pertaining to this world. The Church does not stand against the State, measuring it against the City of God or Divine Law. If a conflict should occur between the State's command and God's law, it will occur in the mind or heart of the individual believer *vis-a-vis* the secular authority. If there is such a conflict between the Christian's conscience (as reflective of God's law) and the State's command, Luther says the believer should follow God's law rather than man's, but only if he is certain that the State's command violates God's law. If the individual Christian has any doubt as to the injustice of the State's command, Luther recommends obedience to the State and assures the believer that if he is not absolutely certain of its injustice, his soul will be safe.

Thus, Luther's arguments for "the priesthood of all believers", justification by faith (over bodily works) and individual salvation through Scripture, led to the tearing down of the institutionalized Roman Catholic Church, the elevation of the State (in all matters pertaining to this world, including the Church) and the removal, thereby, of organized religion from politics. These ideas influenced many Protestant churches' views on the relation of Church and State and laid the theoretical groundwork for the formal separation of religion and politics in modern society. However, as seen in the next section, Luther's views on Church and State were greatly modified by the other leading Reformation theologian, John Calvin.

The following selections include three of Luther's most famous political essays: "The Freedom of a Christian" (1520); "To the Christian Nobility of the German Nation . . . ." (1520); and "Temporal Authority: To What Extent It Should Be Obeyed" (1523). In addition to the radical Protestant content of these pamphlets, they are notable for their democratic tone and evangelical style.[1]

---

[1] These writings are drawn from *Luther: Selected Political Writings*, edited by J. M. Porter (Philadelphia: Fortress Press, 1974).

THE FREEDOM OF A CHRISTIAN

After posting the *Ninety-five Theses* in 1517, the resultant controversy forced Luther into a clear attack on the whole Roman ecclesiastical system and dogma. A threat of excommunication was made in the bull, *Exsurge Domino,* of 15 June 1520. *The Freedom of a Christian,*published in early November, 1520, was among Luther's final efforts to achieve reconciliation with Rome. It was sent with an open letter to Pope Leo X "as a token of peace and good hope." The reaction of the pope is not known. This short essay provides the most eloquent and concise statement of Luther's faith. The text below is from LW 31, 333-77 passim.

To make the way smoother for the unlearned–for only them do I serve–I shall set down the following two propositions concerning the freedom and the bondage of the spirit:

A Christian is a perfectly free lord of all, subject to none.

A Christian is a perfectly dutiful servant of all, subject to all.

These two theses seem to contradict each other. If, however, they should be found to fit together they would serve our purpose beautifully. Both are Paul's own statements, who says in I Cor. 9 [:19], "For though I am free from all men, I have made myself a slave to all," and in Rom. 14 [:8], "Owe no one anything, except to love one another." Love by its very nature is ready to serve and be subject to him who is loved. So Christ, although he was Lord of all, was "born of woman, born under the law" [Gal. 4:4], and therefore was at the same time a free man and a servant, "in the form of God" and "of a servant" [Phil. 2:6-7].

Let us start, however, with something more remote from our subject, but more obvious. Man has a twofold nature, a spiritual and a bodily one. According to the spiritual nature, which men refer to as the soul, he is called a spiritual, inner, or new man. According to the bodily nature, which men refer to as flesh, he is called a carnal, outward, or old man, of whom the APostle writes in II Cor. 4 [:16], "Though our outer nature is wasting away, our inner nature is being renewed every day." Because of this diversity of nature the Scriptures assert contradictory things concerning the same man, since these two men in the same man contradict each other, "for the desires of the flesh are against the Spirit, and the desires of the spirit are against the flesh," according to Gal. 5 [:17].

First, let us consider the inner man to see how a righteous, free, and pious

Christian, that is, a spiritual, new, and inner man, becomes what he is. It is evident that no external thing has any influence in producing Christian righteousness or freedom, or in producing unrighteousness or servitude. A simple argument will furnish the proof of this statement. What can it profit the soul if the body is well, free, and active, and eats, drinks, and does as it pleases? For in these respects even the most godless slaves of vice may prosper. On the other hand, how will poor health or imprisonment or hunger or thirst or any other external misfortune harm the soul? Even the most godly men, and those who are free because of clear consciences, are afflicted with these things. None of these things touch either the freedom or the servitude of the soul. It does not help the soul if the body is adorned with the sacred robes of priests or dwells in sacred places or is occupied with sacred duties or prays, fasts, abstains from certain kinds of good, or does any work that can be done by the body and in the body. The righteousness and the freedom of the soul require something far different since the things which have been mentioned could be done by any wicked person. Such works produce nothing but hypocrites. On the other hand, it will not harm the soul if the body is clothed in secular dress, dwells in unconsecrated places, eats and drinks as others do, does not pray aloud, and neglects to do all the above-mentioned things which hypocrites can do.

Furthermore, to put aside all kinds of works, even contemplation, meditation, and all that the soul can do, does not help. One thing, and only one thing, is necessary for Christian life, righteousness, and freedom. That one thing is the most holy Word of God, the gospel of Christ, as Christ says, John 11 [:25], "I am the resurrection and the life; he who believes in me, though he die, yet shall he live"; and John 8 [:36], "So if the Son makes you free, you will be free indeed"; and Matt. 4 [:4], "Man shall not live by bread alone, but by every word that proceeds from the mouth of God." Let us then consider it certain and firmly established that the soul can do without anything except the Word of God and that where the Word of God is missing there is no help at all for the soul. If it has the Word of God it is rich and lacks nothing since it is the Word of life, truth, light, peace, righteousness, salvation, joy, liberty, wisdom, power, grace, glory, and of every incalculable blessing. This is why the prophet in the entire Psalm [119] and in many other places yearns and sighs for the Word of God and uses so many names to describe it.

On the other hand, there is no more terrible disaster with which the wrath of God can afflict men than a famine of the hearing of his Word, as he says in Amos [8:11]. Likewise there is no greater mercy than when he sends forth his word, as we read in Psalm 107 [:20]; "He sent forth his word, and healed them, and delivered them from destruction." Nor was Christ sent into the world for any other ministry except that of the Word. Moreover, the entire spiritual estate–all the apostles, bishops, and priests–has been called and instituted only for the ministry of the Word.

You may ask, "What then is the Word of God, and how shall it be used, since there are so many words of God?" I answer: The Apostle explains this in Romans 1. The Word is the gospel of God concerning his Son, who was made flesh, suffered, rose from the dead, and was glorified through the Spirit who sanctifies. To preach Christ means to feed the soul, make it righteous, set it free, and save it, provided it believes the preaching. Faith alone is the saving and efficacious use of the Word of God, according to Rom. 10 [:9]: "If you confess with your lips that Jesus is Lord and believe in your heart that God raised him from the dead, you will be saved." Furthermore, "Christ is the end of the law, that every one who has faith may be justified" [Rom. 10:4]. Again, in Rom. 1 [:17], "He who through faith is righteous shall live." The Word of God cannot be received and cherished by any works whatever but only by faith. Therefore it is clear that, as the soul needs only the Word of God for its life and righteousness, so it is justified by faith alone and not any works; for if it could be justified by anything else, it would not need the Word, and consequently it would not need faith.

This faith cannot exist in connection with works–that is to say, if you at the same time claim to be justified by works, whatever their character–for that would be the same as "limping with two different opinions" [I Kings 18:21], as worshiping Baal and kissing one's own hand [Job 31:27-28], which, as Job says, is a very great iniquity. Therefore the moment you begin to have faith you learn that all things in you are altogether blameworthy, sinful, and damnable, as the Apostle says in Rom. 3 [:23], "Since all have sinned and fall short of the glory of God," and, "None is righteous, none, not one; . . . all have turned aside, together they have gone wrong" (Rom. 3:10-12). When you have learned this you will know that you need Christ, who suffered and rose again for you so that, if you believe in him, you may through this faith become a new man in so far as your sins are forgiven and you are justified by the merits of another, namely, of Christ alone.

Since, therefore, this faith can rule only in the inner man, as Rom. 10 [:10] says, "For man believes with his heart and so is justified," and since faith alone justifies, it is clear that the inner man cannot be justified, freed, or saved by any outer work or action at all, and that these works, whatever their character, have nothing to do with this inner man. On the other hand, only ungodliness and unbelief of heart, and no outer work, make him guilty and a damnable servant of sin. Wherefore it ought to be the first concern of every Christian to lay aside all confidence in works and increasingly to strengthen faith alone and through faith to grow in the knowledge, not of works, but of Christ Jesus, who suffered and rose for him, as Peter teaches in the last chapter of his first Epistle (I Pet. 5:10). No other work makes a Christian. Thus when the Jews asked Christ, as related in John 6 [:28], what they must do "to be doing the work of God," he brushed aside the multitude of works which he saw they did in great profusion and suggested one work, saying, "This is the work of God, that you believe in him whom he has sent" [John 6:29]; "for on him has God the Father set his seal" [John 6:27].

Therefore true faith in Christ is a treasure beyond comparison which brings with it complete salvation and saves man from every evil, as Christ says in the last chapter of Mark [16:16]: "He who believes and is baptized will be saved; but he who does not believe will be condemned." Isaiah contemplated this treasure and foretold it in chapter 10: "The Lord will make a small and consuming word upon the land, and it will overflow with righteousness" [Cf. Isa. 10:22]. This is as though he said, "Faith, which is a small and perfect fulfilment of the law, will fill believers with so great a righteousness that they will need nothing more to become righteous." So Paul says, Rom. 10 [:10], "For man believes with his heart and so is justified."

Should you ask how it happens that faith alone justifies and offers us such a treasure of great benefits without works in view of the fact that so many works, ceremonies, and laws are prescribed in the Scriptures, I answer: First of all, remember what has been said, namely, that faith alone, without works, justifies, frees, and saves; we shall make this clearer later on. Here we must point out that the entire Scripture of God is divided into two parts: commandments and promises. Although the commandments teach things that are good, the things taught are not done as soon as they are taught, for the commandments show us what we ought to do but do not give us the power to do it. They are intended to teach man to know himself, that through them he may recognize his inability to do good and may despair of his own ability. That is why they are called the Old Testament and constitute the Old Testament. For example, the commandment, "You shall not covet" [Exod. 20:17], is a command which proves us all to be sinners, for no one can avoid coveting no matter how much he may struggle against it. Therefore, in order not to covet and to fulfil the commandment, a man is compelled to despair of himself, to seek the help which he does not find in himself elswehre and from someone else, as stated in Hosea [13:9]: "Destruction is your own, O Israel: your help is only in me." As we fare with respect to one commandment, so we fare with all, for it is equally impossible for us to keep any one of them.

Now when a man has learned through the commandments to recognize his helplessness and is distressed about how he might satisfy the law–since the law must be fulfilled so that not a jot or tittle shall be lost, otherwise man will be condemned without hope–then, being truly humbled and reduced to nothing in his own eyes, he finds in himself nothing whereby he may be justified and saved. Here the second part of Scripture comes to our aid, namely, the promises of God which declare the glory of God, saying, "If you wish to fulfil the law and not covet, as the law demands, come, believe in Christ in whom grace, righteousness, peace, liberty, and all things are promised you. If you believe, you shall have all things; if you do not believe, you shall lack all things." That which is impossible for you to accomplish by trying to fulfil all the works of the law–many and useless as they all are–you will accomplish quickly and easily through faith. God our Father has made all things depend on faith so that whoever has faith will have everything, and whoever does not have faith will have nothing. "For God has consigned all men to disobedience, that he may have mercy upon all," as it is stated in Rom. 11 [:32]. Thus the promises of God give what the commandments of God demand and fulfil what the law prescribes so that all things may be God's alone, both the commandments and the fulfilling of the commandments. He alone commands, he alone fulfils. Therefore the promises of God belong to the New Testament. Indeed, they are the New Testament.

Since these promises of God are holy, true, righteous, free, and peaceful words, full of goodness, the soul which clings to them with a firm faith will be so closely united with them and altogether absorbed by them that it not only will share in all their power but will be saturated and intoxicated by them. If a touch of Christ healed, how much more will this most tender spiritual touch, this absorbing of the Word, communicate to the soul all things that belong to the Word. This, then, is how through faith alone without works the soul is justified by the Word of God, sanctified, made true, peaceful, and free, filled with every blessing and truly made a child of God, as John 1 [:12] says: "But to all who . . . believed in his name, he gave power to become children of God."

From what has been said it is easy to see from what source faith derives such great power and why a good work or all good works together cannot equal it. No good work can rely upon the Word of God or live in the soul, for faith alone and the Word of God rule in the soul. Just as the heated iron glows like fire because of the union of fire with it, so the Word imparts its qualities to the soul. It is clear, then, that a Christian has all that he needs in faith and needs no works to justify him; and if he has no need of works, he has no need of the law; and if he has no need of the law, surely he is free from the law. It is true that "the law is not laid down for the just" [I Tim. 1:9]. This is that Christian liberty, our faith, which does not induce us to live in idleness or wickedness but makes the law and works unnecessary for any man's righteousness and salvation.

* * *

That we may examine more profoundly that grace which our inner man has in Christ, we must realize that in the Old Testament God consecrated to himself all the first-born males. The birthright was highly prized for it involved a twofold honor, that of priesthood and that of kingship.

* * *

The nature of this priesthood and kingship is something like this: First, with respect to the kingship, every Christian is by faith so exalted above all things that, by virtue of a spiritual power, he is lord of all things without exception, so that nothing can do him any harm. As a matter of fact, all things are made subject to him and are compelled to serve him in obtaining salvation. Accordingly Paul says in Rom. 8 [:28], "All things work together for good for the elect," and in I Cor. 3 [:21-23], "All things are yours whether...life or death or the present or the future, all are yours; and you are Christ's...." This is not to say that every Christian is placed over all things to have and control them by physical power–a madness with which some churchmen are afflicted–for such power belongs to kings, princes, and other men on earth. Our ordinary experience in life shows us that we are subjected to all, suffer many things, and even die. As a matter of fact, the more Christian a man is, the more evils, sufferings, and deaths he must endure, as we see in Christ the first-born prince himself, and in all his brethren, the saints. The power of which we speak is spiritual. It rules in the midst of enemies and is powerful in the midst of oppression. This means nothing else than that "power is made perfect in weakness" [II Cor. 12:9] and that in all things I can find profit toward salvation [Rom. 8:28], so that the cross and death itself are compelled to serve me and to work together with me for my salvation. This is a splendid privilege and hard to attain, a truly omnipotent power, a spiritual dominion in which there is nothing so good and nothing so evil but that it shall work together for good to me, if only I believe. Yes, since faith alone suffices for salvation, I need nothing except faith exercising the power and dominion of its own liberty. Lo, this is the inestimable power and liberty of Christians.

Not only are we the freest of kings, we are also priests forever, which is far more excellent than being kings, for as priests we are worthy to appear before God to pray for others and to teach one another divine things. These are the functions of priests, and they cannot be granted to any unbeliever. Thus Christ has made it possible for us, provided we believe in him, to be not only his brethren, co-heirs, and fellow-kings, but also his fellow-priests. Therefore we may boldly come into the presence of God in the spirit of faith [Heb. 10:19, 22] and cry "Abba, Father!" pray for one another, and do all things which we see done and foreshadowed in the outer and visible works of priests.

* * *

From this anyone can clearly see how a Christian is free from all things and over all things so that he needs no works to make him righteous and save him, since faith alone abundantly confers all these things. Should he grow so foolish, however, as to presume to become righteous, free, saved, and a Christian by means of some good work, he would instantly lose faith and all its benefits, a foolishness aptly illustrated in the fable of the dog who runs along a stream with a piece of meat in his mouth and, deceived by the reflection of the meat in the water, opens his mouth to snap at it and so loses both the meat and the reflection.

You will ask, "If all who are in the church are priests, how do these whom we now call priests differ from laymen?" I answer: Injustice is done those words "priest," "cleric," "spiritual," "ecclesiastic," when they are transferred from all Christians to those few who are now by a mischievous usage called "ecclesiastics." Holy Scripture makes no distinction between them, although it gives the name "ministers," "servants," "stewards" to those who are now proudly called popes, bishops, and lords and who should according to the ministry of the Word serve others and teach them the faith of Christ and the freedom of believers. Although we are all equally priests, we cannot all publicly minister and teach. We ought not do so even if we could. Paul writes accordingly in I. Cor. 4 [1], "This is how one should regard us, as servants of Christ and stewards of the mysteries of God."

* * *

Let this suffice concerning the inner man, his liberty, and the source of his liberty, the righteousness of faith. He needs neither laws nor good works but, on the contrary, is injured by them if he believes that he is justified by them.

Now let us turn to the second part, the outer man. Here we shall answer all those who, offended by the word "faith" and by all that has been said, now ask, "If faith does all things and is alone sufficient unto righteousness, why then are good works commanded? We will take our ease and do no works and be content with faith." I answer: no so, you wicked men, not so. That would indeed be proper if we were wholly inner and perfectly spiritual men. But such we shall be only at the last day, the day of the resurrection of the dead. As long as we live in the flesh we only begin to make some progress in that which shall be perfected in the future life. For this reason the Apostle in Rom. 8 [:23] calls all that we attain in this life "the first fruits of the Spirit" because we shall indeed receive the greater portion, even the fulness of the Spirit, in the future. This is the place to assert that which was said above, namely, that a Christian is the servant of all and made subject to all. Insofar as he is free he does no works, but insofar as he is a servant he does all kinds of works. How this is possible we shall see.

Although, as I have said, a man is abundantly and sufficiently justified by faith inwardly, in his spirit, and so has all that he needs, except insofar as this faith and these riches must grow from day to day even to the future life; yet he remains in this mortal life on earth. In this life he must control his own body and have dealings with men. Here the works begin; here a man cannot enjoy leisure; here he must indeed take care to discipline his body by fastings, watchings, labors, and other reasonable discipline and to subject it to the Spirit so that it will obey and conform to the inner man and faith and not revolt against faith and hinder the inner man, as it is the nature of the body to do if it is not held in check. The inner man, who by faith is created in the image of God, is both joyful and happy because of Christ in whom so many benefits are conferred upon him; and therefore it is his one occupation to serve God joyfully and without thought of gain, in love that is not constrained.

* * *

In order to make that which we have said more easily understood, we shall explain by analogies. We should think of the works of a Christian who is justified and saved by faith because of the pure and free mercy of God, just as we would think of the works which Adam and Eve did in Paradise, and all their children would have done if they had not sinned. We read in Gen. 2 [:15] that "The Lord God took the man and put him in the garden of Eden to fill it and keep it." Now Adam was created righteous and upright and without sin by God so that he had no need of being justified and made upright through his tilling and keeping the garden; but, that he might not be idle, the Lord gave him a task to do, to cultivate and protect the garden. This task would truly have been the freest of works, done only to please God and not to obtain righteousness, which Adam already had in full measure and which would have been the birthright of us all.

* * *

From this it is easy to know how far good works are to be rejected or not, and by what standard all the teachings of men concerning works are to be interpreted. If works are sought after as a means to righteousness, are burdened with this perverse leviathan, and are done under the false impression that through them one is justified, they are made necessary and freedom and faith are destroyed; and this addition to them makes them no longer good but truly damnable works. They are not free, and they blaspheme the grace of God since to justify and to save by faith belongs to the grace of God alone. What the works have no power to do they nevertheless–by a godless presumption through this folly of ours–pretend to do and thus violently force themselves into the office and glory of grace. We do not, therefore, reject good works; on the contrary, we cherish and teach them as much as possible. We do not condemn them for their own sake but on account of this godless addition to them and the perverse idea that righteousness is to be sought through them; for that makes them appear good outwardly, when in truth they are not good. They deceive men and lead them to deceive one another like ravening wolves in sheep's clothing [Matt. 7:15].

* * *

Of the same nature are the precepts which Paul gives in Rom. 13 [:1-7], namely, that Christians should be subject to the governing authorities and be ready to do every good work, not that they shall in this way be justified, since they already are righteous through faith, but that in the liberty of the Spirit they shall be so doing serve others and the authorities themselves and obey their will freely and out of love. The works of all colleges, monasteries, and priests should be of this nature. Each one should do the works of his profession and station, not that by them he may strive after righteousness, but that through them he may keep his body under control, be an example to others who also need to keep their bodies under control, and finally that by such works he may submit his will to that of others in the freedom of love. But very great care must always be exercised so that no man in a false confidence imagines that by such works he will be justified or acquire merit or be saved; for this is the work of faith alone, as I have repeatedly said.

* * *

Our faith in Christ does not free us from works but from false opinions concerning works, that is, from the foolish presumption that justification is acquired by works. Faith redeems, corrects, and preserves our consciences so that we know that righteousness does not consist in works, although works neither can nor ought to be wanting; just as we cannot be without food and drink and all the works of this mortal body, yet our righteousness is not in them, but in faith; and yet those works of the body are not to be despised or neglected on that account. In this world we are bound by the needs of our bodily life, but we are not righteous because of them. "My kingship is not of this world" [John 18:36], says Christ. He does not, however, say, "My kingship is not here, that is, in this world." And Paul says, "Though we live in the world we are not carrying on a worldly war" [II Cor. 10:3], and in Gal. 2 [:20], "The life I now live in the flesh I live by faith in the Son of God." Thus what we do, live, and are in works and ceremonies, we do because of the necessities of this life and of the effort to rule our body. Nevertheless we are righteous, not in these, but in the faith of the Son of God.

TO THE CHRISTIAN NOBILITY OF THE GERMAN NATION CONCERNING THE REFORM OF THE CHRISTIAN ESTATE

In response to colleagues and friends, Luther published this small book in early August, 1520. It contains a general attack on the theology of the Roman Catholic Church and an indictment of ecclesiastical abuses. Luther at this time is concerned with reforming the church, and he suggests that a general council to accomplish the task should be called by the nobility since the church itself is unable to do it. Humanists and reformers needed a spokesman in these matters and Luther filled the need with this widely read and popular treatise. The text below is from LW 44, 123-217 passim.

To His Most Illustrious, Most Mighty, and Imperial Majesty, and to the Christian Nobility of the German Nation, from Doctor Martin Luther.

Grace and power from God, Most Illustrious Majesty, and most gracious and dear lords.

It is not from sheer impertinence or rashness that I, one poor man, have taken it upon myself to address your worships. All the estates of Christendom, particularly in Germany, are now oppressed by distress and affliction, and this has stirred not only me but everybody else to cry out time and time again and to pray for help. It has even compelled me now at this time to cry aloud that God may inspire someone with his Spirit to lend a helping hand to this distressed and wretched nation. Often the councils have made some pretense at reformation, but their attempts have been cleverly frustrated by the guile of certain men, and things have gone from bad to worse. With God's help I intend to expose the wiles and wickedness of these men, so that they are shown up for what they are and may never again be so obstructive and destructive. God has given us a young man of noble birth as head of state, and in him has awakened great hopes of good in many hearts. Presented with such an opportunity we ought to apply ourselves and use this time of grace profitably.

The first and most imporant thing to do in this matter is to prepare ourselves in all seriousness. We must not start something by trusting in great power or human reason, even if all the power in the world were ours. For God cannot and will not suffer that a good work begin by relying upon one's own power and reason. He dashes such works to the ground, they do no good at all. As it says in Psalm 33 [:16], "No king is saved by his great might and no lord is saved by the greatness of his strength." I fear that this is why the good emperors Frederick I and Frederick II and many other German emperors were in former times shamefully oppressed and trodden underfoot by the popes, although all the world feared the emperors. It may be that they relied on their own might more than on God, and therefore had to fall. What was it in our own times that raised the bloodthirsty Julius II to such heights? Nothing else, I fear, except that

France, the Germans, and Venice relied upon themselves. The chldren of Benjamin slew forty-two thousand Israelites because the latter relied on their own strength, Judges 30 [:21].

That it may not so fare with us and our noble Charles, we must realize that in this matter we are not dealing with men, but with the princes of hell. These princes could fill the world with war and bloodshed, but war and bloodshed do not overcome them. We must tackle this job by renouncing trust in physical force and trusting humbly in God. We must seek God's help through earnest prayer and fix our minds on nothing else than the misery and distress of suffering Christendom without regard to what evil men deserve. Otherwise, we may start the game with great prospects of success, but when we get into it the evil spirits will stir up such confusion that the whole world will swim in blood, and then nothing will come of it all. Let us act wisely, therefore, and in the fear of God. The more force we use, the greater our disaster if we do not act humbly and in the fear of God. If the popes and Romanists have hitherto been able to set kings against each other by the devil's help, they may well be able to do it again if we were to go ahead without the help of God on our own strength and by our own cunning.

The Romanists have very cleverly built three walls around themselves. Hitherto they have protected themselves by these walls in such a way that no one has been able to reform them. As a result, the whole of Christendom has fallen abominably.

In the first place, when pressed by the temporal power they have made decrees and declared that the temporal power had no jurisdiction over them, but that, on the contrary, the spiritual power is above the temporal. In the second place, when the attempt is made to reprove them with the Scriptures, they raise the objection that only the pope may interpret the Scriptures. In the third place, if threatened with a council, their story is that no one may summon a council but the pope.

In this way they have cunningly stolen our three rods from us, that they may go unpunished. They have ensconced themselves within the safe stronghold of these three walls so that they can practice all the knavery and wickedness which we see today. Even when they have been compelled to hold a council they have weakened its power in advance by putting the princes under oath to let them remain as they were. In addition, they have given the pope full authority over all decisions of a council, so that it is all the same whether there are many councils or no councils. They only deceive us with puppet shows and sham fights. They fear terribly for their skin in a really free council! They have so intimidated kings and princes with this technique that they believe it would be an offense against God not to be obedient to the Romanists in all their knavish and ghoulish deceits.

May God help us, and give us just one of those trumpets with which the walls of Jericho were overthrown to blast down these walls of straw and paper in the same way and set free the Christian rods for the punishment of sin, [and] bring to light the craft and deceit of the devil, to the end that through punishment we may reform ourselves and once more attain God's favor.

Let us begin by attacking the first wall. It is pure invention that pope, bishop, preists, and monks are called the spiritual estate while princes, lords, artisans, and farmers are called the temporal estate. This is indeed a piece of deceit and hypocrisy. Yet no one need be intimidated by it, and for this reason: all Christians are truly of the spiritual estate, and there is no difference among them except that of office. Paul says in I Corinthians 12 [:12-13] that we are all one body, yet every member has its own work by which it serves the others. This is because we all have one baptism, one gospel, one faith, and are all Christians alike; for baptism, gospel, and faith alone make us spiritual and a Christian people.

The pope or bishop anoints, shaves heads, ordains, consecrates, and prescribes garb different from that of the laity, but he can never make a man into a Christian or into a spiritual man by so doing. He might well make a man into a hypocrite or a humbug and blockhead, but never a Christian or a spiritual man. As far as that goes, we are all consecrated priests through baptism, as St. Peter says in I Peter 2 [:9], "You are a royal priesthood and a priestly realm." The Apocalypse says, "Thou has made us to be priests and kings by thy blood" [Rev. 5:9-10]. The consecration by pope or bishop would never make a priest, and if we had no higher consecration than that which pope or bishop gives, no one could say mass or preach a sermon or give absolution.

Therefore, when a bishop consecrates it is nothing else than that in the place and stead of the whole community, all of whom have like power, he takes a person and charges him to exercise this power on behalf of the others. It is like ten brothers, all king's sons and equal heirs, choosing one of themselves to rule the inheritance in the interests of all. In one sense they are all kings and of equal power, and yet one of them is charged with the responsiblity of ruling. To put it still more clearly: suppose a group of earnest Christian laymen were taken prisoner and set down in a desert without an episcopally ordained priest among them. And suppose they were to come to a common mind there and then in the desert and elect one of their number, whether he was married or not, and charge him to baptize, say mass, pronounce absolution, and preach the gospel. Such a man would be as truly a priest as though he had been ordained by all the bishops and popes in the world. That is why in cases of necessity anyone can baptize and give absolution. This would be impossible if we were not all priests. Through canon law the Romanists have almost destroyed and made unknown the wondrous grace and authority of baptism and justification. In times gone by Christians used to choose their bishops and priests in this way from among their own number, and they were confirmed in their office by the other bishops without all the fuss that goes on nowadays. St. Augustine, Ambrose, and Cyprian each became [a bishop in this way].

Since those who exercise secular authority have been baptized with the same baptism, and have the same faith and the same gospel as the rest of us, we must admit that they are priests and bishops and we must regard their office as one which has a proper and useful place in the Christian community. For whoever comes out of the water of baptism can boast that he is already a consecrated priest, bishop, and pope, although of course it is not seemly that just anybody should exercise such office. Because we are all priests of equal standing, no one must push himself forward and take it upon himself, without our consent and election, to do that for which we all have equal authority. For no one dare take upon himself what is common to all without the authority and consent of the community. And should it happen that a person chosen for such office were deposed for abuse of trust, he would then be exactly what he was before. Therefore, a priest in Christendom is nothing else but an officeholder. As long as he holds office he takes precedence; where he is deposed, he is a peasant or a townsman like anybody else. Indeed, a priest is never a priest when he is deposed. But now the Romanists have invented *characteres indelebiles* and say that a deposed priest is nevertheless something different from a mere layman. They hold the illusion that a priest can never be anything other than a priest, or ever become a layman. All this is just contrived talk, and human regulation.

It follows from this argument that there is no true, basic difference between laymen and priests, princes and bishops, between religious and secular, except for the sake of office and work, but not for the sake of status. They are all of the spiritual estate, all are truly priests, bishops, and popes. But they do not all have the same work to do. Just as all priests and monks do not have the same work. This is the teaching of St. Paul in Romans 12 [:4-5] and I Corinthians 12 [:112] and in I Peter 2 [:9], as I have said above, namely, that we are all one body of Christ the Head, and all members one of another. Christ does not have two different bodies, one temporal, the other spiritual. There is but one Head and one body.

Therefore, just as those who are now called "spiritual," that is, priests, bishops, or popes, are neither different from other Christians nor superior to them, except that they are charged with the administration of the word of God and the sacraments, which is their work and office, so it is with the temporal authorities. They bear the sword and rod in their hand to punish the wicked and protect the good. A cobbler, a smith, a peasant—each has the work and office of his trade, and yet they are all alike consecrated priests and bishops. Further, everyone must benefit and serve every other by means of his own work or office so that in this way man kinds of work may be done for the bodily and spiritual welfare of the community, just as all the members of the body serve one another [I Cor. 12:14-26].

Consider for a moment how Christian is the decree which says that the temporal power is not above the "spiritual estate" and has no right to punish it. That is as much as to say that the hand shall not help the eye when it suffers pain. Is it not unnatural, not to mention un-Christian, that one member does not help another and prevent its destruction? In fact, the more honorable the member, the more the others ought to help. I say therefore that since the temporal power is ordained of God to punish the wicked and protect the good, it should be left free to perform its office in the whole body of Christendom without restriction and without respect to persons, whether it affects pope, bishops, priests, monks, nuns, or anyone else. If it were right to say that the temporal power is inferior to all the spiritual estates (preacher, confessor, or any spiritual office), and so prevent the temporal power from doing its proper work, then the tailors, cobblers, stonemasons, carpenters, cooks, innkeepers, farmers, and all the temporal craftsmen should be prevented from providing pope, bishops, priests, and monks with shoes, clothes, house, meat and drink, as well as from paying them any tribute. But if these laymen are allowed to do their proper work without restriction, what then are the Romanist scribes doing with their own laws, which exempt them from the jurisdiction of the temporal Christian authority? It is just so that they can be free to do evil and fulfil what St. Peter said, "False teachers will rise up among you who will deceive you, and with their false and fanciful talk, they will take advantage of you " [II Pet. 2:1-3].

For these reasons the temporal Christian authority ought to exercise its office without hindrance, regardless of whether it is pope, bishop, or priest whom it affects. Whoever is guilty, let him suffer. All that canon law has said to the contrary is the invention of Romanist presumptions. For thus St. Paul says to all Christians, "Let every soul (I take that to mean the pope's soul also) be subject to the temporal authority; for it does not bear the sword in vain, but serves God by punishing the wicked and benefiting the good" [Rom. 13:11, 4]. St. Peter, too, says, "Be subject to all human ordinances for the sake of the Lord, who so wills it" [I Pet. 2:13, 15]. He has also prophesied in II Peter 2 [:1] that such men would arise and despise the temporal authority. This is exactly what has happened through the canon law.

So, then, I think this first paper wall is overthrown. Inasmuch as the temporal power has become a member of the Christian body it is a spiritual estate, even though its work is physical. Therefore, its work should extend without hindrance to all the members of the whole body to punish and use force whenever guilt deserves or necessity demands, without regard to whether the culprit is pope, bishop, or priest. Let the Romanists hurl threats and bans about as they like. That is why guilty priests, when they are handed over to secular law, are first deprived of their priestly dignities. This would not be right unless the secular sword previously had had authority over these priests by divine right. Moreover, it is intolerable that in canon law so much importance is attached to the freedom, life, and property of the clergy, as though the laity were not also as spiritual and as good Christians as they, or did not also belong to the church. Why are your life and limb, your property and honor, so cheap and mine not, inasmuch as we are all Christians and have the same baptism, the same faith, the same Spirit, and all the rest? If a priest is murdered, the whole country is placed under interdict. Why not when a peasant is murdered? How does this great difference come about between two men who are both Christians? It comes from the laws and fabrications of men.

Moreover, it can be no good spirit which has invented such exceptions and granted sin such license and impunity. For if it is our duty to strive against the words and works of the devil and to drive him out in whatever way we can, as both Christ and his apostles command us, how have we gotten into such a state that we have to do nothing and say nothing when the pope or his cohorts undertake devilish words and works? Ought we merely out of regard for these people allow the suppression of divine commandments and truth, which we have sworn in baptism to support with life and limb? Then we should have to answer to all the souls that would thereby be abandoned and led astray!

It must, therefore, have been the chief devil himself who said what is written in the canon law, that if the pope were so scandalously bad as to lead crowds of souls to the devil, still he could not be deposed. At Rome they build on this accursed and devilish foundation, and think that we should let all the world go to the devil rather than resist their knavery. If the fact that one man is set over others were sufficient reason why he should not be punished, then no Christian could punish another, since Christ commanded that every man should esteem himself as the lowliest and the least [Matt. 18:4].

Where sin is, there is no longer any shielding from punishment. St. Gregory writes that we are indeed all equal, but guilt makes a man inferior to others. Now we see how the Romanists treat Christendom. They take away its freedom without any proof from Scripture, at their own whim. But God, as well as the apostles, made them subject to the temporal sword. It is to be feared that this is a game of the Antichrist, or at any rate that his forerunner has appeared.

The second wall is still more loosely built and less substantial. The Romanists want to be the only masters of Holy Scripture, although they never learn a thing from the Bible all their life long. They assume the sole authority for themselves, and, quite unashamed, they play about with words before our very eyes, trying to persuade us that the pope cannot err in matters of faith, regardless of whether he is righteous or wicked. Yet they cannot point to a single letter. This is why so many heretical and un-Christian, even unnatural, ordinances stand in the canon law. But there is no need to talk about these ordinances at present. Since these Romanists think the Holy Spirit never leaves them, no matter how ignorant and wicked they are, they become bold and decree only what they want. And if what they claim were true, why have Holy Scripture at all? Of what use is Scripture? Let us burn the Scripture and be satisfied with the unlearned gentlemen at Rome who possess the Holy Spirit! And yet the Holy Spirit can be possessed only by pious hearts. If I had not read the words with my own eyes, I would not have believed it possible for the devil to have made such stupid claims at Rome, and to have won supporters for them.

But so as not to fight them with mere words, we will quote the Scriptures. St. Paul sais in I Corinthians 14 [:30], "If something better is revealed to anyone, though he is already sitting and listening to another in God's word, then the one who is speaking shall hold his peace and give place." What would be the point of this commandment if we were compelled to believe only the man who does the talking, or the man who is at the top? Even Christ said in John 6 [:45] that all Christians shall be taught by God. If it were to happen that the pope and his cohorts were wicked and not true Christians, were not taught by God and were without understanding, and at the same time some obscure person had a right understanding, why should the people not follow the obscure man? Has the pope not erred many times? Who would help Christendom when the pope erred if we did not have somebody we could trust more than him, somebody who had the Scriptures on his side?

Therefore, their claim that only the pope may interpret Scripture is an outrageous fancied fable. They cannot produce a single letter [of Scripture] to maintain that the interpretation of Scripture or the confirmation of its interpretation belongs to the pope alone. They themselves have usurped this power. And although they allege that this power was given to St. Peter when the keys were given him, it is clear enough that the keys were not given to Peter alone but to the whole community. Further, the keys were not ordained for doctrine or government, but only for the binding or loosing of sin. Whatever else or whatever more they arrogate to themselves on the basis of the keys is a mere fabrication. But Christ's words to Peter, "I have prayed for you that your faith fail not" [Luke 22:32], cannot be applied to the pope, since the majority of the popes have been without faith, as they must themselves confess. Besides, it is not only for Peter that Christ prayed, but also for all apostles and Christians, as he says in John 17 [:9, 20], "Father, I pray for those whom thou has given me, and not for these only, but for all who believe on me through their word." Is that not clear enough?

Just think of it! The Romanists must admit that there are among us good Christians who have the true faith, spirit, understanding, word, and mind of Christ. Why, then, should we reject the word and understanding of good Christians and follow the pope, who has neither faith nor the spirit? To follow the pope would be to deny the whole faith as well as the Christian church. Again, if the article, "I believe in one holy Christian church," is correct, then the pope cannot be the only one who is right. Otherwise, we would have to confess, " I believe in the pope at Rome." This would reduce the Christian church to one man, and be nothing else than a devilish and hellish error.

Besides, if we are all priests, as was said above, and all have one faith, one gospel, one sacrament, why should we not also have the power to test and judge what is right or wrong in matters of faith? What becomes of Paul's words in I Corinthians 1 [:15], "A spiritual man judges all things, yet he is judged by no one"? Why, then, should not we perceive what is consistent with faith and what is not, just as well as an unbelieving pope does?

We ought to become bold and free on the authority of all these texts, and many others. We ought not to allow the Spirit of freedom (as Paul calls him [II Cor. 3:17]) to be frightened off by the fabrications of the popes, but we ought to march boldly forward and test all that they do, or leave undone, by our believing understanding of the Scriptures. We must compel the Romanists to follow not their own interpretation but the better one. Long ago Abraham had to listen to Sarah, although she was in more complete subjection to him than we are to anyone on earth [Gen. 21:12]. And Balaam's ass was wiser than the prophet himself [Num. 22:21-35]. If God spoke then through an ass against a prophet, why should he not be able even now to speak through a righteous man against the pope? Similarly, St. Paul rebukes St. Peter as a man in error in Galatians 2 [:11-12]. Therefore, it is the duty of every Christian to espouse the cause of the faith, to understand and defend it, and to denounce every error.

The third wall falls of itself when the first two are down. When the pope acts contrary to the Scriptures, it is our duty to stand by the Scriptures, to reprove him and to constrain him, according to the word of Christ, Matthew 18 [:15-17], "If your brother sins against you, go and tell it to him, between you and him alone; if he does not listen to you, then take one or two others with you; if he does not listen to them, tell it to the church; if he does not listen to the church, consider him a heathen." Here every member is commanded to care for every other. How much more should we do this when the member that does evil is responsible for the government of the church, and by his evil-doing is the cause of much harm and offense to the rest! But if I am to accuse him before the church, I must naturally call the church together.

The Romanists have no basis in Scripture for their claim that the pope alone has the right to call or confirm a council. This is just their own ruling, and it is only valid as long as it is not harmful to Christendom or contrary to the laws of God. Now when the pope deserves punishment, this ruling no longer obtains, for not to punish him by authority of a council is harmful to Christendom.

Thus we read in Acts 15 that it was not St. Peter who called the Apostolic Council but the apostles and elders. If then that right had belonged to St. Peter alone, the council would not have been a Christian council, but a heretical *conciliabulum*. Even the Council of Nicaea, the most famous of all councils, was neither called nor confirmed by the bishop of Rome, but by the emperor Constantine. Many other emperors after him have done the same, and yet these councils were the most Christian of all. But if the pope alone has the right to convene councils, then these councils would all have been heretical. Further, when I examine the councils the pope did summon, I find that they did nothing of special importance.

Therefore, when necessity demands it, and the pope is an offense to Christendom, the first man who is able should, as a true member of the whole body, do what he can to bring about a truly free council. No one can do this so well as the temporal authorities, especially since they are also fellow-Christians, fellow-priests, fellow-members of the spiritual estate, fellow-lords over all things. Whenever it is necessary or profitable they ought to exercise the office and work which they have received from God over everyone. Would it not be unnatural if a fire broke out in a city and everyone were to stand by and let it burn on and on and consume everything that could burn because nobody had the authority of the major, or because, perhaps, the fire broke out in the mayor's house? In such a situation is it not the duty of every citizen to arouse and summon the rest? How much more should this be done in the spiritual city of Christ if a fire of offense breaks out, whether in the papal government, or anywhere else! The same argument holds if an enemy were to attack a city. The man who first roused the others deserves honor and gratitude. Why, then, should he not deserve honor who makes known the presence of the enemy from hell and rouses Christian people and calls them together?

But all their boasting about an authority which dare not be opposed amounts to nothing at all. Nobody in Christendom has authority to do injury or to forbid the resisting of injury. There is no authority in the church except to promote good. Therefore, if the pope were to use his authority to prevent the calling of a free council, thereby preventing the improvement of the church, we should have regard neither for him nor for his authority. And if he were to hurl his bans and thunderbolts, we should despise his conduct as that of a madman. On the contrary, we should excommunicate him and drive him out as best we could, relying completely upon God. This presumptuous authority of his is nothing. He does not even have such authority. He is quickly defeated by a single text of Scripture, where Paul says to the Corinthians, "God has given us authority not to ruin Christendom, but to build it up" [II Cor. 10:8]. Who wants to leap over the hurdle of this text? It is the power of the devil and of Antichrist which resists the things that serve to build up Christendom. Such power is not to be obeyed, but rather resisted with life, property, and with all our might and main.

Even though a miracle were to be done against the temporal authority on the pope's behalf, or if somebody were struck down by the plague–which they boast has sometimes happened–it should be considered as nothing but the work of the devil designed to destroy our faith in God. Christ foretold this in Matthew 24 [:24], "False Christs and false prophets shall come in my name, who shall perform signs and wonders in order to deceive even the elect." And Paul says in II Thessalonians 2 [:9] that Antichrist shall, through the power of Satan, be mighty in false wonders.

Let us, therefore, hold fast to this: no Christian authority can do anything against Christ. As St. Paul says, "We can do nothing against Christ, only for Christ" [II Cor. 13:8]. But if an authority does anything against Christ, then that authority is the power of Antichrist and of the devil, even if it were to deluge us with wonders and plagues. Wonders and plagues prove nothing, especially in these evil latter days. The whole of Scripture fortells such false wonders. This is why we must hold fast to the word of God with firm faith, and then the devil will soon drop his miracles!

With this I hope that all this wicked and lying terror with which the Romanists have long intimidated and dulled our conscience has been overcome, and that they, just like all of us, shall be made subject to the sword. They have no right to interpret Scripture merely by authority and without learning. They have no authority to prevent a council, or even worse yet at their mere whim to pledge it, impose conditions on it, or deprive it of its freedom. When they do that they are truly in the fellowship of Antichrist and the devil. They have nothing at all of Christ except the name.

TEMPORAL AUTHORITY: WHO WHAT EXTENT IT SHOULD BE OBEYED

At Worms in 1521 Luther was commanded by the highest temporal authority, the emperor, to recant his works, and he had refused. Several rulers had burned his works and imprisoned his followers, and Luther himself had been excommunicated and was under the ban of the empire. In the midst of these political consequences of the Reformation, Luther gave some sermons on temporal authority in October, 1522, before Duke John of Saxony and others who urged him to publish his thoughts on the subject. Luther then wrote this relatively nonpolemical treatise in order to provide for the Christian a general theory of temporal authority. In it Luther explains the nature of temporal authority, its limitations, and the responsibilities of the Christian subject and the Christian ruler. The text below is from LW 45, 81-129 passim.

First, we must provide a sound basis for the civil law and sword so no one will doubt that it is in the world by God's will and ordinance. The passages which do this are the following: Romans 13, "Let every soul [*seele*] be subject to the governing authority, for there is no authority except from God; the authority which everywhere [*allenthalben*] exists has been ordained by God. He then who resists the governing authority resists the ordinance of God, and he who resists God's ordinance will incur judgment." Again, in I Peter 2 [:14-14], "Be subject to every kind of human ordinance, whether it be to the king as supreme, or to governors, as those who have been sent by him to punish the wicked and to praise the righteous."

The law of this temporal sword has existed from the beginning of the world. For when Cain slew his brother Ael, he was in such great terror of being killed in turn that God even placed a special prohibition on it and suspended the sword for his sake, so that no one was to slay him [Gen. 4:14-15]. He would not have had this fear if he had not seen and heard from Adam that murderers are to be slain. Moreover, after the Flood, God re-established and confirmed this in unmistakable terms when he said in Genesis 9 [:6], "Whoever sheds the blood of man, by man shall his blood be shed." This cannot be understood as a plague or punishment of God upon murderers, for many murderers who are punished in other ways or pardoned altogether continue to live, and eventually die by means other than the sword. Rather, it is said of the law of the sword, that a murderer is guilty of death and in justice is to be slain by the sword. Now if justice should be hindered or the sword have become negligent so that the murderer dies a natural death, Scripture is not on that account false when it says, "Whoever sheds the blood of man, by man shall his blood be shed." The credit or blame belongs to men if this law instituted by God is not carried out; just as other commandments of God, too, are broken.

Afterward it was also confirmed by the law of Moses, Exodus 21 [:14], "If a man wilfully kills another, you shall take him from my altar, that he may die." And again, in the same chapter, "A life for a life, an eye for an eye, a tooth for a tooth, a foot for a foot, a hand for a hand, a wound for a wound, a stripe for a stripe." In addition, Christ also confirms it when he says to Peter in the garden, "He that takes the sword will perish by the sword" [Matt. 26:52], which is to be interpreted exactly like the Genesis 9 [:6] passage, "Whoever sheds the blood of man," etc. Christ is undoubtedly referring in these words to that very passage which he thereby wishes to cite and to confirm. John the Baptist also teaches the same thing. When the soldiers asked him what they should do, he answered, "Do neither violence nor injustice to any one, and be content with your wages" [Luke 3:14]. If the sword were not a godly estate, he should have directed them to get out of it, since he was supposed to make the people perfect and instruct them in a proper Christian way. Hence, it is certain and clear enough that it is God's will that the temporal sword and law be used for the punishment of the wicked and the protection of the upright.

Second. There appear to be powerful arguments to the contrary. Christ says in Matthew 5 [:38-41], "You have heard that it was said to them of old: An eye for an eye, a tooth for a tooth. But I say to you, Do not resist evil; but if anyone strikes you on the right cheek, turn to him the other also. And if anyone would sue you and take your coat, let him have your cloak as well. And if anyone forces you to go one mile, go with him two miles," etc. Likewise Paul in Romans 12 [:19], "Beloved, defend not yourselves, but leave it to the wrath of God; for it is written, 'Vengeance is mine; I will repay, says the Lord.'" And in Matthew 5 [:44], "Love your enemies, do good to them that hate you." And again, in I Peter 2 [3:9], "Do not return evil for evil, or reviling for reviling," etc. These and similar passages would certainly make it appear as though in the New Testament Christians were to have no temporal sword.

Hence, the sophists also say that Christ has thereby abolished the law of Moses. Of such commandments they make "counsels" for the perfect. They divide Christian teaching and Christians into two classes. One part they call the perfect, and assign to it such counsels. The other they call the imperfect, and assign to it the commandments. This they do out of sheer wantonness and caprice, without any scriptural basis. They fail to see that in the same passage Christ lays such stress on his teaching that he is unwilling to have the least word of it set aside, and condemns to hell those who do not love their enemies. Therefore, we must interpret these passages differently, so that Christ's words may apply to everyone alike, be he perfect or imperfect. For perfection and imperfection do not consist in works, and do not establish any distinct external order among Christians. They exist in the heart, in faith and love, so that those who believe and love the most are the perfect ones, whether they be outwardly male or female, prince or peasant, monk or layman. For love and faith produce no sects or outward differences.

Third. Here we must divide the children of Adam and all mankind into two classes, the first belonging to the kingdom of God, the second to the kingdom of the world. Those who belong to the kingdom of God are all the true believers who are in Christ and under Christ, for Christ is King and Lord in the kingdom of God, as Psalm 2 [:6] and all of Scripture says. For this reason he came into the world, that he might begin God's kingdom and establish it in the world. Therefore, he says before Pilate, "My kingdom is not of the world, but every one who is of the truth hears my voice" [John 18:36-37]. In the gospel he continually refers to the kingdom of God, and says, "Amend your ways, the kingdom of God is at hand" [Matt. 4:17, 10:7]; again, "Seek first the kingdom of God and his righteousness" [Matt. 6:33]. He also calls the gospel a gospel of the kingdom of God; because it teaches, governs, and upholds God's kingdom.

Now observe, these people need no temporal law or sword. If all the world were composed of real Christians, that is, true believers, there would be no need for or benefits from prince, king, lord, sword, or law. They would serve no purpose, since Christians have in their heart the Holy Spirit, who both teaches and makes them to do injustice to no one, to love everyone, and to suffer injustice and even death willingly and cheerfully at the hands of anyone. Where there is nothing but the unadulterated doing of right and bearing of wrong, there is no need for any suit, litigation, court, judge, penalty, law, or sword. For this reason it is impossible that the temporal sword and law should find any work to do among Christians, since they do of their own accord much more than all laws and teachings can demand, just as Paul says in I Timothy 1 [:9], "The law is not laid down for the just but for the lawless."

Why is this? It is because the righteous man of his own accord does all and more than the law demands. But the unrighteous do nothing that the law demands; therefore, they need the law to instruct, constrain, and compel them to do good. A good tree needs no instruction or law to bear good fruit; its nature causes it to bear according to its kind without any law or instruction. I would take to be quite a fool any man who would make a book full of laws and statutes for an apple tree telling it how to bear apples and not thorns, when the tree is able by its own nature to do this better than the man with all his books can describe and demand. Just so, by the Spirit and by faith all Christians are so thoroughly disposed and conditioned in their very nature that they do right and keep the law better than one can teach them with all manner of statutes; so far as they themselves are concerned, no statutes or laws are needed.

You ask: Why, then, did God give so many commandments to all mankind, and why does Christ prescribe in the gospel so many things for us to do? Of this I have written at length in the Postils and elsewhere. To put it here as briefly as possible, Paul says that the law has been laid down for the sake of the lawless [I Tim. 1:9], that is, so that those who are not Christians may through the law be restrained outwardly from evil deeds, as we shall hear later. Now since no one is by nature Christian or righteous, but altogether sinful and wicked, God through the law puts them all under restraint so they dare not wilfully implement their wickedness in actual deeds. In addition, Paul ascribes to the law another function in Romans 7 and Galatians 2, that of teaching men to recognize sin in order that it may make them humble unto grace and unto faith in Christ. Christ does the same thing here in Matthew 5 [:39], where he teaches that we should not resist evil; by this he is interpreting the law and teaching what ought to be and must be the state and temper of a true Christian, as we shall hear further on.

Fourth. All who are not Christians belong to the kingdom of the world and are under the law. There are few true believers, and still fewer who live a Christian life, who do not resist evil and indeed themselves do no evil. For this reason God has provided for them a different government beyond the Christian estate and kingdom of God. He has subjected them to the sword so that, even though they would like to, they are unable to practice their wickedness, and if they do practice it they cannot do so without fear or with success and impunity. In the same way a savage wild beast is bound with chains and ropes so that it cannot bite and tear as it would normally do, even though it would like to; whereas a tame and gentle animal needs no restraint, but is harmless despite the lack of chains and ropes.

If this were not so, men would devour one another, seeing that the whole world is evil and that among thousands there is scarcely a single true Christian. No one could support wife and child, feed himself, and serve God. The world would be reduced to chaos. For this reason God has ordained two governments: the spiritual, by which the Holy Spirit produces Christians and righteous people under Christ; and the temporal, which restrains the un-Christian and wicked so that–no thanks to them–they are obliged to keep still and to maintain an outward peace. Thus does St. Paul interpret the temporal sword in Romans 13 [:3], when he says it is not a terror to good conduct but to bad. And Peter says it is for the punishment of the wicked [I Pet. 2:14].

If anyone attempted to rule the world by the gospel and to abolish all temporal law and sword on the plea that all are baptized and Christians, and that, according to the gospel, there shall be among them no law or sword—or need for either—pray tell me, friend, what would he be doing? He would be loosing the ropes and chains of the savage wild beasts and letting them bite and mangle everyone, meanwhile insisting that they were harmless, tame, and gentle creatures; but I would have the proof in my wounds. Just so would the wicked under the name of Christian abuse evangelical freedom, carry on their rascality, and insist that they were Christians subject neither to law nor sword, as some are already raving and ranting.

To such a one we must say: Certainly it is true that Christians, so far as they themselves are concerned, are subject neither to law nor sword, and have need of neither. But take heed and first fill the world with real Christians before you attempt to rule it in a Christian and evangelican manner. This you will never accomplish; for the world and the masses are and always will be un-Christian, even if they are all baptized and Christian in name. Christians are few and far between (as the saying is). Therefore, it is out of the question that there should be a common Christian government over the whole world, or indeed over a single country or any considerable body of people, for the wicked always outnumber the good. Hence, a man who would venture to govern an entire country or the world with the gospel would be like a shepherd who should put together in one fold wolves, lions, eagles, and sheep, and let them mingle freely with one another, saying, "Help yourselves, and be good and peaceful toward one another. The fold is open, there is plenty of good. You need have no fear of dogs and clubs." The sheep would doubtless keep the peace and allow themselves to be fed and governed peacefully, but they would not live long, nor would one beast survive another.

For this reason one must carefully distinguish between these two governments. Both must be permitted to remain; the one to produce righteousness, the other to bring about external peace and prevent evil deeds. Neither one is sufficient in the world without the other.

* * *

Fifth. But you say: if Christians then do not need the temporal sword or law, why does Paul say to all Christians in Romans 13 [:1], "Let all souls be subject to the governing authority," and St. Peter, "Be subject to every human ordinance" [I Pet. 2:13], etc., as quoted above? Answer: I have just said that Christians, among themselves and by and for themselves, need no law or sword, since it is neither necessary nor useful for them. Since a true Christian lives and labors on earth not for himself alone but for his neighbor, he does by the very nature of his spirit even what he himself has no need of, but is needful and useful to his neighbor. Because the sword is most beneficial and necessary for the whole world in order to preserve peace, punish sin, and restrain the wicked, the Christian submits most willingly to the rule of the sword, pays his taxes, honors those in authority, serves, helps, and does all he can to assist the governing authority, that it may continue to function and be held in honor and fear. Although he has no need of these things for himself–to him they are not essential–nevertheless, he concerns himself about what is serviceable and of benefit to others, as Paul teaches in Ephesians 5 [:21-6:9].

Just as he performs all other works of love which he himself does not need–he does not visit the sick in order that he himself may be made well, or feed others because he himself needs food–so he serves the governing authority not because he needs it but for the sake of others, that they may be protected and that the wicked may not become worse.

* * *

Sixth. You ask whether a Christian too may bear the temporal sword and punish the wicked, since Christ's words, "Do not resist evil," are so clear and definite that the sophists have had to make of them a "counsel." Answer: You have now heard two propositions. One is that the sword can have no place among Christians; therefore, you cannot bear it among Christians or hold it over them, for they do not need it. The question, therefore, must be referred to the other group, the non-Christians, whether you may bear it there in a Christian manner. Here the other proposition applies, that you are under obligation to serve and assist the sword by whatever means you can, with body, goods, honor, and soul. For it is something which you do not need, but which is very beneficial and essential for the whole world and for your neighbor. Therefore, if you see that there is a lack of hangmen, constables, judges, lords, or princes, and you find that you are qualified, you should offer your services and seek the position, that the essential governmental authority may not be despised and become enfeebled or perish. The world cannot and dare not dispense with it.

* * *

To prove our position also by the New Testament, the testimony of John the Baptist in Luke 3 [:14] stands unshaken on this point. There can be no doubt that it was his task to point to Christ, witness for him, and teach about him; that is to say, the teaching of the man who was to lead a truly perfected people to Christ had of necessity to be purely New Testament and evangelical. John confirms the soldiers' calling, saying they should be content with their wages. Now if it had been un-Christian to bear the sword, he ought to have censured them for it and told them to abandon both wages and sword, else he would not have been teaching them Christianity aright. So likewise, when St. Peter in Acts 10 [:34-43] preached Christ to Cornelius, he did not tell him to abandon his profession, which he would have had to do if it had prevented Cornelius from being a Christian. Moreover, before he was baptized the Holy Spirit came upon him [Acts 10:44-48]. St. Luke also praises him as an upright man prior to St. Peter's sermon, and does not criticize him for being a soldier, the centurion of a pagan emperor [Acts 10:1-2]. It is only right that what the Holy Spirit permitted to remain and did not censure in the case of Cornelius, we too should permit and not censure.

* * *

Here you see that Christ is not abrogating the law when he says, "You have heard that it was said to them of old, 'An eye for an eye'; but I say to you: Do not resist evil," etc. [Matt. 5:38-39]. On the contrary, he is expounding the meaning of the law as it is to be understood, as if he were to say, "You Jews think that it is right and proper in the sight of God to recover by law what is yours. You rely on what Moses said, 'An eye for an eye,' etc. But I say to you that Moses set this law over the wicked, who do not belong to God's kingdom, in order that they might not avenge themselves or do worse but be compelled by such outward law to desist from evil, in order that by outward law and rule they might be kept subordinate to the governing authority. You, however, should so conduct yourselves that you neither need nor resort to such law. Although the temporal authority must have such a law by which to judge unbelievers, and although you yourselves may also use it for judging others, still you should not invoke or use it for yourselves and in your own affairs. You have the kingdom of heaven; therefore, you should leave the kingdom of earth to anyone who wants to take it."

There you see that Christ does not interpret his words to mean that he is abrogating the law of Moses or prohibiting temporal authority. He is rather making an exception of his own people. They are not to use the secular authority for themselves but leave it to unbelievers. Yet they may also serve these unbelievers, even with their own law, since they are not Christians and no one can be forced into Christianity. That Christ's words apply only to his own is evident from the fact that later on he says they should love their enemies and be perfect like their heavenly Father [Matt. 5:44, 48]. But he who loves his enemies and is perfect leaves the law alone and does not use it to demand an eye for an eye. Neither does he restrain the non-Christians, however, who do not love their enemies and who do wish to make use of the law; indeed, he lends his help that these laws may hinder the wicked from doing worse.

Thus the word of Christ is now reconciled, I believe, with the passages which establish the sword, and the meaning is this: No Christian shall wield or invoke the sword for himself and his cause. In behalf of another, however, he may and should wield it and invoke it to restrain wickedness and to defend godliness. Even as the Lord says in the same chapter [Matt. 5:34-37], "A Christian should not swear, but his word should be Yes, yes; No, no." That is, for himself and of his volition and desire, he shold not swear. When it is needful or necessary, however, and salvation or the honor of God demands it, he should swear. Thus, he uses the forbidden oath to serve another, just as he uses the forbidden sword to serve another. Christ and Paul often swore in order to make their teaching and testimony valuable and credible to others, as men do and have the right to do in covenants and compacts, etc., of which Psalm 63 [:11] says, "They shall be praised who swear by his name."

Here you inquire further, whether constables, hangmen, jurists, lawyers, and others of similar function can also be Christians and in a state of salvation. Answer: If the governing authority and its sword are a divine service, as was proved above, then everything that is essential for the authority's bearing of the sword must also be divine service. There must be those who arrest, prosecute, execute, and destroy the wicked, and who protect, acquit, defend, and save the good. Therefore, when they perform their duties, not with the intention of seeking their own ends but only of helping the law and the governing authority function to coerce the wicked, there is no peril in that; they may use their office like anybody else would use his trade, as a means of livelihood. For, as has been said, love of neighbor is not concerned about its own; it considers not how great or humble,but how profitable and needful the works are for neighbor or community.

You may ask, "Why may I not use the sword for myself and for my own cause, so long as it is my intention not to seek my own advantage but to punish evil?" Answer: Such a miracle is not impossible, but very rare and hazardous. Where the Spirit is so richly present it may well happen. For we read thus of Samson in Judges 15 [:11], that he said, "As they did to me, so have I done to them," even though Proverbs 24 [:29] says to the contrary, "Do not say I will do to him as he has done to me," and Proverbs 20 [:22] adds, "Do not say, I will repay him his evil." Samson was called of God to harass the Philistines and deliver the children of Israel. Although he used them as an occasion to further his own cause, still he did not do so in order to avenge himself or to seek his own interests, but to serve others and to punish the Philistines [Judg. 14:4]. No one but a true Christian, filled with the Spirit, will follow this example. Where reason too tries to do likewise, it will probably contend that it is not trying to seek its own, but this will be basically untrue, for it cannot be done without grace. Therefore first become like Samson, and then you can also do as Samson did.

Part Two
How Far Temporal Authority Extends

We come now to the main part of this treatise. Having learned that there must be temporal authority on earth, and how it is to be exercised in a Christian and salutary manner, we must now learn how far its arm extends and how widely its hand stretches, lest it extend too far and encroach upon God's kingdom and government. It is essential for us to know this, for where it is given too wide a scope, intolerable and terrible injury follows; on the other hand, injury is also inevitable where it is restricted too narrowly. In the former case, the temporal authority punishes too much; in the latter case, it punishes too little. To err in this direction, however, and punish too little is more tolerable, for it is always better to let a scoundrel live than to put a godly man to death. The world has plenty of scoundrels anyway and must continue to have them, but godly men are scarce.

It is to be noted first that the two classes of Adam's children–the one in God's kingdom under Christ and the other in the kingdom of the world under the governing authority as was said above–have two kinds of law. For every kingdom must have its own laws and statutes; without law no kingdom or government can survive, as everyday experience amply shows. The temporal government has laws which extend no further than to life and property and external affairs on earth, for God cannot and will not permit anyone but himself to rule over the soul. Therefore, where the temporal authority presumes to prescribe laws for the soul, it encroaches upon God's government and only misleads souls and destroys them. We want to make this so clear that everyone will grasp it, and that our fine gentlemen, the princes and bishops, will see what fools they are when they seek to coerce the people with their laws and commandments into believing this or that.

* * *

Furthermore, every man runs his own risk in believing as he does, and he must see to it himself that he believes rightly. As nobody else can go to heaven or hell for me, so nobody else can believe or disbelieve for me; as nobody else can open or close heaven or hell to me, so nobody else can drive me to belief or unbelief. How he believes or disbelieves is a matter for the conscience of each individual, and since this takes nothing away from the temporal authority the latter should be content to attend to its own affairs and let me believe this or that as they are able and willing, and constrain no one by force. For faith is a free act, to which no one can be forced. Indeed, it is a work of God in the spirit, not something which outward authority should compel or create. Hence arises the common saying, found also in Augustine, "No one can or ought to be forced to believe."

Moreover, the blind, wretched fellows fail to see how utterly hopeless and impossible a thing they are attemtping. For no matter how harshly they law down the law, or how violently they rage, they can do no more than force an outward compliance of the mouth and the hand; the heart they cannot compel, though they work themselves to a frazzle. For the proverb is true: "Thoughts are tax-free." Why do they persist in trying to force people to believe from the heart when they see that it is impossible: In so doing they only compel weak consciences to lie, to disavow, and to utter what is not in their hearts. They hereby load themselves down with dreadful alien sins, for all the lies and false confessions which such weak consciences utter fall back upon him who compels them. Even if their subjects were in error, it would be much easier simply to let them err than to compel them to lie and to utter what is not in their hearts. In addition, it is not right to prevent evil by something even worse.

* * *

If your prince or temporal ruler commands you to side with the pope, to believe thus and so, or to get rid of certain books, you should say, "It is not fitting that Lucifer should sit at the side of God. Gracious sir, I owe you obedience in body and property; command me within the limits of your authority on earth, and I will obey. But if you command me to believe or to get rid of certain books, I will not obey; for then you are a tyrant and overreach yourself, commanding where you have neither the right nor the authority," etc. Should he seize your property on account of this and punish such disobedience, then blessed are you; thank God that you are worthy to suffer for the sake of the divine word. Let him rage, fool that he is; he will meet his judge. For I tell you, if you fail to withstand him, if you give in to him and let him take away your faith and your books, you have truly denied God.

* * *

You must know that since the beginning of the world a wise prince is a mighty rare bird, and an upright prince even rarer. They are generally the biggest fools or the worst scoundrels on earth; therefore, one must constantly expect the worst from them and look for little good, especially in divine matters which concern the salvation of souls. They are God's executioners and hangmen; his divine wrath uses them to punish the wicked and to maintain outward peace. Our God is a great lord and ruler; this is why he must also have such noble, highborn, and rich hangmen and constables. He desires that everyone shall copiously accord them riches, honor, and fear in abundance. It pleases his divine will that we call his hangmen gracious lords, fall at their feet, and be subject to them in all humility, so long as they do not ply their trade too far and try to become shepherds instead of hangmen. If a prince should happen to be wise, upright, or a Christian, that is one of the great miracles, the most previous token of divine grace upon that land. Ordinarily the course of events is in accordance with the passage from Isaiah 3 [:4], "I will make boys their princes, and gaping fools shall rule over them"; and in Hosea 13 [:11], "I will give you a king in my anger, and take him away in my wrath." The world is too wicked, and does not deserve to have many wise and upright princes. Frogs must have their storks.

Again you say, "The temporal power is not forcing men to believe; it is simply seeing to it externally that no one deceives the people by false doctrine; how could heretics otherwise be restrained?" Answer: This the bishops should do; it is a function entruested to them and not to the princes. Heresy can never be restrained by force. One will have to tackle the problem in some other way, for heresy must be opposed and dealt with otherwise than with the sword. Here God's word must do the fighting. If it does not succeed, certainly the temporal power will not succeed either, even if it were to drench the world in blood. Hersey is a spiritual matter which you cannot hack to pieces with iron, consume with fire, or drown in water. God's word alone avails here, as Paul says in II Corinthians 10 [:4-5], "Our weapons are not carnal, but mighty in God to destroy every argument and proud obstacle that exalts itself against the knowledge of God, and to take every thought captive in the service of Christ."

* * *

But you might say, "Since there is to be no temporal sword among Christians, how then are they to be ruled outwardly? There certainly must be authority even among Christians." Answer: Among Christians there shall and can be no authority; rather all are alike subject to one another, as Paul says in Romans 12: "Each shall consider the other his superior"; and Peter says in I Peter 5 [:5], "All of you be subject to one another." This is also what Christ means in Luke 14 [:10], "When you are invited to a wedding, go and sit in the lowest place." Among Christians there is no superior but Christ himself, and him alone. What kind of authority can there be where all are equal and have the same right, power, possession, and honor, and where no one desires to be the other's superior, but each the other's subordinate? Where there are such people, one could not establish authority even if he wanted to, since in the nature of things it is impossible to have superiors where no one is able or willing to be a superior. Where there are no such people, however, there are no real Christians either.

What, then, are the priests and bishops? Answer: Their government is not a matter of authority or power, but a service and an office, for they are neither higher or better than other Christians. Therefore, they should impose no law or decree on others without their will and consent. Their ruling is rather nothing more than the inculcating of God's word, by which they guide Christians and overcome heresy. As we have said, Christians can be ruled by nothing except God's word, for Christians must be ruled in faith, not with outward works. Faith, however, can come through no word of man, but only through the word of God, as Paul says in Romans 10 [:17], "Faith comes through hearing, and hearing through the word of God." Those who do not believe are not Christians; they do not belong to Christ's kingdom, but to the worldly kingdom where they are constrained and governed by the sword and by outward rule. Christians do every good thing of their own accord and without constraint, and find God's word alone sufficient for them. Of this I have written frequently and at length elsewhere.

Part Three

Now that we know the limits of temporal authority, it is time to inquire also how a prince should use it. We do this for the sake of those very few who would also like very much to be Christian princes and lords, and who desire to enter into the life in heaven.

* * *

First. He must give consideration and attention to his subjects, and really devote himself to it. This he does when he directs his every thought to making himself useful and beneficial to them; when instead of thinking, "The land and people belong to me, I will do what best pleases me," he think rather, "I belong to the land and the people, I shall do what is good for them . . .

* * *

Second. He must beware of the high and mighty and of his counselors, and so conduct himself toward them that he despises none, but also trusts none enough to leave everything to him. God cannot tolerate either course.

* * *

Third. He must take care to deal justly with evildoers. Here he must be very wise and prudent, so he can inflict punishment without injury to others. . . .Therefore, he must not follow the advice of those counselors and fire-eaters who would stir and incite him to start a war, saying, "What, must he suffer such insult and injustice?' He is a mighty poor Christian who for the sake of a single castle would put the whole land in jeopardy.

In short, here one must go by the proverb, "He cannot govern who cannot wink at faults." Let this be his rule: Where wrong cannot be punished without greater wrong, there let him waive his rights, however just they may be. He should not have regard to his own injury, but to the wrong others must suffer in consequence of the penalty he imposes. What have the many women and children done to deserve being made widows and orphans in order that you may avenge yourself on a worthless tongue or an evil hand which has injured you?

Here you will ask: "Is a prince then not to go to war, and are his subjects not to follow him into battle?" Answer: This is a far-reaching question, but let me answer it very briefly. To act here as a Christian, I say, a prince should not go to war against his overlord–king, emperor, or other liege lord–but let him who takes, take. For the governing authority must not be resisted by force, but only by confession of the truth. If it is influenced by this, well and good; if not, you are excused, you suffer wrong for God's sake. If, however, the antagonist is your equal, your inferior, or of a foreign government, you should first offer him justice and peace, as Moses taught the children of Israel. If he refuses, then–mindful of what is best for you–defend yourself against force by force, as Moses so well describes it in Deuteronomy 20 [:10-12]. But in doing this you must not consider your personal interests and how you may remain lord, but those of your subjects to whom you owe help and protection, that such action may proceed in love. Since your entire land is in peril you must make the venture, so that with God's help all may not be lost. If you cannot prevent some from becoming widows and orphans as a consequence, you must at least see that no everything goes to ruin until there is nothing left except widows and orphans.

In this matter subjects are in duty bound to follow, and to devote their life and property, for in such a case one must risk his goods and himself for the sake of others. In a war of this sort it is both Christian and an act of love to kill the enemy without hesitation, to plunder and burn and injure him by every method of warfare until he is conquered (except that one must beware of sin, and not violate wives and virgins). And when victory has been achieved, one should offer mercy and peace to those who surrender and humble themselves...

What if a prince is in the wrong? Are his people bound to follow him then too? Answer: No, for it is no one's duty to do wrong; we must obey God (who desires the right) rather than men [Acts 5:29]. What is the subjects do not know whether their prince is in the right or not? Answer: So long as they do not know, and cannot with all possible diligence find out, they may obey him without peril to their souls. For in such a case one must apply the law of Moses in Exodus 21, where he writes that a murderer who has unknowingly and unintentionally killed a man shall through flight to a city of refuge and by judgment of a court be declared acquitted. Whichever side then suffers defeat, whether it be in the right or in the wrong, must accpet it as a punishment from God. Whichever side rights and wins in such ignorance, however, must regard its battle as though someone fell from a roof and killed another, and leave the matter to God. It is all the same to God whether he deprives you of life and property by a just or by an unjust lord. You are His creature and He can do with you as He wills, just so your conscience is clear. Thus in Genesis 20 [:2-7] God himself excuses Abimelech for taking Abraham's wife; not because he had done right, but because he had not known that she was Abraham's wife.

Fourth. Here we come to what should really have been placed first, and of which we spoke above. A prince must act in a Christian way toward his God also; that is, he must subject himself to him in entire confidence and pray for wisdom to rule well, as Solomon did [I Kings 3:9]. But of faith and trust in God I have written so much that it is not necesary to say more here. Therefore, we will close with this brief summation, that a prince's duty is fourfold: First, toward God there must be true confidence and earnest prayer; second, toward his sujects there must be love and Christian service third, with respect to his counselors and officials he must maintain an untrammeled reason and unfettered judgment; fourth, with respect to evildoers he must manifest a restrained severity and firmness. Then the prince's job will be done right, both outwardly and inwardly; it will be pleasing to God and to the people. But he will have to expect much envy and sorrow on account of it; the cross will soon rest on the shoulders of such a prince.

Finally, I must add an appendix in answer to those who raise questions about restitution, that is, about the return of goods wrongfully acquired. This is a matter about which the temporal sword is commonly concerned; much has been written about it, and many fantastically severe judgments have been sought in cases of this sort. I will put it all in a few words, however, and at one fell swoop dispose of all such laws and of the harsh judgments based upon them, thus: No surer law can be found in this matter than the law of love. In the first place, when a case of this sort is brought before you in which one is to make restitution to another, if they are both Christians the matter is soon settled; neither will withhold what belongs to the other, and neither will demand that it be returned. If only one of them is a Christian, namely, the one who whom restitution is due, it is again easy to settle, for he does not care whether restitution is ever made to him. The same is true if the one who is supposed to make restitution is a Christian, for he will do so.

But whether one be a Christian or not a Christian, you should decide the question of restitution as follows. If the debtor is poor and unable to make restitution, and the other party is not poor, then you should let the law of love prevail and acquit the debtor; for according to the law of love the other party is in any event obliged to relinquish the debt and, if necessary, to give him something besides. But if the debtor is not poor, then have him restore as much as he can, whether it be all, a half, a third, or a fourth of it, provided that you leave him enough to assure a house, food, and clothing for himself, his wife, and his children. This much you would owe him in any case, if you could afford it; so much the less ought you to take it away now, since you do not need it and he cannot get along without it.

* * *

A good and just decision must not and cannot be pronounced out of books, but must come from a free mind, as though there were no books. Such a free decision is given, however, by love and by natural law, with which all reason is filled; out of the books come extravagant and untenable judgments. Let me give you an example of this.

This story is told of Duke Charles of Burgundy. A certain nobleman took an enemy prisoner. The prisoner's wife came to ransom her husband. The nobleman promised to give back the husband on condition that she would lie with him. The woman was virtuous, yet wished to set her husband free; so she goes and asks her husband whether she should do this thing in order to set him free. The husband wished to be set free and to save his life, so he gives his wife permission. After the nobleman had lain with the wife, he had the husband beheaded the next day and gave him to her as a corpse. She laid the whole case before Duke Charles. He summoned the nobleman and commanded him to marry the woman. When the wedding day was over he had the nobleman beheaded, gave the woman possession of his property, and restored her to honor. Thus he punished the crime in a princely way.

Observe: No pope, no jurist, no lawbook could have given him such a decision. It sprang from untrammeled reason, above the law in all the books, and is so excellent that everyone must approve of it and find the justice of it written in his own heart. St. Augustine relates a similar story in *The Lord's Sermon on the Mount*. Therefore, we should keep written laws subject to reason, from which they originally welled forth as from the spring of justice. We should not make the spring dependent on its rivulets, or make reason a captive of letters.

CHAPTER IV Church Polity and Christian Politics

JOHN CALVIN

John Calvin

INTRODUCTION

John Calvin (1509-1564) was a French theologian and a leading figure in the Protestant Reformation. He studied theology at the University of Paris and law at Orleans. In 1533, Calvin broke with the Roman Catholic Church and in 1536 published his *Institutes of the Christian Religion,* vindicating Reformation principles. He applied those principles to the strict governance of Geneva and greatly influenced the Scottish Presbyterians, French Hughenots, Dutch Reformed and English Puritan Churches.

Calvin's formulation of proper Church-State relations is unique in the Christian tradition. While the major Catholic theologians connected religion and politics by placing the State below the Church in the universal hierarchy and Luther separated religion and politics by placing the State above the Church in this world, Calvin separates Church and State by placing them at equal levels in this world under God's rule and related them by making the Church political (through the policy of Presbyters, Elders and Deacons) and the State religious (through its proper concern with justice, charity and godliness).

In asserting that Church and State are at once separate and related, Calvin insists that "the spiritual kingdom of Christ and civil government are things very different," but "this distinction does not lead us to consider the whole system of civil government as a polluted thing which has nothing to do with Christian men." Church and State are interrelated as the earthly governments properly strive for the peace and justice of the Heavenly Kingdom, while being reminded by the Church that they remain in this World.

". . .this civil government is designed, as long as we live in this world, to cherish and support the external worship of God, to preserve the pure doctrine of religion, to defend the constitution of the Church, to regulate our lives in a manner requisite for the society of men, to form our manners to civil justice, to promote our concord with each other, and to establish general peace and tranquility. . . ."

The sequence of these duties of civil government are interesting: for Calvin, if the State supports religion and forms citizens' "manners to civil justice" (its positive, ethical role), it will not be required to expend as much effort in crime and punishment ("establishing general peace"–its negative, worldly role), because its populace will be less inclined to criminality. Thus the religious tenor of Calvin's politics contributes to its worldly duty of controlling and punishing sin. If the State educates its citizens in Godly conduct, it will reduce its role as policeman and "hangman" as the people will have greater self-control and be less likely to break the law.

Because the state contains this religious dimension, Calvin regards government service as "the most sacred and honorable in human life," and the magistrates, consequently, ought to "watch with all care, earnestness, and diligence, that in their administration they may exhibit to men an image, as it were, of the providence, care, goodness, benevolence, and justice of God." The City of God is not manifest in the civil government, but it is not irrelevant to it either. Rather it is a model towards which the State strives, knowing it will never fully attain it, but regarding it as a standard against which to measure earthly imperfection.

For Calvin, the Civil authorities, as God's ministers, deserve subjects' obedience, but only if they do not violate God's trust. The Church is the best determiner of that trust and therefore it resumes its role as a check on the State, in this world.

It has been suggested[6] that John Calvin's theology, while classically Protestant in its emphasis on the Scriptural basis of knowledge, justification by faith, original sin and God's Grace, corrects some of the Reformation excesses found in Luther, by restoring the Church institution (albeit along Protestant lines) and re-establishing the place of religion (and the Church) in the politics of this world.

The following selection is Calvin's chapter "On Civil Government" in his *Institutes of the Christian Religion*.[7]

---

[6] In Sheldon Wolins' essay "Calvin: The Political Education of Protestantism" in *Politics and Vision* (Boston: Little, Brown, 1960).

[7] This selection is drawn from *On God and Political Duty,* edited by John T. McNeil (Indianapolis: Bobbs-Merrill, 1956) which uses the 1813 translation of the *Institutes,* translated by John Allen, published by Westminster Press, Philadelphia, PA.

ON CIVIL GOVERNMENT

Having already stated that man is the subject of two kinds of government, and having sufficiently discussed that which is situated in the soul, or the inner man, and relates to eternal life–we are, in this chapter, to say something of the other kind which relates to civil justice and the regulation of the external conduct. For, though the nature of this argument seems to have no connection with the spiritual doctrine of faith which I have undertaken to discuss, the sequel will show that I have sufficient reason for connecting them togehter, and, indeed, that necessity obliges me to it, especially since, on the one hand, infatuated and barbarous men madly endeavor to subvert this ordinance established by God, and, on the other hand, the flatterers of princes, extolling their power beyond all just bounds, hesitate not to oppose it to the authority of God himself. Unless both these errors be resisted, the purity of the faith will be destroyed.

Yet this distinction does not lead us to consider the whole system of civil government as a polluted thing which has nothing to do with Christian men. Some fanatics who are pleased with nothing but liberty, or rather licentiousness without any restraint, do indeed boast and vociferate, that since we are dead with Christ to the elements of this world and, being translated into the kingdom of God, sit among the celestials, it is a degradation to us and far beneath our dignity to be occupied with those secular and impure cares which relate to things altogether uninteresting to a Christian man. Of what use, they ask, are laws without judgments and tribunals? But what have judgments to do with a Christian man? And if it be unlawful to kill, of what use are laws and judgments to us? But as we have just suggested that this kind of government is distinct from that spiritual and internal reign of Christ, so it ought to be known that they are in no respect at variance with each other. For that spiritual reign, even now upon earth, commences within us some preludes of the heavenly kingdom, and in this mortal and transitory life affords us some prelibations of immortal and incorruptible blessedness; but this civil government is designed, as long as we live in this world, to cherish and support the external worship of God, to preserve the pure doctrine of religion, to defend the constitution of the Church, to regulate our lives in a manner requisite for the society of men, to form our manners to civil justice, to promote our concord with each other, and to establish general peace and tranquility–all of which I confess to be superfluous if the kingdom of God, as it now exists in us, extinguishes the present life. But if it is the will of God that while we are aspiring toward our true country, we be pilgrims on the earth, and if such aids are necessary to our pilrimage, they who take them from man deprive him of his human nature.

The Lord has not only testified that the function of magistrates has his approbation and acceptance, but has eminently commended it to us, by dignifying it with the most honorable titles. We will mention a few of them. When all who sustain the magistracy are called "gods," it ought not to be considered as an appellation of trivial importance, for it implies that they have their command from God, that they are invested with his authority and are altogether his representatives, and act as his viceregents. This is not an invention of mine, but the interpretation of Christ, who says, "If he called them gods, unto whom the word of God came, and the Scripture cannot be broken."

This consideration ought continually to occupy the magistrates themselves, since it is calculated to furnish them with a powerful stimulus by which they may be excited to their duty, and to afford them peculiar consolation by which the difficulties of their office, which certainly are many and arduous, may be alleviated. For what an ardent pursuit of integrity, prudence, clemency moderation, and innocence ought they to prescribe to themselves who are conscious of having been constituted ministers of the Divine justice! With what audacity will they pronounce an unjust sentence with that mouth which they know to be the destined organ of Divine truth? With what conscience will they subscribe to impious decrees with that hand which they know to be appointed to register the edicts of God? In short, if they remember that they are the viceregents of God, it behooves them to watch with all care, earnestness, and diligence, that in their administration they may exhibit to men an image, as it were, of the providence, care, goodness, benevolence, and justice of God. And they must constantly bear this in mind that if in all cases "he be cursed that doeth the word of the Lord deceitfully," a far heavier curse awaits those who act fraudulently in a righteous calling.

And this admonition is entitled to have considerable weight with them; for if they fail in their duty, they not only injure men by criminally distressing them, but even offend God by polluting his sacred judgments. On the other hand, it opens a source of peculiar consolation to them to reflect that they are not employed in profane things, or occupations unsuitable to a servant of God, but in a most sacred function, inasmuch as they execute a Divine commission.

Those who are not restrained by so many testimonies of Scripture, but still dare to stigmatize this sacred ministry as a thing incompatible with religion and Christian piety, do they not offer an insult to God himself, who cannot but be involved in the reproach cast upon his ministry?

Moreover, though there are various forms of magistracy, yet there is no difference in this respect, but we ought to receive them all as ordinances of God. For Paul comprehends them all together when he says that "there is no power but of God"; and that which was furthest from giving general satisfaction is recommended to us in a remarkable manner beyond all others–namely, the government of one man, which, as it is attended with the common servitude of all, except the single individual to whose will all others are subjected, has never been so highly approved by heroic and noble minds. But the Scripture, on the contrary, to correct these unjust sentiments, expressly affirms that it is by the providence of Divine wisdom that kings reign, and particularly commands us to "honor the king."

The first duty of subjects toward their magistrates is to entertain the most honorable sentiments of their function, which they know to be a jurisdiction delegated to them from God, and on that account to esteem and reverence them as God's minsiters and viceregents. For there are some persons to be found who show themselves very obedient to their magistrates and have not the least wish that there were no magistrates for them to obey, because they know them to be so necessary to the public good, but who, nevertheless, consider the magistrates themselves as no other than necessary evils. But something more than this is required of us by Peter when he commands us to "honor the king"; and by Solomon, when he says, "Fear thou the Lord and the king"; for Peter, under the term "honor," comprehends a sincere and candid esteem; and Solomon, by connecting the king with the Lord, attributes to him a kind of sacred veneration and dignity. It is also a remarkable commendation of magistrates which is given by Paul, when he says that we "must needs be subject, not only for wrath, but also for conscience' sake"; by which he means that subjects ought to be induced to submit to princes and governors, not merely from a dread of their power, as persons are accustomed to yield to an armed enemy, who they know will immediately take vengeance upon them if they resist; but because the obedience which is rendered to princes and magistrates is rendered to God, from whom they have received their authority. I am not speaking of the persons as if the mask of dignity ought to palliate or excuse folly, ignorance, or cruelty, and conduct the most nefarious and flagitious, and so to acquire for vices the praise due to virtues; but I affirm that the station itself is worthy of honor and reverence, so that, whoever our governors are, they ought to possess our esteem and veneration on account of the office which they fill.

Hence follows another duty–that, with minds disposed to honor and reverence magistrates, subjects approve their obedience to them in submitting to their edicts, in paying taxes, in discharging public duties, and bearing burdens which relate to the common defense, and in fulfilling all their other commands. Paul says to the Romans, "Let every soul be subject unto the higher powers. Whosoever resisteth the power, resisteth the ordinance of God." He writes to Titus, "Put them in mind to be subject to principalities and powers, to obey magistrates, to be ready to every good work." Peter exhorts, "Submit yourselves to every ordinance of man for the Lord's sake; whether it be to the king, as supreme; or unto governors, as unto them that are sent by him for the punishment of evildoers, and for the praise of them that do well." Moreover, that subjects may testify that theirs is not a hypocritical but a sincere and cordial submission Paul teaches that they ought to pray to God for the safety and prosperity of those under whose government they live. "I exhort," he says, "that supplications, prayers, intercessions, and giving of thanks be made for all men; for kings, and for all that are in authority; that we may lead a quiet and peaceable life in all godliness and honesty." Here let no man deceive himself. For as it is impossible to resist the magistrate without at the same time resisting God himself, though an unarmed magisrate may seem to be despised with impunity, yet God is armed to inflict exemplary vengeance on the contempt offered to himself. Under this obedience I also include the moderation which private persons ought to prescribe to themselves in relation to public affairs, that they do not, without being called upon, intermeddle with affairs of state or rashly intrude themselves into the office of magistrates, or undertake anything of a public nature. If there be anything in the public administration which requires to be corrected, let them not raise any tumults or take the business into their own hands, which ought to be all bound in this respect, but let them refer it to the cognizance of the magistrate, who is alone authorized to regulate the concerns of the public. I mean that they ought to attempt nothing without being commanded; for when they have the command of a governor, then they also are invested with public authority. For, as we are accustomed to call the counsellors of a prince "his eyes and ears," so they may not unaptly be called "his hands" whom he has commissioned to execute his commands.

    Now, as we have hitherto described a magistrate who truly answers to his title–who is the father of his country and, as the poet calls him, the pastor of his people, the guardian of peace, the protector of justice, the avenger of innocence; he would justly be deemed insane who disapproved of such a government. But, as it has happened, in almost all ages, that some princes, regardless of everything to which they ought to have directed their attention and provision, give themselves up to their pleasures in indolent exemption from every care; others, absorbed in their own inteest, expose to sale all laws privileges, rights, and judgments; others plunder the public wealth which they afterwards lavish in mad prodigality; others commit flagrant outrages, pillaging houses, violating virgins and matrons, and murdering infants; many persons cannot be persuaded that such ought to be acknowledged as princes whom, as far as possible, they ought to obey. For in such enormities and actions so completely incompatible, not only with the office of a magistrate, but with the duty of every man, they discover no appearance of the image of God, which ought to be conspicuous in a magistrate; while they perceive no vestige of that minister of God who is "not a terror to good works, but to the evil," who is sent "for the punishment of evildoers, and for the praise of them that do well"; nor recognize that governor whose dignity and authority the Scripture recommends to us. And certainly the minds of men have always been naturally disposed to hate and execrate tyrants as much as to love and reverence legitimate kings.

But, if we direct our attention to the word of God, it will cary us much farther: even to submit to the government, not only of those princes who discharge their duty to us with becoming integrity and fidelity, but of all who possess the sovereignty, even though they perform none of the duties of their function. For, though the Lord testifies that the magistrate is an eminent gift of his liberality to preserve the safety of men, and prescribes to magistrates themselves the extent of their duty, yet he at the same time declares that whatever be their characters, they have their government only from him; that those who govern for the public good are true specimens and mirrors of his eneficence; and that those who rule in an unjust and tyrannical manner are raised up by him to punish the iniquity of the people.

But in the obedience which we have shown to be due to the authority of governors, it is always necessary to make one exception, and that is entitled to our first attention–that it do not seduce us from obedience to him to whose will the desires of all kings ought to be subject, to whose decrees all their commands ought to yield, to whose majesty all their scepters ought to submit. And, indeed, how preposterous it would be for us, with a view to satisfy men, to incur the displeasure of him on whose account we yield obedience to men! The Lord, therefore, is the King of kings; who, when he has opened his sacred mouth, is to be heard alone, above all, for all, and before all; in the next place, we are subject to those men who preside over us, but no otherwise than in him. If they command anything against him, it ought not to have the least attention, nor, in this case, ought we to pay any regard to all that dignity attahed to magistrates, to which no injury is done when it is subjected to the unrivaled and supreme power of God. On this principle Daniel denied that he had committed any crime against the king. . . .

CHAPTER V Liberal Anglicanism
WILLIAM TEMPLE

William Temple

INTRODUCTION

William Temple (1881-1944) was Archbishp of Canterbury and considered a classic representative of liberal theology and politics in the twentieth century. He studied Neo-Hegelian philosophy at Oxford, and served as Canon Westminster, Bishop of Manchester, and Archbishop of York before assuming the Primacy of the Anglican Church. He was known as "the People's Archbishop," for his liberal views on social and economic issues, but was never identified with any particular party or movement.

Temple insisted that the Church must be involved in politics, but always as the Church–applying general Christian principles to social problems, but not giving specific technical solutions. He endorsed many "social welfare" programs in England (public housing, health care, unemployment relief, educational reforms, etc.) on the grounds that the problems they addressed damaged the spiritual growth of individuals and their dignity as creatures of God. The Church, therefore, has a duty to advise the State on social matters affecting citizens' spiritual health, including economic matters, and to move the world towards a Christian social order where exists "the fullest possible development of individual personality in the widest and deepest possible fellowship."[8]

So, for example, Temple participated with other Bishops in attempting to resolve a major coal strike in Britain, not by siding with management or labour, or by offering specific terms of contract, but by emphasizing the Christian principles of love and unity to both sides in the dispute, hoping for a fair and just reconciliation. The Church, Temple believed, should address all social ills similarly.

"The method of the Church's impact upon society as large should be twofold. The Church must announce Christian principles and point out where the existing social order at any time is in conflict with them. It must then pass on to Christian citizens, acting in their civic capacity, the task of re-shaping the existing order in closer conformity to the principles, for at this point technical knowledge may be required and judgements of practical expedi- ency are always required. If a bridge is to be built, the Church may remind the engineer that it is his obligation to provide a really safe bridge; but it is not entitled to tell him whether, in fact, his design meets this requirement. . . ."[9]

Thus, Temple separates the general aims of a Christian society, which the

---

[8] William Temple, *Christianity and the Social Order,* (Baltimore, 1942), p. 100.

[9] *Ibid.,* p. 50.

Church must articulate, for the specific means of achieving it, which the Church is not always competent to judge. The Church, therefore is obliged to advise and criticize the world but not to prescribe specific policies or directly rule the world. Temple summarized the proper role of the Church in society this way:

"So we answer the question, 'How should the Church interfere?' by saying: In three ways–(1) its members must fulfill their moral responsibilities and functions in a Christian spirit; (2) its members must exercise their purely civic rights in a Christian spirit; (3) it must itself supply them with a systematic statement of principles to aid them in doing these two things, and this will carry with it a denunciation of customs or institutions in contemporary life and practice which offend against those principles."[10]

The following selections are from Archbishop Temple's last book, *Christianity and the Social Order* (1942), and include his general theological approach to Religion and Politics and some specific "social welfare" policy suggestions to the Britain of his time.

---

[10] *Ibid.*, pp. 31-32.

WHAT RIGHT HAS THE CHURCH TO INTERFERE?

The claim of the Christian Church to make its voice heard in matters of politics and economics is very widely resented, even by those who are Christian in personal belief and in devotional practice. It is commonly assumed that Religion is one department of life, like Art or Science, and that it is playing the part of a busybody when it lays down principles for the guidance of other departments, whether Art and Science or Business and Politics. When a group of Bishops attempted to bring Government, coal-owners, and miners together in a solution of the disastrous Coal Strike of 1926, Mr. Baldwin, then Prime Minister, asked how the Bishops would like it if he referred to the Iron and Steel Federation the revision of the Athanasian Creed, and this was acclaimed as a legitimate score.

I

Few people read much history. In an age when it is tacitly assumed that the Church is concerned with another world than this, and in this with nothing but individual conduct as bearing on prospects in that other world, hardly any one reads the history of the Church in its exercise of political influence. It is assumed that the Church exercises little influence and ought to exercise none; it is further assumed that this assumption is self-evident and has always been made by reasonable men. As a matter of fact it is entirely modern and extremely questionable.

Of course, it has a real foundation. No assumption is commonly made without one. The foundation is two-fold, and consists, first, in a perfectly sound conviction that each main department of life is independent and autonomous as regards its own technique, and secondly that the Church in the days of its power, and Christian theorists of a later time, have often ignored this. Just as the theologians interfered with the autonomy of Natural Science on its own ground in the case of Galileo, so they have at times interfered with action in the economic field where technical as well as moral questions were involved. The attempts made by Archbishop Laud to use the Star Chamber as a means of preventing the oppression of the common people by 'engrossing' corn or his eagerness to promote the work of the Commissions established to check 'enclosures', illustrate this. Laud was petulant and arrogant; but he was a friend of the poor with a genuine passion for justice, and a stalwart opponent of that 'progress' which enslaves them. He has been too harshly judged. 'If his vices made him intolerable to the most powerful forces of his own age, his virtues were not of a kind to commend him to those of its successor, and history has been hardly more merciful to him than were his political opponents.'

Laud was no innovator. He was a die-hard conservative. He was trying to conserve the medieval tradition which the great Reformers did not repudiate but rather tried to re-establish. Latimer was quite as much a prophetic upholder of the old moral principles in political economy as a reformer of ecclesiastical doctrine and worship. The control of the Church in this field has never been fully effective, but its law was not a dead letter. 'Florence was the financial capital of medieval Europe; but even at Florence the secular authorities fined bankers right and left for usury in the middle of the fourteenth century.' Two centuries later 'Archbishop Grindal's injunctions to the laity of the Province of York (1571) expressly emphasized the duty of presenting to the Ordinary those who lend and demand back more than the principal, whatever the guise under which the transaction may be concealed.'

It was not till after the Restoration that the Church in England ceased to claim moral control in the field of business. Then there was a rapid retreat upon the central citadel of religion, and during most of the eighteenth century theology and the direct relation of the soul to God were alone regarded as the Church's concern. This could not last. John Wesley had no intention of bringing the Church back into politics; but his revival had that effect. The abolition of the slave trade and of slavery itself were political projects; but they were carried through by Evangelicals in the fervour of their Evangelical faith. It is reported of Lord Melbourne, Queen Victoria's first Prime Minister, that after hearing an Evangelical preacher he remarked that, if religion was going to interfere with the affairs of private life, things were come to a pretty pass; later Prime Ministers have felt and said the same about the interference of religion with the affairs of public life; but the interference steadily increases and will increase.

It is interesting to note the stages of the recovery. First came the long campaign for the abolition of the slave trade and emancipation of the slaves. This was prompted by human sympathy and care for the individuals affected. It was shortly afterwards followed by the movement for the reform of prisons associated at successive stages with the names of John Howard and Elizabeth Fry. Still the concern was for individuals. Then came the series of Factory Acts; and still the motive was concern for individuals; but now, not only was the action taken political, but it was such as affected the relations between employer and employed, and, to that extent, the structure of society. While that series of Acts was being passed, James Ludlow, soon to be followed by F. D. Maurice and Charles Kingsley, launched the Christian Social Movement, which subjected the whole order of society to criticism in the light of Christian beliefs about God and man. This was carried on Westcott, Gore, and Scott Holland up to the eve of the Four Years' War and into the period following it. Its fullest expression, perhaps, was the Conference on Christian Politics, Economics, and Citizenship (Copec) held at Birmingham in

1924.

This rapid survey of history shows that the claim of the Church to-day to be heard in relation to political and economic problems is no new usurpation, but a reassertion of a right once universally admitted and widely regarded. But it also shows that this right may be compromised by injudicious exercise, especially when the 'autonomy of technique' in the various departments of life is ignored. Religion may rightly censure the use of artistic talents for making money out of men's baser tastes, but it cannot lay down laws about perspective or the use of a paint-brush. It may insist that scientific enquiry be prompted by a pure love of truth and not distorted (as in Nazi Germany) by political considerations. It may declare the proper relation of the economic to other activities of men, but it cannot claim to know what will be the purely economic effect of particular proposals. It is, however, entitled to say that some economic gains ought not to be sought because of the injuries involved to interests higher than economic; and this principle of the subordination of the whole economic sphere is not yet generally accepted. We all recognize that in fact the exploitation of the poor, especially of workhouse children, in the early days of power-factories was an abomination not to be excused by any economic advantage thereby secured; but we fail to recognize that such an admission in a particular instance carries with it the principle that economics are properly subject to a non-economic criterion.

II

The approach to the problem in our own time is to be made along four distinct lines: (1) the claims of sympathy for those who suffer; (2) the educational influence of the social and economic system; (3) the challenge offered to our existing system in the name of justice; (4) the duty of conformity to the 'Natural Order' in which is to be found the purpose of God.

(1) The suffering caused by existing evils makes a claim upon our sympathy which the Christian heart and conscience cannot ignore. Before the outbreak of war there were three main causes of widespread suffering–bad housing, malnutrition, and unemployment. The varied forms of suffering which bad housing causes are easy to imagine in part, but few who have had no personal knowledge of it are able to imagine the whole–the crushing of a woman's pride in her home through the ceaseless and vain struggle against dirt and squalor; the nervous fret; the lack of home comforts for the tired worker; the absence of any space for children to play. The bad conditions in slum quarters are not chiefly due to the people living there. When they are moved to new housing estates, more than half of them rise fully to the fresh opportunity, and three-quarters of them make a reasonable use of it. The toleration of bad housing is a wanton and callous cruelty.

Malnutrition is a direct result of poverty and ignorance. It produces enfeebled bodies, embittered minds and irritable spirits; thus it tells against good citizenship and good fellowship. Children are the most obvious sufferers, but those who have suffered in this way as children seldom come later to full strength or to physical and spiritual stability. It was found, when attempts were made to organize physical training classes for the unemployed, that most of these could not take advantage of the training offered; it made them too hungry.

Unemployment is the most hideous of our social evils, and has lately seemed to have become established in a peculiarly vicious form. We have long been acquainted with transitional, seasonal, and cyclical unemployment–in which catalogue the adjectives represent a *crescendo* of evil; but now we have also to face long-term unemployment.

Transitional unemployment is no more than a period of inactivity between the completion of one job and the beginning of the next. With a reasonable scheme of Insurance it is no great evil, provided the period is short. It does not sap away a man's humanity.

Seasonal unemployment is necessarily incidental to some occupations in which, at certain seasons of the year, there is little work to be done. The seasons are known and it is possible to make provisions for them. The Danes are the pioneers in this matter; it was part of the scheme of the People's High Schools that they would provide educational courses for periods of seasonal unemployment. The courses provided–in Danish history and literature and in the principles of co-operative farming–played a large part in securing for Denmark its high level of agricultural prosperity. By these and other devices, with a sound Insurance scheme, seasonal unemployment can be converted into valuable leisure.

Cyclical unemployment is a far more serious matter. The history of trade, since the Industrial Revolution and the introduction of power-production, has shown alternating periods of prosperity and depression, 'boom' and 'slump'. Before 1914 a 'slump' caused suffering of appalling intensity; charitable people organized soup-kitchens and in other ways tried to save families from hunger and despair. The special problem caused by demobilization alike of soldiers and of munition-workers led to the establishment of what is unfairly called 'the dole', apart from which a revolution could hardly have been avoided. But still the volume of suffering caused by cyclical unemployment is fearful; for the period of inactivity is often long, so that the problem approximates to that of the worst form of the trouble, which is of comparatively recent origin and is now chronic.

This is long-term unemployment, which seems to be incurable under our present system except by the drastic remedy of war. For a study of this terrible social evil I must refer to *Men Without Work,* a survey financed by the Pilgrim

Trust and published by the Cambridge University Press. The main points to notice are these:

(a) The worst evil of such unemployment, whether due to cyclical or to more permanent conditions, is its creating in the unemployed a sense that they have fallen out of the common life. However much their physical needs may be supplied (and before the war this supply was in many cases inadequate) the gravest part of the trouble remains; they are not wanted! That is the thing that has power to corrupt the soul of any man not already far advanced in saintliness. Because the man has no opportunity of service, he is turned in upon himself and becomes, according to his temperament, a contented loafer or an embittered self-seeker. It has not been sufficiently appreciated that this moral isolation is the heaviest burden and most corrosive poison associated with unemployment: not bodily hunger but social futility. Consequently it is no remedy to pay the unemployed man as much as the employed; unless he has intellectual interests with which to occupy his leisure and is able to turn these into a means of service by study resulting in books or lectures, this will only make him content with idleness; and we have enough people suffering from that form of deadly sin (technically called Sloth) at the other end of the social scale. Nothing will touch the real need except to enable the man to do something which is needed by the community. For it is part of the principle of personality that we should live for one another.

(b) Much depends on the history and experience of the particular individuals concerned. A recent enquiry disclosed the disquieting fact that in a town where long-term unemployment was rife, the older men, who had formerly had experience of full employment, preferred to go back to work even at a wage less than their unemployment benefit, while the younger, who had never had regular employment, preferred to be idle 'on the dole' even if they could earn a larger weekly sum. This does not mean that they were happy in idleness; most of them were conscious of futility and frustration (though they would not use those words about it), and they were bitter against a world which had no use for them and made no room for them; but they had a strong distaste for the drudgery of regular work. They were degraded into a condition of universal dissatisfaction.

The only real cure for unemployment is employment–beginning from the time when school-education is complete and continuing, with no longer intervals than can be appreciated as holidays, till strength begins to fail. In other words we are challenged to find a social order which provides employment, steadily and generally, and our consciences should be restive till we succeed. Christian sympathy demands this.

(2) What has been said about unemployment has already carried us on to the second ground for the Church's concern in social questions–the educational influence of the social and economic system in which men live. This was first set

forth by Plato in Books VIII and IX of the *Republic*. The social order at once expresses the sense of values active in the minds of citizens and tends to reproduce the same sense of values in each new generation. If the State is so ordered as to give great prominence to military leaders, as Sparta was, as Prussia was, as Nazi Germany is, this must represent the fact that the effective body of citizens, which may be a compact minority, regards the military qualities as specially honourable or specially important; and the system expressing that estimate impresses it by perpetual suggestion upon every growing generation. So it is if wealth receives conspicuous honour.

The Nazis take all young Germans into the *Hitler-Jugend* and train them in the qualities admired and needed by the Nazi *regime*. We throw most young Englishmen out into a world of fierce competition where each has to stand on his own feet (which is good) and fight for his own interest (which is bad), if he is not to be submerged. Our system is not deliberately planned, but it produces effects just the same. It offers a perpetual suggestion in the direction of combative self-assertiveness. It is recognized on all hands that the economic system is an educative influence, for good or ill, of immense potency. Marshall, the prince of orthodox economists of the last generation, ranks it with the religion of a country as the most formative influence in the moulding of a people's character. If so, then assuredly the Church must be concerned with it. For a primary concern of the Church is to develop in men a Christian character. When it finds by its side an educative influence so powerful it is bound to ask whether that influence is one tending to develop Christian character, and if the answer is partly or wholly negative the Church must do its utmost to secure a change in the economic system so that it may find in that system an ally and not an enemy. How far this is the situation in our country to-day we shall consider later. At present it is enough to say that the Church cannot, without betraying its own trust, omit criticism of the economic order, or fail to urge such action as may be prompted by that criticism.

(3) The existing system is challenged on moral grounds. It is not merely that some who 'have not' are jealous of some who 'have'. The charge against our social system is one of injustice. The banner so familiar in earlier unemployed or socialist processions–'Damn your charity; we want justice'–vividly exposes the situation as it was seen by its critics. If the present order is taken for granted or assumed to be sacrosanct, charity from the more or less fortunate would seem virtuous and commendable; to those for whom the order itself is suspect or worse, such charity is blood-money. Why should some be in the position to dispense and others to need that kind of charity?

An infidel could ignore that challenge, for apart from faith in God there is really nothing to be said for the notion of human equality. Men do not seem to be equal in any respect, if we judge by available evidence. But if all are children of one Father, then all are equal heirs of a status in comparison with which the apparent differences of quality and capacity are unimportant; in the deepest and most important of all–their relationship to God–all are equal. Why should some of God's children have full opportunity to develop their capacities in freely-chosen occupations, while others are confined to a stunted form of existence, enslaved to types of labour which represent no personal choice but the sole opportunity offered? The Christian cannot ignore a challenge in the name of justice. He must either refuse it or, accepting it, devote himself to removal of the stigma. The moral quality of the accusation brought against the economic and social order involves the Church in interference' on pain of betraying the trust committed to it.

(4) For the commission given to the Church is that it carry out the purpose of God. That is what is meant by the description of it as 'the Body of Christ'. It is to be the instrument or organ of His will, as His fleshly Body was in the days of His earthly ministry. That Body has many functions to fulfil, and one of them is suffering. The members of the Church do not, or should not, belong to it for what they can get in this world or in any other world; they–we–should belong to it in order to take our share in the great work, the fulfilment of God's purpose in the world and beyond it.

We know in outline what that is. God could make, and did make, multitudes of things which always obey His law for them–suns and planets, molecules and atoms, all that is studied in the 'natural sciences'. But He also made men and women, with hearts and wills that cannot be coerced but can respond freely, in order that there might be a fellowship of love answering the love with which He made them. But they used their freedom for self-seeking; so He came Himself to share our life and our death, in order that He might show that love which prompted the activity of creation in a form intelligible to men and women, the form of a human life. Thereby He gathered together a fellowship of those who respond to that appeal, to be at once the nucleus of the universal fellowship of love and the chief means to its establishment. (All this is a paraphrase of the Epistle to the Ephesians read from one angle. St. Paul is there wheeling round and round his theme, like an eagle in flight, and seeing it from many angles; but the theme is the purpose of God in creation, manifested in Jesus the Messiah, accomplished through the Church.)

If we belong to the Church with such a purpose and hope as this, we are obliged to ask concerning every field of human activity what is the purpose of God for it. If we find this purpose it will be the true and proper nature of that activity, and the relation of the various activities to one another in the divine purpose will be the 'Natural Order' of those activities. To bring them into that Order, if they have in fact departed from it, must be one part of the task of the Church as the Body of Christ. If what has true value as a means to an end beyond itself is in fact being sought as an end in itself, the Church must rebuke this dislocation of the structure of life and if possible point out the way of recovery. It is bound to 'interfere' because it is by vocation the agent of God's purpose, outside the scope of which no human interest or activity can fall.

HOW SHOULD THE CHURCH INTERFERE?

When people talk about Church History they usually have in mind a record of theological controversies, General or other Councils, and the formulation of doctrines. All that is immensely important. But Church History is a vastly bigger thing than that; it is the story of the impact made by the Spirit of Christ upon the life of mankind.

The Church never gets credit for the greater part of what it does. That does not very much matter, because credit (like merit in Lord Melbourne's dictum) is 'only what one gentleman thinks of another gentleman'; and Christians are warned not to concern themselves about that. No doubt some people would attend more to the Church and therefore also to its Gospel if they knew all that it really does in the world; that would be a gain as far as it goes; but each heart must know its need before it finds the satisfaction of that need in Christ. It is not so much to gain for the Church the credit and influence to which it is entitled that I emphasize the importance of clear thinking about the way in which the Church does its work, but rather for the avoidance of confusion of thought tending to calamitous results in practice.

Nine-tenths of the work of the Church in the world is done by Christian people fulfilling responsibilities and performing tasks which in themselves are not part of the official system of the Church at all. For example, the abolition of the Slave Trade and, later, of Slavery itself, was carried through by Wilberforce and his friends in the inspiration of their Christian faith and by means of appeal to the Christian principles professed by their fellow-citizens. The far-reaching reform of our penal system in the interval between the two wars has been effected by a group of men who, being concerned with its administration, thought out the question how, on Christian principles, a community ought to treat its own offenders. And apart from specific achievements like these there is the pervasive sweetening of life and of all human relationships by those who carry with them something of the Mind of Christ, received from Christian upbringing, from prayer and meditation, and from communion. No particular enterprises, nor all of them together, can compare in importance with the influence so exerted. To this extent they are justified who say that the task of the Church in face of social problems is to make good Christian men and women. That is by far its most important contribution. But (as I shall contend in a moment) it has others, less important and yet for their own purpose indispensable.

Next to the work of the Church done through its members in ordinary human relationships and in ordinary avocations, we may consider its work done through its members in their capacity as citizens shaping the political decisions which affect the national life and destiny. It is of crucial importance that the Church acting corporately should not commit itself to any particular policy. A policy always depends on technical decisions concerning the actual relations of cause and effect in the political and economic world; about these a Christian as such has no more reliable judgement than an atheist, except so far as he should be more immune to the temptations of self-interest. After the last war most Christian leaders in England strongly supported the principle of the League of Nations. The Bishop of Gloucester always dissented from this, and now holds that the League and its supporters are largely responsible for the outbreak of this present war, because they lured men to rely upon a security which in fact did not exist. It would be monstrous to suggest that this sincerely held judgement on the actual process of history proves him who holds it to be a less loyal or less whole-hearted Christian than the Bishops with whom he disagreed. The Church must not corporately be committed to either view. This refusal to adopt a particular policy is partly a matter of prudence, for the policy may turn out to be mistaken, as indeed every policy always turns out to have been less than perfectly adapted to the situation, and the Church must not be involved in its failure; still more is it a matter of justice, for even though a large majority of Christians hold a particular view, the dissentient minority may well be equally loyal to Christ and equally entitled to be recognized as loyal members of His Church. At the end of this book I shall offer, in my capacity as a Christian citizen, certain proposals for definite action which would, in my private judgement, conduce to a more Christian ordering of society; but if any member of the Convocation of York should be so ill-advised as to table a resolution that these proposals be adopted as a political programme for the Church, I should in my capacity as Archbishop resist that proposal with all my force, and should probably, as President of the Convocation, rule it out of order. The Church is committed to the everlasting Gospel and to the Creeds which formulate it; it must never commit itself to an ephemeral programme of detailed action.

But this repudiation of direct political action does not exhaust its political responsibility. It must explicitly call upon its members to exercise their citizenship in a Christian spirit. After the great Conference on Christian Politics, Economics and Citizenship ('Copec'), held in Birmingham in 1924, the Christian ratepayers of a London Borough approached their Borough Council with a demand that their rates should be increased in order that some very bad housing in the Borough might be improved. When it became apparent, after the 'economic blizzard', that the Chancellor of the Exchequer would, for the first time in several years, have a surplus to dispose of, a great number of Christian income-tax payers wrote to their Members of Parliament to urge that restoration of the 'cuts' in unemployment relief should take precedence of any reduction in the rate of income-tax. There are frequently occasions when there is opportunity for generous action in the political field; Christians should take advantage of these and ought to be able to feel that they have the support of the whole Church in doing so. To a considerable extent, though not by any means completely, the Conservative and Labour Parties represent the 'haves' and the 'have-nots' respectively. That is politically unwholesome and ethically un- Christian. The Church must constantly press upon its members that the only question they should ask before casting their votes is the question–not 'What will best suit ME?' but 'What will be best for the country?'–and even then to take care that the standard of 'best' and 'worst' is the Christian standard. For it is tragically easy to be even fanatically devoted to a purely pagan ideal for one's nation; the Nazi movement has taught us that.

So far there is probably little dispute among Christians who have given serious thought to the subject. It is recognized that Christian men and women in the various walks of life should bring the spirit of Christ to bear upon their work, as well as on their purely personal relationships; and it is recognized, though perhaps not frequently enough asserted, that Christians should vote in a Christian spirit at least to the extent of preferring the public advantage to their own, and ob subordinating the interest of their own section of society to that of a section evidently in greater need. But is this all? Is each individual Christian citizen to be left to work out by his own unaided effort what is the good of the community to which his own interest is to be subordinated? Can we, in face of the Nazi combination of complete personal self-dedication with absolute national egoism, still say it is no business of the Church to work out a scale of values for the political field?

I am to do what is best for my country? Very well. There is an opportunity to acquire for it additional wealth and power by merely expropriating some small State whose citizens are happy in their independence, or again by some successful diplomatic deception. Is it 'good' for my country to gain power or wealth by those means? Is it 'good' for a country to gain the whole world and to lose its own soul? If not, why not? Must there not be some ordered system of principles which represents the real 'good', and which is outraged by such conduct, however patriotic its motive or however successful its accomplishment?

It is here, as I contend, that the Church has to recover lost ground. It has in the past concerned itself very actively with these questions. It developed what was for the needs of the period a very complete system of principles by which those who were responsible for the public ordering of life might be guided. For a variety of reasons, at which we shall glance in the next chapter, this whole area of human activity was evacuated by the Church. Yet duties recognized as incumbent on the individual can scarcely be performed unless the Church recovers this lost territory.

In this enterprise we shall be censured for departure from our own contention that the Church is concerned with principles and not with policy. For the framing of policy knowledge of contemporary facts, and that power to estimate tendencies which comes only from specialist study, are indispensable. But a statement of principles will carry us on to ground commonly left during the last three centuries to purely secular forces; it is bound to seem like an intrusion into practical politics, even when it scrupulously stops short. And the line of demarcation is not very clear. It may be possible to draw it with more definiteness when we have reviewed the history of the Church's enterprise or lack of it in this field, and have set out some of the principles concerned. The aim, however, is clear throughout. The Christian citizen is required in his civic action (e.g. voting) to promote the best interest of his country, with a Christian interpretation of the word 'best'; the aim of any formulation of Christian social principles is to provide that Christian interpretation or at least the means of reaching it.

So we answer the question 'How should the Church interfere?' by saying: In three ways—(1) its members must fulfil their moral responsibilities and functions in a Christian spirit; (2) its members must exercise their purely civic rights in a Christian spirit; (3) it must itself supply them with a systematic staement of principles to aid them in doing these two things, and this will carry with it a denunciation of customs or institutions in contemporary life and practice which offend against those principles.

There remains the question whether or not the Church should ever interfere in a particular issue, such as, for example, an actual trade dispute which has broken out. It can be answered with almost complete assurance that the Church, acting officially, should stand aside. It has its own witness to give; and if this were heeded, no dispute would arise. It is very seldom that Christianity offers a solution of practical problems; what it can do is to lift the parties to a level of thought and feeling at which the problem disappears. In parts of South-Eastern Europe there are regions in which different races and cultures are so intermingled that there is no hope of establishing justice among them so long as each asserts its claim against the other. So long as that condition exists, the problem to which it gives rise is insoluble. If, on the other hand, all could be brought to love their neighbours as themselves, there would be no problem. It would not be solved; it would be abolished.

So it was that our Lord refused to settle a dispute about an inheritance. One of two brothers had a grievance; he thought he was not getting the share due to him; so he came with the request: 'Master, bid my brother divide the inheritance with me.' But He refused to settle the dispute–'Man, who made Me a judge or a divider over you?' Instead, He tells them how to avoid having a dispute to settle: 'Take heed, and keep yourselves from all covetousness.' For, of course, if there had been no covetousness in either brother, there would have been no dispute.

But though the Church, and its agents acting in its name, cannot undertake to give judgement between contending parties, they may, as promoters of goodwill, try to bring the contending parties together. So Bishop Westcott secured a settlement of a Durham coal-strike by pleading with each side to recognize what was fair in the contention of the other, till they came in fact to an agreement. No one questions the propriety of the Bishop's action in that case. Let me illustrate the principle further by reference to the action of a group of Bishops, of whom I was one, in 1926–the action which led to Lord Baldwin's comment quoted near the beginning of this book. The coal-strike, which had been the occasion of the general strike, had lasted several months. These Bishops decided to try to bring the parties together. They had no proposals of their own to make–that would have been to go beyond their province. But there had been a Royal Commission and its recommendations had not been adopted. We decided to see how far the representatives of the coal-owners and the representatives of the miners would be willing to come towards agreement in acceptance of those recommendations. Both parties were willing to meet us. At that date the miners were ready to accept the proposals of the Commission as a basis of negotiation; the owners were not. But as the owners had at first been willing to do so if the miners would do so as well, it seemed right to report to the Prime Minister what we had found. Our effort was a failure. It is arguable that nothing but success (such as Bishop Westcott achieved) justified any intervention. My plea is that it could hardly ever be right for the Church or ecclesiastical persons as such to propose terms for the solution of a dispute, because they lack the specialist knowledge required; it is certainly right for them to urge the spirit and method of conciliation; and it very well may be right for them to recall the parties to proposals made by competent persons, such as a Royal Commission appointed for the purpose, with a view to seeing whether or not these may supply the basis for a solution.

Yet even if such action is occasionally justified, the main task of the Church must be to inculcate Christian principles and the power of the Christian spirit.

CHRISTIAN SOCIAL PRINCIPLES:
(A) PRIMARY

The method of the Church's impact upon society at large should be twofold. The

Church must announce Christian principles and point out where the existing social order at any time is in conflict with them. It must then pass on to Christian citizens, acting in their civic capacity, the task of re-shaping the existing order in closer conformity to the principles. For at this point technical knowledge may be required and judgements of practical expediency are always required. If a bridge is to be built, the Church may remind the engineer that it is his obligation to provide a really safe bridge; but it is not entitled to tell him whether, in fact, his design meets this requirement; a particular theologian may also be a competent engineer, and, if he is, his judgement on this point is entitled to attention; but this is altogether because he is a competent engineer and his theological equipment has nothing whatever to do with it. In just the same way the Church may tell the politician what ends the social order should promote; but it must leave to the politician the devising of the precise means to those ends.

This is a point of first-rate importance, and is frequently misunderstood. If Christianity is true at all it is a truth of universal application; all things should be done in the Christian spirit and in accordance with Christian principles. 'Then,' say some, 'produce your Christian solution for unemployment.' But there neither is nor could be such a thing. Christian faith does not by itself enable its adherent to foresee how a vast multitude of people, each one partly selfish and partly generous, and an intricate economic mechanism, will in fact be affected by a particular economic or political innovation–'social credit', for example. 'In that case,' says the reformer–or, quite equally, the upholder of the *status quo*–'keep off the turf. By your own confession you are out of place here.' But this time the Church must say 'No; I cannot tell you what is the remedy; but I can tell you that a society of which unemployment (in peace time) is a chronic feature, is a diseased society, and that if you are not doing all you can to find and administer the remedy, you are guilty before God.' Sometimes the Church can go further than this and point to features in the social structure itself which are bound to be sources of social evil because they contradict the principles of the Gospel.

So the Church is likely to be attacked from both sides if it does its duty. It will be told that it has become 'political' when in fact it has been careful only to state principles and point to breaches of them; and it will be told by advocates of particular policies that it is futile because it does not support these. If it is faithful to its commission it will ignore both sets of complaints, and continue so far as it can to influence all citizens and permeate all parties.

Before going on to state in outline the chief principles of Christian social doctrine, it may be wise, in the prevailing temper of our age, to add a further word of caution. For it is sometimes supposed that what the Church has to do is to sketch a perfect social order and urge men to establish it. But it is very difficult to know what a 'perfect social order' means. Is it the order that would work best if we were all perfect? Or is it the order that would work best in a world of men and women such as we actually are? If it is the former, it certainly ought not to be established; we should wreck it in a fortnight. If it is the latter, there is no reason for expecting the Church to know what it is.

Here we are dealing with what is at this moment the least popular part of traditional Christianity: the doctrine of Original Sin. No doubt this has often been put forward in ways which men to-day find peculiar difficulty in accepting. It would be quite out of place to deal with the whole topic here. Quite enough for our present purpose may be expressed as follows. When we open our eyes as babies we see the world stretching out around us; we are in the middle of it; all proportions and perspectives in what we see are determined by the relation–distance, height, and so forth–of the various visible objects to ourselves. This will remain true of our bodily vision as long as we live. I am the centre of the world I see; where the horizon is depends on where I stand. Now just the same thing is true at first of our mental and spiritual vision. Some things hurt us; we hope they will not happen again; we call them bad. Some things please us; we hope they will happen again; we call them good. Our standard of value is the way things affect ourselves. So each of us takes his place in the centre of his own world. But I am not the centre of the world, or the standard of reference as between good and bad; I am not, and God is. In other words, from the beginning I put myself in God's place. This is my original sin. I was doing it before I could speak, and everyone else has been doing it from early infancy. I am not 'guilty' on this account because I could not help it. But I am in a state, from birth, in which I shall bring disaster on myself and everyone affected by my conduct unless I can escape from it. Education may make my self-centredness less disastrous by widening my horizon of interest; so far it is like the climbing of a tower, which widens the horizon for physical vision while leaving me still the centre and standard of reference. Education may do more than this if it succeeds in winning me into devotion to truth or to beauty; that devotion may effect a partial deliverance from self-centredness. But complete deliverance can be effected only by the winning of my whole heart's devotion, the total allegiance of my will–and this only the Divine Love disclosed by Christ in His Life and Death can do.

The political problem is concerned with men as they are, not with men as they ought to be. Part of the task is so to order life as to lead them nearer to what they ought to be; but to assume that they are already this, will involve certain failure and disaster. It is not contended that men are utterly bad, or that they are more bad than good. What is contended is that they are not perfectly good, and that even their goodness is infected with a quality–self-centredness–which partly vitiates it, and exposes tem to temptations so far as they achieve either freedom or power. This does not mean that freedom or power should be denied to them; on the contrary, it is fundamental to the Christian position that men should have freedom even though they abuse it; but it is also to be recognized that they certainly will abuse it except so far as they are won by devotion to truth or to beauty to that selfless outlook, which is only perfectly established in men by love which arises in them in answer to the redemptive love of God.

In any period worth considering, and probably to the end of earthly history, statesmen will themselves be men, and will be dealing with men, who abuse freedom and power. Now the most fundamental requirement of any political and economic system is not that it shall express love, though that is desirable, nor that it shall express justice, though that is the first ethical demand to be made upon it, but that it shall supply some reasonable measure of security against murder, robbery, and starvation. If it can be said with real probability that a proposed scheme would in fact, men being what they are, fail to provide that security, that scheme is doomed. Christians have some clues to the understanding of human nature which may enable them to make a more accurate estimate than others of these points. But they will not, if they are true to their own tradition, approach the question with rosy-tinted spectacles. Its assertion of Original Sin should make the Church intensely realistic and conspicuously free from Utopianism.

There is no such thing as a Christian social ideal, to which we should conform our actual society as closely as possible. We may notice, incidentally, about any such ideals from Plato's *Republic* onwards, that no one really wants to live in the ideal state as depicted by anyone else. Moreover, there is the desperate difficulty of getting there. When I read any description of an Ideal State and think how we are to begin transforming our own society into that, I am reminded of the Englishman in Ireland who asked the way to Roscommon. 'Is it Roscommon you want to go to?' asked the Irishman. 'Yes,' said the Englishman; 'that's why I asked the way.' 'Well,' said the Irishman, 'if I wanted to go to Roscommon, I wouldn't be starting from here.'

But though Christianity supplies no ideal in this sense, it supplies something of far more value–namely, principles on which we can begin to act in every possible situation.

CHAPTER VI   Christian Responsibility

DIETRICH BONHOEFFER

Dietrich Bonhoeffer

INTRODUCTION

Dietrich Bonhoeffer (1906-1945) was a German theologian and Lutheran pastor. He was educated at Tubingen, Berlin, and Union Theological Seminary in New York. Bonhoeffer was active in the Ecumenical movement and the Confessing Church that resisted Hitler's Nazi regime. For his outspoken criticisms of the Nazis, he was arrested in 1943 and executed in 1945.

Bonhoeffer developed a systematic theory of Religion and Politics by clarifying the categories of Church and State, and distinguishing them from Government and the body of Christians. Yet he warned against attempts to impose a single formula for Church-State relations in all circumstances. In the section on Religion and Politics in his *Ethics,* Bonhoeffer describes the classical Catholic (Thomist) view of Church-State relations based in reason and the hierarchy of Laws, and the classical Protestant (Lutheran) view premised upon human sin and the primacy of "The Sword" in this world, and rejects both. Bonhoeffer's placing of Church and State on an even plane in this world, wherein they are at once separate and related, is more reminiscent of St. Augustine and John Calvin.

Church and State are unified, for Bonhoeffer, in both being under the rule of one God: Christ is the head of both Civil and Ecclesiastical authorities; but they are separate in exercising different, if complementary, roles in this world.

The duty of the State, for Bonhoeffer, is to punish evil and promote good. Its primary role is the former, through "The Sword", but this is not isolated from the latter, or moral education, as the second will diminish the need for the first. But, in order to promote good, the State must know what the good is, which it cannot know through its primary earthly value of the sword. The State learns what the good is from the Church, which teaches ultimate moral truth. Hence, the Church (or "spiritual office") remains distinct from the State, but is necessary to the State. The Church advises the State on matters of moral truth and conduct.

The Government, for Bonhoeffer, demands obedience from its subjects, and deserves to get it, so long as it properly performs its duty. Furthermore, the State rightfully expects support from the Church, but only so long as the Government acknowledges its true ruler in Christ and respects the autonomy of the Church and its right to advise the State on moral issues.

These doctrines caused Bonhoeffer to run afoul of the Nazi authorities: his insistence that the State respect the autonomy and sanctity of the Church resisted the Nazi's attempt to impose "Aryan Christianity" on the German Church, and his insistence that Christ is the head of the Government and the Church is to openly bear witness to that fact, frustrated the Nazis' pretensions to absolute truth and moral authority. Especially Bonhoeffer's claim that the Church must "call sin by its name," resisting the Nazis' attempts to mask evil with virtue, caused him to be intolerable to the Third Reich. His insistence that the Church, as the Body of Christ, must suffer the consequences of such moral witness, as shown in the quote below, caused some anxiety and discomfort in many members of the German clergy as well.

"It is part of the Church's office of guardianship that she call sin by its name and that she shall warn men against sin; for 'righteousness exalteth a nation', both in time and in eternity, 'but sin is perdition for the people', both temporal and eternal perdition (Prov. 14, 34). If the Church did not do this, she would be incurring part of the guilt for the blood of the wicked (Ezek. 3, 17 ff.). This warning against sin is delivered to the congregation openly and publically. . .not to improve the world, but to summon it to believe in Jesus Christ and to bear witness to the reconciliation which has been accomplished through Him and to His dominion."

Thus, unlike the founder of his denomination, Martin Luther, Bonhoeffer conceived of the State as more than merely a "hangman" and the Church as more than merely a spiritual entity. Much of his writing on Religion and Politics is more Calvinist than Lutheran. Thus, in a case where the individual Christian finds himself in a conflict between earthly and Godly values, Bonhoeffer admits a Church to advise him rather than leaving the individual alone to judge the accuracy of the State's claims to justice. He implies that the Church, being closer to God's ultimate truth, and God being the head of the State, in matters of morals, the individual should follow the Church before the State.

The following selections are from Bonhoeffer's *Ethics,* published posthumously.[11]

---

[11] Translated by Neville Horton Smith, edited by Eberhard Bethge (New York: Macmillan Publishing Company, 1965).

STATE AND CHURCH

I. The Concepts Involved

The concept of the state is foreign to the New Testament. It has its origin in pagan antiquity. Its place is taken in the New Testament by the concept of government ('power'). The term 'state' means an ordered community; government is the power which creates and maintains order. The term 'state' embraces both the rulers and the ruled; the term 'government' refers only to the rulers. The concept of the *polis,* which is a constituent of the concept of the state, is not necessarily connected with the concept of *exousia.* For the New Testament the *polis* is an eschatological concept; it is the future city of God, the new Jerusalem, the heavenly society under the rule of God. The term government does not essentially refer to the earthly *polis;* it may go beyond it; it is, for example, applicable even in the smallest form of community, in the relation of father and child or of master and servant. The term government does not, therefore, imply any particular form of society or any particular form of state. Government is divinely ordaned authority to exercise worldly dominion by divine right. Government is deputyship for God on earth. It can be understood only from above. Government does not proceed from society, but it orders society from above. If it is exegetically correct to regard it as an angelic power, this would still serve only to define its position between God and the world. Only the concept of government, and not the concept of the state, can have a theological application. Nevertheless, in a concrete study the concept of state naturally cannot be avoided.

In using the term 'church', and especially in clarifying its relation to the terms 'government' and 'state', we have to distinguish between the spiritual office or ministry and the congregation or the Christians. The spiritual office is the divinely ordained authority to exercise spiritual dominion by divine right. It does not proceed from the congregation, but from God. A clear distinction must be drawn between the secular and the spiritual authority, but the Christians are, nevertheless, at the same time citizens, and the citizens, whether they be believers or not, are at the same time subject to the claim of Jesus Christ. Consequently the relationship of the spiritual office to the government differs from that of the Christians. In order to avoid constant misunderstandings this difference should be kept clearly in view.

2. The Basis of Government

A. *In the Nature of Man.* The ancients, especially Aristotle, base the state on the character of man. The state is the supreme consummation of the rational character of men, and to serve it is the supreme purpose of human life. All ethics is political ethics. Virtues are political virtues. This theory of the state was taken over in principle by Catholic theology. The state is a product of human nature. Man's ability to live in society derives from the Creation, as does also the relation of rulers and ruled. The state fulfils the assigned purpose of the human character within the sphere of the natural and creaturely. The state is the 'highest development of the natural society' (Schilling, *Moraltheologie,*II, p. 609). This Aristotelian and Thomist doctrine is found in a somewhat modified form in Anglican theology. And indeed it has also penetrated into modern Lutheranism. With the Anglicans the connexion between natural theology and incarnational theology opens up the possibiility of a peculiar natural-cum-Christian theory of the state. (Incidentally, the questionableness of this combination of natural and incarnational theology is now clearly perceived by the young Anglo-Catholics, who provide the corrective of a *theologia crucis.*) Modern Lutheranism acquired the notion of the natural state through Hegel and romanticism. In this case the state is the fulfilment not of the universally human and rational character of man, but of the creative will of God in the people. The state is essentially a nation-state. The people fulfils its divinely-willed destiny in such a state. The detailed contents are of no significance here. The Ancient Greek concept of the state persists in the forms of the rational state, the nation-state, the culture-state, the social state, and finally, as the decisive factor, the Christian state. The state is the executor of certain given contents, and indeed, when this theory is carried to its ultimate conclusion, the state becomes the actual subject or originator of these contents, *i.e.* of the people, the culture, the economy or the religion. It is 'the real god' (Hegel). All these theories alike regard the state as a community, so that it is only with difficulty and by indirect means that they admit of the idea of government. Fundamentally it is necessary in these cases to derive government, too, from the natural character of man. It consequently becomes difficult to understand it at the same time as the coercive power which directs itself against man, for it is precisely this coercive power which essentially distinguishes the government of the state from that voluntary priority and subordination which is to be found in every community. Whenever the basis of the state is sought in the created nature of man, the concept of government is broken up and is then reconstructed from below, even when this is not at all intended. Whenever the state becomes the executor of all the vital and cultural activities of man, it forfeits its own proper dignity, its specific authority as government.

B. *In Sin.* The Reformation, by taking up ideas of St. Augustine, broke away from the ancient Greek concept of the state. The Reformation does not represent the state as a community arising from the created nature of man, although traces of this idea, too, can be found in the writings of some of the Reformers; it places the origin of the state, as government, in the Fall. It was sin that made necessary the divine institution of government. The sword which God has given to government is to be used by it in order to protect men against the chaos which is caused by sin. Government is to punish the criminal and to safeguard life. Thus a reason is provided for the existence of government both as a coercive power and as the protector of an outward justice. The Reformation attached equal importance to both of these aspects, but its thinking subsequently developed along two divergent lines. Some thinkers subordinated the concept of justice to the concept of coercive force, and were thus led on to the concept of the state which is founded on power; others subordinated power to justice, and so attained to the concept of the state which is founded on law and order. The former believed that there was *exousia* only where there was power, the latter only where there was justice. In this way both parties failed to give its full meaning to the Reformation concept of *exousia*.Both parties perceived that the state is not a consummation of creaturely characteristics but an institution of God which is ordained from above. They did not understand the state 'from below', on the basis of the people, the culture, etc., but from above, that is to say, in the true sense, as government. In this way the original idea of the Reformation and of the Bible was faithfully followed out. Thus the state is not essentially a culture-state, etc. These are only possible, divinely permitted forms of political society, and there may well be an abundance of other such forms which have hitherto remained unknown to us. Unlike these forms of society, which are merely permitted by God, government is actually established and ordained by God himself. People, culture, social organization, etc., are of the world. Government is order in the world, an order which bears the authority of God. Government is not itself of the world, but of God. On this basis the notion of the Christian state is also untenable; for the state possesses its character as government independently of the Christian character of the persons who govern. There is government also among the heathen.

C. *In Christ.* It becomes clear from these last remarks, and indeed from everything that we have said so far on this subject, that the basing of the state on sin or on the nature of man leads to a conception of the state as a self-contained entity, a conception which fails to take account of the relation of the state to Jesus Christ. Whether it be as an institution of creation or as an institution of preservation, the state exists here by itself, more or less independently of the revelation of God in Jesus Christ. This conclusion cannot be avoided even in the case of the second theory, which is in many ways superior to the first. But now the question arises, what basis can there be for a theologically tenable assertion (as distinct from a philosophy in general Christian terms) with regard to Paradise and the Fall–what basis can there be other than Jesus Christ? It is through Jesus Christ and for Jesus Christ that all things are created (John 1.3; I Cor. 8.6; Heb. 1.2), and in particular 'thrones, dominions, principalities and powers' (Col. i.16). It is only in Jesus Christ that all these things 'consist' (Col. 1.17). And it is He who is 'the head of the church' (Col. 1.1). A theological proposition with regard to government, with regard, that is to say, to the government which is instituted by God and not to some general philosophical idea of government, is therefore in no circumstances possible without reference to Jesus Christ, and to Jesus Christ as the head of His Church; no such proposition is possible without reference to the Church of Jesus Christ. The true basis of government is therefore Jesus Christ Himself. The relation of Jesus Christ to government can be expressed under seven headings.

a As the Mediator of Creation, 'through whom' government,too, is created, Jesus Christ is the sole and necessary medium between government and the Creator. There is no immediate relation between government and God. Christ is its Mediator.

b Government, like all created things, 'consists only in Jesus Christ'; in other words, it is only in Him that it has its essence and being. If Jesus Christ did not exist there would be no created things; all created things would be annihilated in the wrath of God.

c Government, like all created things, is designed and directed 'towards Jesus Christ'. Its goal is Jesus Christ Himself. Its purpose is to serve him.

d Jesus Christ possesses all power in heaven and on earth (Matt. 28.18), and He is, therefore, also the Lord of government.

e Through the atonement on the cross Jesus Christ has restored the relation between government and God (Col. 1.20).

f In addition to these relations to Jesus Christ which government shares with all created things, there is also a special relation in which government stands with respect to Jesus Christ.

I Jesus Christ was crucified with the permission of government.

II By acknowledging and openly declaring the innocence of Jesus (John 18.38; cf. also the part played by Lysias, Felix, Festus and Agrippa in the trial of St. Paul), government gave evidence of its proper character.

III When government did not dare to exercise its governmental power in maintaining its own knowledge and judgement, it abandoned its office under pressure from the people. This does not constitute a condemnation of the office, but only of the faulty discharge of this office.

IV Jesus submitted to government; but He reminded government that its power is not human arbitrary will, but a 'gift from above' (John 19.10).

V With this Jesus showed that government can only serve Him, precisely because it is a power which comes down from above, no matter whether it discharges its office well or badly. Both in acquitting Him of guilt and in delivering Him up to be crucified, government was obliged to show that it stands in the service of Jesus Christ. Thus it was precisely through the cross that Jesus won back His dominion over government (Col. 2.15), and, at the end of all things, 'all dominion and government and power' will be both abolished and preserved through Him.

g So long as the earth continues, Jesus will always be at the same time Lord of all government and Head of the Church, without government and Church ever becoming one and the same. But at the end there will be a holy city *(polis)* without temples, for God and the Lamb will Themselves be the Temple (Rev. 21), and the citizens of this city will be the faithful of the congregation of Jesus throughout all the world, and dominion in this city will be exercised by God and the Lamb. In the heavenly *polis* state and Church will be one.

Only the derivation of government from Jesus Christ can supersede the derivations in terms of natural law which are the ultimate consequences of the derivations from the nature and the sin of man. The derivation from the nature of man regards the actual conditions of peoples, etc., as providing the basis for the state in terms of natural law. This argument affords a justification for imperialism and for revolution (for both inward and outward revolution). The derivation from sin has to devise natural-law standards in order to restrict the concept of power by means of the concept of justice; these standards will imbue it with a more strongly conservative tendency. But both the concept and the contents of natural law are equivocal (depending on whether this natural law is derived from certain particular data or from certain particular standards); and it therefore fails to provide an adequate basis for the state. Natural law can furnish equally cogent arguments in favour of the state which is founded on force and the state which is founded on justice, for the nation-state and for impérialism, for democracy and for dictatorship. A solid basis is afforded only by the biblical derivation of government from Jesus Christ. Whether and to what extent a new natural law can be established on this foundation is a theological question which still remains open.

3. The Divine Character of Government

A. *In its Being*. Government is given to us not as an idea or a task to be fulfilled but as a reality and as something which 'is' (Rom. 13.1c). It is in its being that it is a divine office. The persons who exercise government are God's 'ministers', servants and representatives (Rom. 13.4). The being of government is independent of the manner of its coming into being. No matter if man's path to governmental office repeatedly passes through guilt, no matter if almost every crown is stained with guilt (*cf.* Shakespeare's histories), the being of government lies beyond its earthly coming into being; for government is an institution of God, not in its coming into being but in its being. Like all existing things, government, too, stands in a certain sense beyond good and evil; that is to say, it possesses not only an office but also a historical existence. An ethical failure does not *eo ipso* deprive it of its divine dignity. This situation is clearly expressed in the saying 'my country, right or wrong'. This is that historical relationship of one actual entity to another which is found again in the relationship between father and child, between brother and brother, and between master and servant, and which is immediately obvious in these cases. There can be no ethical isolation of the son from his father, and indeed, on the basis of actual being, there is a necessity of sharing in the assuming and carrying of the guilt of a father or a brother. There is no glory in standing amid the ruins of one's native town in the consciousness that at least one has not oneself incurred any guilt. That is rather the self-glorification of the moral legalist in the face of history. The clearest expression of this dignity of government, one source of which is its historical existence, is its power, the sword which it wields. Even when the government incurs guilt and is open to ethical attack, its power is from God. It has its existence solely in Jesus Christ, and through the cross of Christ it is reconciled with God *(vide supra).*

B. *In its Task.* The being of government is linked with a divine commission. Its being is fulfilled only in the fulfilment of the commission. A total apostasy from its commission would jeopardize its being. But by God's providence this total apostasy is possible only as an eschatological event, and as such it leads amidst grievous torments to a total separation of the congregation from the government as the embodiment of Antichrist. The mission of government consists in serving the dominion of Christ on earth by the exercise of the worldly power of the sword and of justice. Government serves Christ by establishing and maintaining an outward justice by means of the sword which is given to it, and to it alone, in deputyship for God. And it has not only the negative task of punishing the wicked, but also the positive task of praising the good or 'them that do well' (I Pet. 2.14). It is therefore endowed, on the one hand, with a judicial authority, and on the other hand, with a right to educate for goodness, *i.e.* for outward justice or righteousness. The way in which it exercises this right of education is, of course, a question which can be considered only in the context of the relation of government to the other divine mandates. The much-discussed question of what constitutes this goodness or outward justice which government is charged with promoting is easily resolved if one keeps in view the derivation of government from Jesus Christ. This good cannot in any case be in conflict with Jesus Christ. Good consists in allowance being made in every action of government for the ultimate purpose, namely, the service of Jesus Christ. What is intended here is not a Christian action, but an action which does not exclude Christ. Government achieves such an action if it takes the contents of the second table as its criterion in its various particular historical situations and decisions. But whence does government derive its knowledge of these contents? Primarily from the preaching of the Church. But for pagan government the answer is that there is a providential congruity between the contents of the second table and the inherent law of historical life itself. Failure to observe the second table destroys the very life which government is charged with preserving. Thus, if it is properly understood, the task of protecting life will itself lead to observance of the second table. Does this mean that the state is after all based on natural law? No; for in fact it is a matter here only of the government which does not understand itself but which now is, nevertheless, providentially enabled to acquire the same knowledge, of crucial significance for its task, as is disclosed to the government which does understand itself in the true sense in Jesus Christ. One might, therefore, say that in this case natural law has its foundation in Jesus Christ.

Consequently, whether or not govrnment is aware of its own true basis, its task consists in maintaining by the power of the sword an outward justice in which life is preserved and is thus held open for Christ.

Does the task of government also include observance of the first table, that is to say, the decision for the God and Father of Jesus Christ? We intend to consider this question in the section on government and Church, and at this point we will say only that the knowledge of Jesus Christ is part of the assignment of all men, including, therefore, those persons who exercise government. But the praise and the protection of the righteous (I. Pet. 2.14) is an integral part of the mission of government, independently of the decision of faith of the persons who exercise government. Indeed it is only in protecting the righteous that government fulfils its true mission of serving Christ.

The mission of government to serve Christ is at the same time its inescapable destiny. Government serves Christ no matter whether it is conscious or unconscious of this mission or even whether it is true or untrue to it. If it is unwilling to fulfil this mission, then, through the suffering of the congregation, it renders service to the witness of the name of Christ. Such is the close and indissoluble relation of government to Christ. It cannot in either case evade its task of serving Christ. It serves Him by its very existence.

C. *In its Claim*. The claim of government, which is based on its power and its mission,is the claim of God and is binding upon conscience. Government demands obedience 'for conscience' sake' (Rom. 13.5), which may also be interpreted as 'for the Lord's sake' (I Pct. 2.13). This obedience is combined with deference (Rom.

13.7; I Pet. 2.17). In the exercise of the mission of government the demand for obedience is unconditional and qualitatively total; it extends both to conscience and to bodily life. Belief, conscience and bodily life are subject to an obligation of obedience with respect to the divine commission of government. A doubt can arise only when the contents and the extend of the commission of government become questionable. The Christian is neither obliged nor able to examine the rightfulness fo the demand of government in each particular case. His duty of obedience is binding on him until government directly compels him to offend against the divine commandment, that is to say, until government openly denies its divine commission and thereby forfeits its claim. In cases of doubt obedience is required; for the Christian does not bear the responsibility of government. But if government violates or exceeds its commission at any point, for example by making itself master over the belief of the congregation, then at this point, indeed, obedience is to be refused, for conscience' sake, for the Lord's sake. It is not, however, permissible to generalize from this offence and to conclude that this government now possesses no claim to obedience in some of its other demands, or even in all its demands. Disobedience can never be anything but a concrete decision in a single particular case. Generalizations lead to an apocalyptic diabolization of government. Even an anti-Christian government is still in a certain sense government. It would, therefore, not be permissible to refuse to pay taxes to a government which persecuted the Church. Conversely, the fact of obedience to government in its political functions, payment of taxes, acceptance of loyalty oaths and military service, is always a proof that this government is not yet understood in the sense of the apocalypse. An apocalyptic view of a particular concrete government would necessarily have total disobedience as its consequence; for in that case every single act of obedience obviously involves a denial of Christ (Rev. 13.7). In all political decisions the historical entanglement in the guilt of the past is too great to be assessed, and it is therefore generally impossible to pass judgement on the justice of a single particular decision. It is here that the venture of responsibility must be undertaken, but the responsibility for such a venture on the part of the government can be borne *in concreto* (*i.e.*apart from the general share in responsibility for political action which is borne by individuals) only by the government. Even in cases where the guilt of the government is extremely obvious, due consideration must still be given to the guilt which has given rise to this guilt. The refusal of obedience in the case of a particular historical and political decision of government must therefore, like this decision itself, be a venture undertaken on one's own responsibility. A historical decision cannot be entirely resolved into ethical terms; there remains a residuum, the venture of action. That is true both of the government and of its subjects.

4. Government and the Divine Institutions in the World

Government has the divine task of preserving the world, with its institutions which are given by God, for the purpose of Christ. For this purpose government alone bears the sword. Everyone is subject to an obligation of obedience towards government. But, both with its task and with its claim, government always presupposes the created world. Government maintains created things in their proper order, but it cannot itself engender life; it is not creative. However, it finds already in the world which it governs two institutions through which God the Creator exercises His creative power, and upon which it must therefore, in the nature of things, rely; these are marriage and labour. The Bible discloses both of these to us already in Paradise, and thereby shows that they are part of God's creation, which is through and for Jesus Christ. Even after the Fall, *i.e.* in the only form in which we know them, both are still divine institutions of discipline and grace, because God desires to show Himself even to the fallen world as the Creator, and because He causes the world to consist in Christ and makes it Christ's own. Marriage and labour are from the beginning subject to a definite divine mandate which must be executed in faith and obedience towards God. Marriage and labour, therefore, possess their own origin in God, an origin which is not established by government, but which requires to be acknowledged by government. Through marriage bodily life is propagated and men are brought into being for the glorification and service of Jesus Christ. But this implies also that marriage is there not only for begetting children but also for educating them in obedience to Jesus Christ. The parents are for the child the deputies of God, both as its begetters and as its educators. Through labour a world of values is created for the glorification and service of Jesus Christ. Here, too, as in the case of marriage, there is not a divine creation out of nothing, but on the basis of the first creation there is a creation of new things, in marriage of new life and in labour of new values. Labour embraces here the whole range of work which extends from agriculture by way of industry and commerce to science and art (*cf.*Gen. 4.17ff.). Thus, for the sake of Jesus Christ, a right of their own is conferred both upon marriage, together with the family, and upon labour, together with economic life, culture, science and art. This means that for these fields the significance of government is regulative and not constitutive. Marriage is performed not by government but in the presence of government. Industry and commerce, science and art, are not cultivated by government itself, but they are subject to its supervision, and within certain limits (which cannot be discussed in detail here) to its direction. But government never becomes the subject or originator of these fields of labour. If it asserts its authority beyond the limits of its assigned task it will in the long run forfeit its genuine authority over these fields.

Distinct from the order or institution of marriage and that of labour is the order or institution of the people. According to Scripture, its origin lies neither in Paradise nor in an explicit divine mandate. The people is, on the one hand (according to Gen. 10), a natural consequence of the spreading of the succeeding generations; on the other hand (Gen. 11), it is a divine institution which causes mankind to live in dissension and mutual incomprehension, and which thereby reminds men that their unity does not lie in their own achievements of complete power but solely in God, the Creator and Redeemer. Yet in Scripture there is no special commission of God for the people. Marriage and labour are divine offices, but the people is a historical reality, which in a special sense has reference to the divine reality of the one people of God, the Church. Scripture offers no indication with regard to the relation between people and government; it does not demand the nation-state; it recognizes the possibility that several peoples may be united under one government. It knows that the people grows from below, but that government is instituted from above.

5. Government and Church

Government is instituted for the sake of Christ; it serves Christ, and consequently it also serves the Church. Yet the dominion of Christ over all government does not by any means imply the dominion of the Church over government. But the same Lord, whom government serves, is the Head of the congregation, the Lord of the Church. The service of government to Christ consists in the exercise of its commission to secure an outward justice by the power of the sword. This service is thus an indirect service to the congregation, which only by this is enabled to 'lead a quiet and peaceable life' (I TIm. 2.2). Through its service towards Christ, government is ultimately linked with the Church. If it fulfils its mission as it should, the congregation can live in peace, for government and congregation serve the same Master.

A. *Government's Claim on the Church.* The claim of government to obedience and deference extends also to the Church. With respect to the spiritual office, government can indeed only demand that this office shall not interfere in the secular office, but that it shall fulfil its own mission, which does, in fact, include the admonition to obey government. Government possesses no authority over this mission itself, as it is exercised in the pastoral office and in the office of Church management. So far as the spiritual office is an office which is exercised publicly, government has a claim to supervise it, to see that everything is done in an orderly manner, that is to say, in accordance with outward justice. It is only in this connexion that it has a claim to intervene in the question of appointments and organization within the office. The spiritual office itself is not subject to government. Yet government possesses a full claim to obedience with regard to the Christian members of the congregation. In this it does not appear as a second authority side by side with the authority of Christ, but its own authority is only a formof the authority of Christ. In his obedience to government the Christian is obedient to Christ. As a citizen the Christian does not cease to be a Christian, but he serves Christ in a different way. This in itself also provides an adequate definition of the contents of the authentic claim of government. It can never lead the Christian against Christ; on the contrary, it helps him to serve Christ in the world. The person who exercises government thus becomes for the Christian a servant of God.

B. *The Church's claim on Government.* The Church has the task of summonng the whole world to submit to the dominion of Jesus Christ. She testifies before government to their common Master. She calls upon the persons who exercise government to believe in Christ for the sake of their own salvation. She knows that it is in obedience to Jesus Christ that the commission of government is properly executed. Her aim is not that government should pursue a Christian policy, enact Christian laws, etc., but that it should be true government in accordance with its own special task. Only the Church brings government to an understanding of itself. For the sake of their common Master the Church claims to be listened to by government; she claims protection for the public Christian proclamation against violence and blasphemy; she claims protection for the institution of the Church against arbitrary interference, and she claims protection for Christian life in obedience to Jesus Christ. The Church can never abandon these claims; and she must make them heard publicly so long as government itself maintains its claim to acknowledge the Church. Of course, if government opposes the Church, explicitly or in fact, there may come a time when the Church no longer wastes her words, even though she still does not give up her claim; for the Church knows that, whether government performs its mission well or badly, it must always serve only its Master, and therefore also the Church. The government which denies protection to the Church thereby places the Church all the more patently under the protection of her Master. The government which blasphemes its Master testifies thereby all the more evidently to the power of this Master who is praised and glorified in the torments and martyrdoms of the congregation.

C. *The Ecclesiastical Responsibility of Government.* To the claim of the Church there corresponds the responsibility of government. Here it becomes necessary to answer the question of the attitude of government to the first commandment. Must government make a religious decision, or does its task lie in religious neutrality? Is government responsible for maintaining the ttue Christian service of God, and has it the right to prohibit other kinds of divine service? Certainly the persons who exercise government ought also to accept belief in Jesus Christ, but the office of government remains independent of the religious decision. Yet it pertains to the responsibility of the office of government that it should protect the righteous, and indeed praise them, in other words that it should support the practice of religion. A government which fails to recognize this undermines the root of the true obedience and, therefore, also its own authority (*e.g.*France in 1905). At the same time the office of government as such remains religiously neutral and attends only to its own task. And it can, therefore, never become the originator in the foundation of a new religion; for if it does so it disrupts itself. It affords protection to every form of service of God which does not undermine the office of government. It takes care that the differences between the various forms of service of God do not give rise to a conflict which endangers the order of the country. But it achieves this purpose not by suppressing one form of service of God, but by a clear adherence to its own governmental commission. It will thereby become evident that the true Christian service of God does not endanger this commission, but, on the contrary, continually establishes it anew. If the persons who exercise government are Christian they must know that the Christian proclamation is delivered not by means of the sword but by means of the word. The idea of *cuius regio eius religio* was possible only in certain quite definite political circumstances: namely, the agreement of the princes to admit each other's exiles; as a general principle it is incompatible with the office of government. In the case of some special situation of ecclesiastical emergency it would be the responsibility of the Christians who exercise government to make their power available, if the Church requests it, in order to remove the source of the disorder. This does not mean, however, that in such circumstances government as such would take over the functions of ecclesiastical control. It is here exclusively a matter of restoring the rightful order within which the spiritual office can be rightfully discharged and both government and Church can perform their own several tasks. Government will fulfil its obligation under the first commandment by being government in the rightful manner and by discharging its governmental responsibility also with respect to the Church. But it does not possess the office of confessing and preaching faith in Jesus Christ.

D. *The Political Responsibility of the Church.* If political responsibility is understood exclusively in the sense of governmental responsibility, then it is clearly only upon government that this responsibility devolves. But if the term is taken to refer quite generally to life in the *polis,*then there are a number of senses in which it is necessary to speak of political responsibility of the Church in answer to the claim of government upon the Church. Here again we distinguish between the responsibility of the spiritual office and the responsibility of the Christians. It is part of the Church's office of guardianship that she shall call sin by its name and that she shall warn men against sin; for 'righteousness exalteth a nation', both in time and in eternity, 'but sin is perdition for the people', both temporal and eternal perdition (Prov. 14.34). If the Church did not do this, she would be incurring part of the guilt for the blood of the wicked (Ezek. 3.17ff.). This warning against sin is delivered to the congregation openly and publicly, and whoever will not hear it passes judgement upon himself. The intention of the preacher here is not to improve the world, but to summon it to belief in Jesus Christ and to bear witness to the reconciliation which has been accomplished through Him and to His dominion. The theme of the proclamation is not the wickedness of the world bu the grace of Jesus Christ. It is part of the responsibility of the spiritual office that it shall devote earnest attention to the proclamation of the reign of Christ as King, and that it shall with all due deference address government directly in order to draw its attention to shortcomings and errors which must otherwise imperil its governmental office. If the word of the Church is, on principle, not received, then the only political responsibility which remains to her is in establishing and maintaining, at least among her own members, the order of outward justice which is no longer to be found in the *polis,*for by so doing she serves government in her own way.

Is there a political responsibility on the part of individual Christians? Certainly the individual Christian cannot be made responsible for the action of government, and he must not make himself responsible for it; but because of his faith and his charity he is responsible for his own calling and for the sphere of his own personal life, however large or however small it may be. If this responsibility is fulfilled in faith, it is effectual for the whole of the *polis*. According to Holy Scripture, there is no right to revolution; but there is a responsibility of every individual for reserving the purity of his office and mission in the *polis*. In this way, in the true sense, every individual serves government with his responsibility. No one, not even government itself, can deprive him of this responsibility or forbid him to discharge it, for it is an integral part of his life in sanctification, and it arises from obedience to the Lord of both Church and government.

E. *Conclusions*. Government and Church are connected in such various ways that their relationship cannot be regulated in accordance with any single general principle. Neither the separation of state and Church, nor the form of the state church can in itself constitute a solution of the problem. Nothing is more dangerous than to draw theoretical conclusions by generalizing from single particular experiences. The recommendation for a withdrawal of the Church from the world and from the relations which she still maintains with the state under the impact of an apocalyptic age is, in this general aspect, nothing but a somewhat melancholy interpretation of the times in terms of the philosophy of history. If it were really acted upon in earnest, it would necessarily lead to the most drastic consequences, which are described in Rev. 13. But, conversely, a philosophy of history may equally easily be the source for a scheme for a state church or a national church. No constitutional form can as such exactly represent the actual relative closeness and remoteness of government and Church. Government and Church are bound by the same Lord and are bound together. In their task government and Church are separate, but government and Church have the same field of action, man. No single one of these relationships must be isolated so as to provide the basis for a particular constitutional form (for example in the sequence state church, free church, national church); the true aim is to provide room within every given form for the relationship which is, in fact, instituted by God and to entrust the further development to the Lord of both government and Church.

6. The Church and the Form of the State

In both Protestant and Catholic political theory the question of the form of the state is always treated as a secondary problem. Certainly, so long as government fulfils its assigned mission, the form in which it does so is of no great importance for the Church. Still, there is justification for asking which form of the state offers the best guarantee for the fulfilment of the mission of govenment and should, therefore, be promoted by the Church. No form of the state is in itself an absolute guarantee for the proper discharge of the office of government. Only concrete obedience to the divine commisison justifies a form of the state. It is, nevertheless, possible to formulate a few general propositions in order to discern those forms of the state which provide a relatively favourable basis for rightful governmental action and, therefore, also for a rightful relationship between church and state; precisely these relative differences may be of great practical consequence.

a That form of the state will be relatively the best in which it becomes most evident that government is from above, from God, and in which the divine origin of government is most clearly apparent. A properly understood divine right of government, in its splendour and in its responsibility, is an essential constituent of the relatively best form of the state. (Unlike other western royalty, the kings of the Belgians called themselves kings 'by the grace of the people'.)

b That form of the state will be relatively the best which sees that its power is not endangered but is sustained and secured

I by the strict maintenance of an outward justice,

II by the right of the family and of labour, a right which has its foundation in God, and

III by the proclamation of the gospel of Jesus Christ.

c That form of state will be relatively the best which does not express its attachment to its subjects by restricting the divine authority which has been conferred upon it, but which attaches itself to its subjects in mutual confidence by just action and truthful speech. It will be found here that what is best for government is also best for the relationship between government and church.

CHAPTER VII Christian Realism

REINHOLD NIEBUHR

Reinhold Niebuhr

INTRODUCTION

Reinhold Niebuhr (1892-1971) was an American theologian born in Missouri and educated at Yale Divinity School. After serving a pastorate in Detroit, Michigan, Niebuhr joined the faculty at Union Theological Seminary in New York. There he taught Christian Ethics and wrote extensively on Religion and Politics. His ideas, which came to be known as "Christian Realism," greatly influenced twentieth-century politics.

Christian Realism emphasizes man's sinful nature, as displayed in his pride, egoism and will-to-power. Man's sin is most dangerous when it is masquerading as virtue, superficial goodness often disguising self-interest. Niebuhr notes that this human capacity to deceive others (and even oneself), as to the virtue of one's actions, renders sin more complex and difficult to control.

Modern sin often assumes "idealistic" pretenses: the striving for "progress," "humanity," "social justice," etc., which Niebuhr claims, often mask man's sinful desire to control and manipulate the world, putting himself before God. His critique of Enlightenment liberalism, with its optimistic faith in progress through man's reason and technology, follows from this indictment of man's prideful pretenses. While temporarily attracted to Marxist sociology, Niebuhr later sees Communism as merely an extension of that Enlightenment faith in human perfectability through economic progress. While Marxism sees the source of all human evil and misery in a social structure (capitalism), Niebuhr identifies evil and misery with man's pride, especially that pride of Marxism which claims man can save himself through his own devices. All human actions are tainted with sin and man's only hope lies in humility towards God and God's Grace.

Thus, Niebuhr was often equally critical of Soviet Socialism and Western democracies, as both agreed on the salvation of the world through man-made technological progress. Technology, for Niebuhr can be used equally for evil, destructive ends as for good, constructive ones; so, the faith in "historical progress" is an illusion. Technology, as with political and nationalist movements, may just amplify the individual's egoistic pride.

Niebuhr's Christian Realism, then, insists on identifying "the ideal" with God's Heavenly Kingdom, rather than with any human creation. That ideal is to be striven for, but never attained, because of man's fallen, imperfect condition. Niebuhr revives St. Augustine's Two Cities, insisting on acknowledging the continual tension between them, avoiding both the despair of the absence of a Heavenly Kingdom and the foolish optimism that says we can attain it on earth through human means. Niebuhr is critical of those churches that preach easy salvation through simple beliefs, ignoring the reality of sin and often identifying salvation with trivial, worldly attainments.

The Church, for Niebuhr, is obliged to remind the world that perfection resides only in the transcendent Kingdom of God and that, therefore, *all* individuals and *all* nations are unjust when compared with His Kingdom. The Church is to work for greater justice, love and peace, using God's Kingdom as a standard; but it is not to be taken over by secular political movements, nor to pretend that those movements, or the Church, constitute the Kingdom of Heaven.

Given man's sinful nature, Niebuhr commended a system of Madisonian "checks and balances" in domestic politics and a "balance of power" in international politics: both controlling man's selfish wills by pitting them against each other. This style of politics was congenial with American pluralism.

Niebuhr's "Neo-orthodoxy" self-consciously models itself on St. Augustine's and John Calvin's theology concerning human sin and the "co-mingling" of the Two Cities in this world. The Church has a role in politics, as advisor and critic; but it must be true to its own ideal and guard against the "spiritual pride" of forgetting its own imperfections.

The following selections are taken from several of Reinhold Niebuhr's writings, and illustrate the Christian Realist view of human nature, politics and religion.[12]

---

[12] Drawn from *Reinhold Niebuhr on Politics,* edited by Harry R. Davis and Robert C. Good (New York: Charles Scribner's Sons, 1960).

The Relevance of Christian Realism:
An Orientation

The terms "idealism" and "realism" are not analogous in political and in metaphysical theory; and they are certainly not as precise in political, as in metaphysical, theory. In political and moral theory "realism" denotes the disposition to take into account all factors in a social and political situation which offer resistance to established norms, particularly the factors of self-interest and power. In the words of a notorious "realist," Machiavelli, the purpose of the realist is "to follow the truth of the matter rather than the imagination of it; for many have pictures of republics and principalities which have never been seen." This definition of realism implies that idealists are subject to illusions about social realities, which indeed they are.

"Idealism" is, in the extreme of its proponents, characterized by loyalty to moral norms and ideals, rather than to self-interest, whether individual or collective. The idealists believe that self-interest should be brought under the discipline of a higher law, which is correct, for evil is always the assertion of some self-interest without regard to the whole, whether the whole be conceived as the immediate community, or the total community of mankind, or the total order of the world. The good is, on the other hand, always the harmony of the whole on various levels. Devotion to a subordinate and premature "whole" such as the nation, may of course become evil, viewed from the perspective of a larger whole, such as the community of mankind. The idealist may thus be defined as the person who seeks to bring self-interest under the discipline of a more universal law and in harmony with a more universal good.

In the opinion of its critics, however, idealism is characterized by a disposition to ignore or be indifferent to the forces in human life which offer resistance to universally valid ideals and norms. This disposition, to which Machiavelli refers, is general whenever men are inclined to take the moral pretensions of themselves or their fellow men at face value; for the disposition to hide self-interest behind the facade of pretended devotion to values transcending self-interest is well-nigh universal. Man is a curious creature with so strong a sense of obligation to his fellows that he cannot pursue his own interests without pretending to serve his felow men. The definitions of "realists" and "idealists" emphasize disposition, rather than doctrines; and they are therefore bound to be inexact. It must remain a matter of opinion whether or not a man takes adequate account of all the various factors and forces in a social situation.

At the level of political policy, realistic and idealistic approaches may be identified in analogous, but somewhat different, terms. For the realist, all plans for the future are dominated by the question: Where do we go from *here?* The broken process of history is emphasized and it is believed that new ventures in political organization, however broad their field and bold their purpose, remain under certain conditions and limitations which human history never transcends. For the idealist, the primary concern is not with perennial conditions but with new possibilities, and not with the starting point but with the goal.

The realists understand that certain perennial problems of political organization emerge in new forms, but are of the same essence on each level of the political integration of human society. The idealists are more conscious of novel and radical elements in a new situation and are inclined to believe and hope that old problems and vexations will disappear in the new level of political achievement.

These differences of temper and viewpoint are finally focussed upon a crucial issue: the problem of power. The realists know that history is not a simple rational process but a vital one. All human societies are organizations of diverse vitalities and interests. Some balance of power is the basis of whatever justice is achieved in human relations. Where the disproportion of power is too great and where an equilibrium of social forces is lacking, no mere rational or moral demands can achieve justice.

The idealists are inclined to view history from the standpoint of the moral and social imperatives which a rational analysis of a situation generates. Thus, for example, they look at the world and decide that its social and economic problems demand and require a "federation of the world." They think of such a federation not primarily in terms of the complex economic and social interest and vitalities, which must be brought into and held in a tolerable equilibrium. Least of all do they think of the necessity of some dominant force or power as the organizing center of the equilibrium. They are on the whole content to state the ideal requirements of the situation in as rigorous terms as possible.

Augustine was, by general consent, the first great "realist" in Western history. He deserves this distinction because his picture of social reality in his *Civitas Dei* gives an adequate account of the social facitons, tensions, and competitions which we know to be well-nigh universal on every level of community; while the classical age conceived the order and justice of its *polis* to be a comparatively simple achievement, which would be accomplished when reason had brought all subrational forces under its dominion.

This difference in the viewpoint of Augustine and the classical philosophers lies in Augustine's Biblical, rather than rationalistic or idealistic conception of human selfhood with the ancillary conception of the seat of evil being in the self. According to Augustine the self is an integral unity of mind and body. It is something more than mind and is able to use mind for its purposes. The self has, in fact, a mysterious identity and integrity transcending its functions of mind, memory, and will. It must be observed that the transcendant freedom of this self, including its capacity to defy any rational or natural system into which someone may seek to coordinate it (its capacity for evil) makes it difficult for any philosophy, whether ancient or modern, to comprehend its true dimension. This conception of selfhood is drawn from the Bible, rather than from philosophy, because the transcendent self which is present in, though it transcends, all of the functions and effects, is comprehensible only in the dramatic-historical mode of apprehension which characterizes Biblical faith.

Augustine's conception of the evil which threatens the human community on every level is a corollary of his doctrine of selfhood. "Self-love" is the source of evil rather than some residual natural impulse which mind has not yet completely mastered. This excessie love of self, sometimes also defined as pride or *superbia,* is explained as the consequence of the self's abandonment of God as its true end and of making itself "a kind of end." It is this powerful self-love or, in a modern term, "egocentricity," this tendency of the self to make itself its own end, or even to make itself the false center of whatever community it inhabits, which sows confusion in every human community.

Augustine's description of the social effects of human egocentricity or self-love is contained in his definition of the life of the "city of this world," the *civitas terrena,* which he sees as commingled with the *civitas dei.* The "city of this world" is dominated by self-love to the point of contempt of God; and is distinguished from the *civitas dei* which is actuated by the "love of God" to the point of contempt of self. This "city" is not some little city-state, as it is conceived in classical thought. It is the whole human community on its three levels of the family, the commonwealth, and the world.

The *civitas terrena* is described as constantly subject to an uneasy armistice between contending forces, with the danger that factional disputes may result in "bloody insurrection" at any time. Augustine's realism prompts him to challenge Cicero's conception of a commonwealth as rooted in a "compact of justice." No so, declares Augustine. Commonwealths are bound together by a common love, or collective interest, rather than by a sense of justice; and they could not maintain themselves without the imposition of power. "Without injustice the republic would neither increase nor subsist. The imperial city to which the republic belongs could not rule over provinces without recourse to injustice. For it is unjust for some men to rule over others."

This realism has the merit of describing the power realities which underlie all large-scale social integrations whether in Egypt or Babylon or Rome, where a dominant city-state furnished the organizing power for the Empire. It also describes the power realities of national states, even democratic ones, in which a group, holding the dominant form of social power, achieves oligarchic rule, no matter how much modern democracy may bring such power under social control. This realism in regard to the facts which underlie the organizing or governing power refutes the charge of modern liberals that a realistic analysis of social forces makes for state absolutism, so that a mild illusion in regard to human virtue is necessary to validate democracy. Realistic pessimism did indeed prompt both Hobbes and Luther to an unqualified endorsement of state power; but that is only because they were not realistic enough. They saw the dangers of anarchy in the egoism of the citizens but failed to perceive the dangers of tyranny in the selfishness of the ruler. Therefore they obscured the consequent necessity of placing checks upon the ruler's self-will.

If Augustine's realism is contained in his analysis of the *civitas terrena,* his refutation of the idea that realism must lead to cynicism or relativism is contained in his definition of the *civitas dei,* which he declares to be "commingled" with the "city of this world" and which has the "love of God" rather than the "love of self" as its guiding principle. The tension between the two cities is occasioned by the fact that, while egoism is "natural" in the sense that it is universal, it is not natural in the sense that it does not conform to man's nature who transcends himself indeterminately and can only have God rather than self for his end. A realism becomes morally cynical or nihilistic when it assumes that the universal characteristic in human behavior must also be regarded as normative. The Biblical account of human behavior, upon which Augustine bases his thought, can escape both the illusions of a too consistent idealism and the cynicism of a too consistent realism because it recognizes that the corruption of human freedom may make a behavior pattern universal without making it normative. Good and evil are not determined by some fixed structure of human existence. Man, according to the Biblical view, may use his freedom to make himself falsely the center of existence; but this does not change the fact that love rather than self-love is the law of his existence in the sense that man can only be healthy and his communities at peace if man is drawn out of himself and saved from the self-defeating consequences of self-love.

At the same time any Christian political thought which exploits the law of love without considering the power of the law of self-love is betrayed into sentimentality. As David Hume observed: "Politics must assume the selfishness of men, however we may speculate on the degree of their unselfishness and however much we may seek to increase that degree above the level of our political arrangements." Indeed, Augustine's doctrine of love as the final norm must be distinguished from modern sentimental versions of Christianity which regard love as a simple possibility and which think it significant to assert the obvious proposition that all conflicts in the community would be avoided if only people and nations would love one another. Augustine's approach differs from modern forms of sentimental perfectionism in the fact that he takes account of the power and persistence of egoism, both individual and collective, and seeks to establish the most tolerable form of peace and justice under conditions set by human sin.

It must be equally emphasized that the Augustinian formula for the leavening influence of a higher upon a lower loyalty or love, is effective in preventing the lower loyalty from involving itself in self-defeat. It corrects the "realism" of those who are myopically realistic, who see only their own interests and fail thereby to do justice to their interests where they are involved with the interests of others. There are modern realists, for instance, who, in their reaction to abstract and vague forms of international idealism, counsel the nation to consult only its own interests. In a sense collective self-interest is so consistent that it is superfluous to advise it. But a consistent self-interest on the pat of a nation will work against its interests because it will fail to do justice to the broader and longer interests, which are involved with the interests of other nations. A narrow national loyalty on our part, for instance, will obscure our long range interests where they are involved with those of a whole alliance of free nations. Thus the loyalty of a leavening portion of a nation's citizens to a value transcending national interest will save a realistic nation from defining its interests in such narrow and short range terms as to defeat the real interests of the nation.

Whatever the defects of Augustine's approach may be, we must acknowledge his immense superiority both over those who preceded him and who came after him. As has already been pointed out, a part of that superiority was due to his reliance upon Biblical rather than idealistic or naturalistic conceptions of selfhood. But that could not have been the only cause, else Christian systems before and after him would not have been so inferior. Or were they inferior either because they subordinated the Biblical-dramatic conception of human selfhood too much to the rationalistic scheme, as was the case with medieval Christianity culminating in the thought of Thomas Aquinas? or because they did not understand that the corruption of human freedom could not destroy the original dignity of man, as was the case with the Reformation with its doctrines of sin, bordering on total depravity and resulting in Luther's too pessimistic approach to political problems? As for secular thought, it has difficulty in approaching Augustine's realism without falling into cynicism or in avoiding nihilism without falling into sentimentality. Hobbes' realism was based on an insight which he shared with Augustine, namely, that in all historical encounters the mind is the servant and not the master of the self. But he failed to recognize that the self which thus made the mind its instrument was a corrupted and not a "normal" self. Modern realists know the power of collective self-interest as Augustine did; but they do not understand its blindness. Modern pragmatists understand the irrelevance of fixed and detailed norms; but they do not understand that love as the final norm must take the place of these inadequate norms. Modern liberal Christians know that love is the final norm for man; but they fall into sentimentality because they fail to measure the power and persistence of self-love. A generation which finds its communities imperiled and in decay from the smallest and most primordial community, the family, to the largest and most recent, the potential world community, might well take counsel of Augustine in solving its perplexities.

* * *

The following pages are devoted to the task of analyzing the moral resources and limitations of human nature, of tracing their consequences and cumulative effect in the life of human groups, and of weighing political strategies in the light of the ascertained facts. The ultimate purpose of this task is to find political methods which will offer the most promise of achieving ethical social goals for society. Such methods must always be judged by two criteria: first, do they do justice to the moral resources and possibilities in human nature and provide for the exploitation of every latent moral capacity in man? Second, do they take account of the limitations of human nature, particularly those which manifest themselves in man's collective behavior?

Modern optimists would argue that the second question, with its implied pessimistic reservations upon their utopian dreams, is predicated upon the assumption that human nature does not change, while it is their own belief that human nature is surprisingly malleable and is to a large degree the product of its environment. The question is whether they have not confused human nature with human behavior. Human behavior is constantly changing under the influence of various stimuli. The differences in the behavior of a Chinese Buddhist monk, a British aristocrat, a Prussian general, an American go-getter, an expatriated artist, and a Russian worker are very considerable. But a certain common human nature underlies all this varied behavior. Its common characteristics have been obscured by the rationalistic illusions which began in the eighteenth century, and which lost sight of common human traits in their emphasis upon the variable factors of education and environment.

Recently a considerable number of political scientists have become aware of the relevance of Christian conceptions of human nature for the assessment of man's collective capacities and incapacities for justice and civic virtue. In secular political theory the tendency is to elaborate cynical and undemocratic social theories upon the basis of pessimistic interpretations of human nature; or to expound sentimental political theories upon the basis of a too optimistic interpretation of human nature. This contradiction between cynicism and sentimentality in political theory is partly derived from the separation of two elements in the Christian doctrine of man, the cynics emphasizing the sinful egoism of man and the sentimentalists emphasizing his dignity and greatness.

* * *

Western civilization rests upon two sources–Greek classical thought and Biblical, Hebraic-Christian faith. These two sources are in agreement in their common appreciation of and emphasis upon the dignity and uniqueness of man. The alliance between them is, however, always uneasy, because they disagree on the character of man's unique gifts. For classical, as for modern secular, humanism, the emphasis lies heavily upon man's rational endowments, his logical and analytical faculties–in short, his "reason"–as the mark of his uniqueness. The Biblical view regards man's reason as only a part of his unique endowment, which it defines as the "image of God" and which it describes as a radical form of freedom in the human person. It is the total person, in the unity of will, memory, and understanding, which bears the "image of God."

According to the classical and modern secular view every extension and development of the human mind represents a clear gain. This is why, in the modern period, man's rational conquest of nature increased the prestige of rational humanism so significantly, and why this humanism had such an optimistic view of the moral consequences of man's conquest of nature, and of the development of technical civilization.

According to the Christian view the dignity of man and the "misery" of man are inextricably interwoven in his freedom. Every extension of freedom therefore involves the possibility of both good and evil; for evil is never merely the inertia of "nature" against the operation of "mind." Evil is in the person and not in nature. It is man's inclination to "self-love," his undue concern for himself. This defect is not overcome by any extension of mind; for if the center of personality is not changed, the mind still remains the servant of the self.

One reason why the Christian view has achieved a new relevance today is because modern developments have proved that there is a more intimate relation between what Madison called man's reason and self-love than the rationalists have assumed. The force of sin is stronger than humanism understands; and therefore the necessity of "grace" is greater. By "grace" we must understand every force in life and history which persuades and beguiles self-centered man to forget himself and to realize himself by letting go of himself and seeking the good of his fellows.

Modern, like classical, humanism removes every mystery from human selfhood. Christianity, on the other hand, declares that man stands so far above and beyond all relations of nature and reason that he can understand himself only in his relation to God. Modern humanism tends to equate the "dignity" of man with his virtue. Christianity, on the other hand, recognizes that the "dignity" of man consists precisely of that freedom which makes it possible for man to sin.

* * *

As the classical view of man is determined by Greek metaphysical presuppositions, so the Christian view is determined by the ultimate presuppositions of the Christian faith. The Christian faith in God as Creator of the world transcends the canons and antinomies of rationality, particularly the antinomy between mind and matter, between consciousness and extension. God is not merely mind who forms a previously given formless stuff. God is both vitality and form and the source of all existence. He creates the world. This world is not God; but it is not necessarily evil simply because it is not God. Indeed, being God's creation, it is good.

The consequence of this conception of the world upon the view of human nature in Christian thought is to allow an appreciation of the unity of body and soul in human personality which idealists and naturalists have sought in vain. Furthermore it prevents the idealistic error of regarding the mind as essentially good or essentially eternal and the body as essentially evil. But it also obviates the romantic error of seeking for the good in man-as-nature and for evil in man-as-spirit or as reason. Man is, according to the Biblical view, a created and finite existence in both body and spirit.

Thus, the Christian faith teaches that the world is not evil because it is temporal, that the body is not the source of sin in man, that individuality as separate and particular existence is not evil by reason of being distinguished from undifferentiated totality, and that death is no evil though it is an occasion for evil, namely the fear of death. The Biblical view is that the finiteness, dependence and the insufficiency of man's mortal life are facts which belong to God's plan of creation and must be accepted with reverence and humility.

Another characteristic of the Christian view of man is that he is understood primarily from the standpoint of God, rather than from the uniqueness of his rational faculties or his relation to nature. He is made in the "image of God." It has been the mistake of many Christian rationalists to assume that this term is no more than a religious-pictorial expression of what philosophy intends when it defines man as a rational animal. Whereas in fact the human spirit has the special capacity of standing continually outside itself in terms of indefinite regression. Consciousness is a capacity for surveying the world and determining action from a governing center. Self-consciousness represents a further degree of transcendence in which the self makes itself its own object in such a way that the ego is finally always subject and not object. The rational capacity of surveying the world, of forming general concepts and analyzing the order of the world, is thus but one aspect of what Christianity knows as "spirit." The self knows the world, insofar as it knows the world, because it stands outside both itself and the world, which means that it cannot understand itself except as it is understood from beyond itself and the world.

The essential homelessness of the human spirit is the ground of all religion; for the self which stands outside itself and the world cannot find the meaning of life in itself or the world. It cannot identify meaning with causality in nature; for its freedom is obviously something different from the necessary causal links of nature. Nor can it identify the principle of meaning with rationality, since it transcends its own rational processes, so that it may, for instance, ask the question whether there is a relevance between its rational forms and the recurrences and forms of nature. It is this capacity of freedom which finally prompts great cultures and philosophies to transcend rationalism and to seek for the meaning of life in an unconditioned ground of existence.

While these paradoxes of human self-knowledge are not easily reduced to simpler formulae, they all point to two facts about man. The obvious fact is that man is a child of nature, subject to its vicissitudes, compelled by its necessities, driven by its impulses, and confined within the brevity of the years which nature permits its varied organic forms, allowing them some, but not too much, latitude. The other less obvious fact is that man is a spirit who stands outside of nature, life, himself, his reason and the world.

The behavior of collective man naturally has its course in this anatomy of human nature. If we examine the constants and variables in that behavior, the most apparent constant factors are obviously derived from those aspects of human nature which constitute man a creature of nature, namely his natural hungers and needs, and the natural forces of cohesion in his communities, such as the sense of kinship. But natural necessity is not the only source of the constant factors. Some are derived from the unvarying way in which man's unique freedom manifests itself, such as his yearning for an ultimate good and his inevitable abuse of his freedom. However, freedom is, of course, also the source of the unique and variable factors in social behavior and therefore of the unpredictable character of historical events.

In the Christian view, then, for man to understand himself truly means to begin with a faith that he is understood from beyond himself, that he is known and loved of God and must find himself in terms of obedience to the divine will. This relation of the divine to the human will makes it possible for man to relate himself to God without pretending to be God; and to accept his distance from God as a created thing, without believing that the evil of his nature is caused by this finiteness. Man's finite existence in the body and in history can be essentially affirmed, as naturalism wants to affirm it. Yet the uniqueness of man's spirit can be appreciated even more than idealism appreciates it, though always preserving a proper distinction between the human and the divine. Also the unity of spirit and body can be emphasized in terms of its relation to a Creator and Redeemer who created both mind and body. These are the ultra-rational foundations and presuppositions of Christian wisdom about man.

* * *

This conception of man's stature is not, however, the complete Christian picture of man. The high estimate of the human stature implied in the concept of "image of God" stands in paradoxical juxtaposition to the low estimate of human virtue in Christian thought. Man is a sinner.

Indeed, it is man's radical and boundless freedom which is the basis of the self's destructive as well as creative powers; and there is no simple possibility of making nice distinctions between human destructiveness and creativity. In the words of Pascal, the "dignity of man and his misery" have the same source. Man stands perpetually outside and beyond every social, natural, communal, and rational cohesion. He is not bound by any of them, which makes for his creativity. He is tempted to make use of all of them for his own ends; that is the basis of his destructiveness. One may go further and declare that the limitless character of man's ideals of perfection and the inordinancy of human lusts and ambitions have their common root in the capacity of man to stand out of, and survey, any historical or natural situation which surrounds him.

While the Bible consistently maintains that sin cannot be excused by, or inevitably derived from, any other element in the human situation than man himself, it does admit that man was tempted. In the myth of the Fall the temptation arises from the serpent's analysis of the human situation. The serpent depicts God as jealously guarding his prerogatives against the possibility that man might have his eyes opened and become "as God, knowing good and evil." Man is tempted, in other words, to break and transcend the limits which God has set for him. The temptation thus lies in his situation of finiteness and freedom.

That is, the occasion for man's temptation lies in the two facts taken together: his greatness and his weakness, his unlimited and his limited knowledge. Man is both strong and weak, both free and bound, both blind and far-seeing. He stands at the juncture of nature and spirit; and is involved in both freedom and necessity. His sin is never the mere ignorance of his ignorance. It is always partly an effort to obscure his blindness by overestimating the degree of his sight and to obscure his insecurity by stretching his power beyond its limits.

In short, man is anxious. Anxiety is the inevitable concomitant of the paradox of freedom and finiteness in which man is involved. Anxiety is the internal precondition of sin, the internal description of the state of temptation.

It is not possible to make a simple separation between the creative and destructive elements in anxiety; and for that reason it is not possible to purge moral achievement of sin as easily as moralists imagine. The same action may reveal a creative effort to transcend natural limitations, and a sinful effort to give an unconditioned value to contingent and limited factors in human existence. Man may, in the same moment, be anxious because he has not become what he ought to be, and also anxious lest he cease to be at all.

The parent is anxious about his child and this anxiety reaches beyond the grave. Is the effort of the parent to provide for the future of the child creative or destructive? Obviously it is both.

The statesman is anxious about the order and security of the nation. But he cannot express this anxiety without an admixture of anxiety about his prestige as a ruler and without assuming unduly that only the kind of order and security which he establishes is adequate for the nation's health.

The philosopher is anxious to arrive at the truth; but he is also anxious to prove that his particular truth is the truth. He is never as completely in possession of the truth as he imagines. That may be the error of being ignorant of one's ignorance. But it is never simply that. The pretensions of final truth are always partly an effort to obscure a darkly felt consciousness of the limits of human knowledge. Man is afraid to face the problem of his limited knowledge, lest he fall into the abyss of meaninglessness. Thus fanaticism is always a partly conscious, partly unconscious attempt to hide the fact of ignorance and to obscure the problem of skepticism.

Anxiety, of course, must not be identified with sin because there is always the ideal possibility that faith will purge anxiety of the tendency toward sinful self-assertion. The ideal possibility is that faith in the ultimate security of God's love will overcome all immediate insecurities of nature and history. That is why Christian orthodoxy has consistently defined unbelief as the root of sin, or as the sin which precedes pride. It is significant that Jesus justifies his injunction, "Be not anxious" with the observation, "For your heavenly Father knoweth that ye have need of these things." The freedom from anxiety which he enjoins is a possibility only if perfect trust in divine security has been achieved.

Thus man's sin is defined as rebellion against God. The Christian estimate of human evil is so serious precisely because it places evil at the very center of human personality: in the will. This evil cannot be regarded complacently as the inevitable consequence of his finiteness or the fruit of his involvement in the contingencies and necessities of nature. Sin is occasioned precisely by the fact that man refuses to admit his "creatureliness" and to acknowledge himself as merely a member of a total unity of life. He pretends to be more than he is. Nor can he, as in both rationalistic and mystic dualism, dismiss his sins as residing in that part of himself which is not his true self, that is, that part of himself which is involved in physical necessity. In Christianity it is not the eternal man who judges the finite man; but the eternal and holy God who judges sinful man. Nor is redemption in the power of the eternal man who gradually sloughs off finite man. Man is not divided against himself so that the essential man can be extricated from the non-essential. Man contradicts himself within the terms of his true essence. His essence is free self-determination. His sin is the wrong use of his freedom and its consequent destruction.

Man is an individual but he is not self-sufficing. The law of his nature is love, a harmonious relation of life to life in obedience to the divine center and source of his life. THis law is violated when man seeks to make himself the center and source of his own life. His sin is therefore spiritual and not carnal, though the infection of rebellion spreads from the spirit to the body and disturbs its harmonies also. Man, in other words, is a sinner not because he is one limited individual within a whole but rather because he is betrayed by his very ability to survey the whole to imagine himself the whole.

* * *

The Bible defines sin in moral as well as religious terms. The religious dimension of sin is man's rebellion against God, his effort to usurp the place of God. The moral and social dimension of sin is injustice. The ego which falsely makes itself the center of existence in its pride and will-to-power inevitably subordinates other life to its will and thus does injustice to other life. Man is insecure and involved in natural contingency; he seeks to overcome his insecurity by a will-to-power which overreaches the limits of human creatureliness. Man is ignorant and involved in the limitations of a finite mind; but he pretends that he is not limited. He assumes that he can gradually transcend finite limitations until his mind becomes identical with universal mind. All of his intellectual and cultural pursuits, therefore, become infected with the sin of pride. Man's pride and will-to-power disturb the harmony of creation. We must now examine more carefully the ways in which sin expresses itself as both pride and the lust for power, and the consequences of these evils for social relations.

The most significant distinction between the human and the animal world is that the impulses of the latter are "spiritualized" in the human world. Human capacities for evil as well as for good are derived from this spiritualization. There is of course always a natural survival impulse at the core of all human ambition. But this survival impulse cannot be neatly disentangled from two forms of its spiritualization.

The one form is the desire to fulfill the potentialities of life and not merely to maintain its existence. Man is the kind of animal who cannot merely live. If he lives at all he is bound to seek the realization of his true nature; and to his true nature belongs his fulfillment in the lives of others.

The will-to-live is thus transmuted into the will to self-realization; and self-realization involves self-giving in relations to others. When this desire for self-realization is fully explored it becomes apparent that it is subject to the paradox that the highest form of self-realization is the consequence of self-giving, but that it cannot be the intended consequence without being prematurely limited. Thus the will-to-live is finally transmuted into its opposite in the sense that only in self-giving can the self be fulfilled, for: "He that findeth his life shall lose it; and he that loseth his life for my sake shall find it."

On the other hand the will-to-live is also spiritually transmuted into the will-to-power or into the desire for "power and glory." Man, being more than a natural creature, is not interested merely in physical survival but in prestige and social approval. Having the intelligence to anticipate the perils in which he stands in nature and history, he invariably seeks to gain security against these perils by enhancing his power, individually and collectively. Possessing a darkly unconscious sense of his insignificance in the total scheme of things, he seeks to compensate for his insignificance by pretensions of pride.

The conflicts between men are thus never simple conflicts between competing survival impulses. They are conflicts in which each man or group seeks to guard its power and prestige against the peril of competing expressions of power and pride. Since the very possession of power and prestige always involves some encroachment upon the prestige and power of others, this conflict is by its very nature a more stubborn and difficult one than the mere competition between various survival impulses in nature.

Since the survival impulse in nature is transmuted into two different and contradictory spiritualized forms, which we may briefly designate as the will-to-live-truly and the will-to-power, man is at variance with himself. The power of the second impulse places him more fundamentally in conflict with his fellow man than liberalism realizes. The fact that he cannot realize himself, except in organic relation with his fellows, makes the community more important than bourgeois individualism understands. The fact that the two impulses, though standing in contradiction to each other, are also mixed and compounded with each other on every level of human life, makes the simple distinctions between good and evil, between selfishness and altruism, with which liberal idealism has tried to estimate moral and political facts, invalid. The fact that the will-to-power inevitably justifies itself in terms of the morally more acceptable will to realize man's true nature means that the egoistic corruption of universal ideals is a much more persistent fact in human conduct than any moralistic creed is inclined to admit.

If we survey any period of history, and not merely the present tragic era of world catastrophe, it becomes quite apparent that human ambitions, lusts and desires are more inevitably inordinate, that both human creativity and human evil reach greater heights, and that conflicts in the community between varying conceptions of the good and between competing expressions of vitality are of more tragic proportions than was anticipated in the basic philosophy which underlies liberal civilization.

* * *

The Biblical and distinctively Christian conception of sin as pride and self-love finds various expressions in the observable behavior of men. Besides pride of power, two other types may be distinguished: pride of knowledge and pride of virtue. The third type, the pride of self-righteousness, rises to a form of spiritual pride, which is at once a fourth type and yet not a specific form of pride at all but pride and self-glorification in its inclusive and quintessential form.

The intellectual pride of man is of course a more spiritual sublimation of his pride of power. Sometimes it is so deeply involved in the more brutal and obvious pride of power that the two cannot be distinguished. Every ruling oligarchy of history has found ideological pretensions as important a bulwark of authority as its police power. But intellectual pride is confined neither to the political oligarchs nor to the savants of society. All human knowledge is tainted with an "ideological" taint. It pretends to be more true than it is. It is finite knowledge, gained from a particular perspective; but it pretends to be final and ultimate knowledge. Exactly analogous to the cruder pride of power, the pride of intellect is derived on the one hand from ignorance of the finiteness of the human mind and on the other hand from an attempt to obscure the known conditioned character of human knowledge and the taint of self-interest in human truth.

Moral pride is revealed in all "self-righteous" judgments in which the other is condemned because he fails to conform to the highly arbitrary standards of the self. Since the self judges itself by its own standards it finds itself good. It judges others by its own standards and finds them evil, when their standards fail to conform to its own. This is the secret of the relationship between cruelty and self-righteousness. When the self mistakes its standards for God's standards it is naturally inclined to attribute the very essence of evil to non-conformists.

One might add that the sin of self-righteousness is not only the final sin in the subjective sense but also in the objective sense. It involves us in the greatest guilt. It is responsible for our most serious cruelties, injustices and defamations against our fellow men. The whole history of racial, national, religious and other social struggles is a commentary on the objective wickedness and social miseries which result from self-righteousness.

The sin or moral pride, when it has conceived, brings forth spiritual pride. The ultimate sin is the religious sin of making the self-deification implied in moral pride explicit. This is done when our partial standards and relative attainments are explicitly related to the unconditioned good, and claim divine sanction. For this reason religion is not simply, as is generally supposed, an inherently virtuous human quest for God. It is merely a final battleground between God and man's self-esteem. In that battle even the most pious practices may be instruments of human pride. The same man may in one moment regard Christ as his judge and in the next moment seek to prove that the figure, the standards and the righteousness of Christ bear a greater similarity to his own righteousness than to that of his enemy. The worst form of class domination is religious class domination in which, as for instance in the Indian caste system, a dominant priestly class not only subjects subordinate classes to social disabilities but finally excludes them from participation in any universe of meaning. The worst form of intolerance is religious intolerance, in which the particular interests of the contestants hide behind religious absolutes. The worst form of self-assertion is religious self-assertion in which under the guise of contrition before God, He is claimed as the exclusive ally of our contingent self.

Christianity rightly regards itself as a religion, not so much of man's search for God, in the process of which he may make himself God; but as a religion of revelation in which a holy and loving God is revealed to man as the source and end of all finite existence against whom the self will of man is shattered and his pride abased. But as soon as the Christian assumes that he is, by virtue of possessing this revelation, more righteous, because more contrite, than other men, he increases the sin of self-righteousness and makes the forms of a religion of contrition the tool of his pride.

Indeed the final mystery of human sin cannot be understood if it is not recognized that the greatest teachers of this Reformation doctrine of the sinfulness of all men used it on occasion as the instrument of an arrogant will-to-power against theological opponents. There is no final guarantee against the spiritual pride of man. Even the recognition in the sight of God that he is a sinner can be used as a vehicle of that very sin. If that final mystery of the sin of pride is not recognized the meaning of the Christian gospel cannot be understood.

It must be added that it is not necessary to be explicitly religious in order to raise moral pride to explicit religious proportions. Stalin can be as explicit in making unconditioned claims as the pope; and a French revolutionist of the eighteenth century can be as cruel in his religious fervor as the "God-ordained" feudal system which he seeks to destroy. The hope of modern culture that the elimination of religion might result in the elimination of religious intolerance is fallacious. Religion, by whatever name, is the inevitable fruit of the spiritual stature of man; and religious intolerance and pride is the final expression of his sinfulness. A religion of revelation is grounded in the faith that God speaks to man from beyond the highest pinnacle of the human spirit; and that this voice of God will discover man's highest not only to be short of the highest but involved in the dishonesty of claiming that it is the highest.

* * *

Christianity is a religion with an ethic so pure that it has difficulty in coming to terms with political realities; for in politics moral ideas are inevitably compounded with the practical necessities of conflict and coercion. With its religio-moral ideal of perfect love, it is not quite certain how to approach and what to do with the stubborn realities of the political order; whether it should compromise with them, flee them or be indifferent to them.

Yet Christians must find ways of bringing the love ethic to bear on their political decisions. If the Christian humility which has no illusions about our ideals and structures or about any of the realities of the community is the negative precondition of a Christian social ethic, the positive form of it is the application of the law of love to man's collective relations.

The problem of the application of the law of love to the collective relationships of mankind contains within itself the whole question of the possibility of a Christian social ethic. When Catholic thought embodies the law of love into counsels of perfection and relegates these to the realm of ultimate possibilities of the "supernatural" life in the individual, and when it seeks to regulate the collective relations of mankind by the standards of "justice" which are given in the natural law, it is seeking to come to terms with the realities of the social order which seem to make the law of love inapplicable. This is also behind the logic of the thought of Protestant theologians who, following Luther, relegate love and forgiveness to the heavenly kingdom, as distinguished from the "earthly" one, where "the sword and the law," that is power and coercion, prevail. On the other hand, we have long since learned to recognize the sentimentality of Christian liberalism and other forms of liberalism which regard the establishment of "motives of service" in contrast to the "profit motive" as a simple possibility.

The question is therefore how, if love is not a simple possibility, it may yet be relevant to our political decisions. This question really involves the relevance of our final Christian insights as individuals to our actions as members of the group. As individuals we know the law of love to be final, if we view life through the revelation of Christ. The real problem of a Christian social ethic, then, is to derive from the Gospel a clear view of the realities with which we must deal in our common or social life, and also to preserve a sense of responsibility for achieving the highest measure of order, freedom and justice despite the hazards of man's collective life. We must establish tentative harmonies and provisional equities in a world from which sin cannot be eliminated, and yet hold these provisional and tentative moral achievements under the perspective of the Kingdom of God.

Of course, when the Church proclaims the love commandment to the world as the law of God it must guard against the superficial moralism of telling the world that it can save itself if men will only stop being selfish and learn to be loving. We dare not forget that in us, as well as in those who do not acknowledge the Christian gospel, there is a law in our members that wars against the law that is in our mind. The law of love is not kept simply by being preached. Yet it is the law of life and must be both preached and practiced. It is a terrible heresy to suggest that, because the world is sinful, we have a right to construct a Machiavellian politics or a Darwinian sociology as normative for Christians.

What is significant about the Christian ethic is precisely this: that it does not regard the historic as normative. Man may be, as Thomas Hobbes observed, a wolf to his fellowman. But this is not his essential nature. Let realistic Christians beware that they do not accept the habits of a sinful world as the norms of a Christian collective life. For the Christian only the law of love is normative. He would do well to remember that he is a sinner who has never perfectly kept the law of God. But neither must he forget that he is a child of God who stands under that law.

Frequently, believing Christians are tempted by their recognition of the sinfulness of human existence to disavow their own responsibility for a tolerable justice in the world's affairs. A Christian pessimism which becomes a temptation to irresponsibility toward all those social tasks which constantly confront the life of men and nations–tasks of ordering the productive labor of men, of adjudicating their conflicts, of arbitrating their divergent desires, of raising the level of their social imagination and increasing the range of their social sympathies–such a pessimism cannot speak redemptively to a world constantly threatened by anarchy and suffering from injustice. The Christian gospel which transcends all particular and contemporary social situations can be preached with power only by a Church which ears its share of the burdens of immediate situations in which men are involved, burdens of establishing peace, of achieving justice, and of perfecting justice in the spirit of love. Thus is the Kingdom of God which is not of this world made relevant to every problem of the world.

* * *

The Christian faith ought to persuade us that political controversies are always conflicts between sinners and not between righteous men and sinners. It ought to mitigate the self-righteousness which is an inevitable concomitant of all human conflict. The spirit of contrition is an important ingredient in the sense of justice. If it is powerful enough it may be able to restrain the impulse of vengeance sufficiently to allow a decent justice to emerge. The recognition of the law of love as an indiscriminate principle of criticism over all attempts at social and international justice is actually a resource of justice, for it prevents the pride, self-righteousness and vindictiveness of men from corrupting their efforts at justice.

* * *

To look at human communities from the perspective of the Kingdom of God is to know that there is a sinful element in all the expedients which the political order uses to establish justice. But it must also be recognized that it is not possible to eliminate the sinful element in the political expedients. They are, in the words of St. Augustine, both the consequence of, and the remedy for, sin. If they are the remedy for sin, the ideal of love is not merely a principle of indiscriminate criticism upon all approximations of justice. It is also a principle of discriminate criticism among forms of justice.

* * *

The heedlessness of love, which sacrifices the interests of the self, enters into calculations of justice principally by becoming the spirit of contrition which issues from the self's encounter with God. In that encounter it is made aware of the contingent character of all human claims and the tainted character of all human pretensions and ideals. This contrition is the socially relevant counterpart of love. It breaks the pride of the implacable contestants and competitors in all human encounters and persuades them to be "kindly affectioned one with another, forgiving one another, even also as God in Christ has forgiven you" (Ephesians 4:32). This spirit lies at the foundatin of what we define as democracy. For democracy cannot exist if there is no recognition of the fragmentary character of all systems of thought and value which are allowed to exist together within the democratic frame. Thus the *Agape* of forgiveness as well as the *Agape* of sacrificial love become a leaven in the lump of the spirit of justice. Or rather it would be better to use the other Gospel symbol and define them as the "salt" which arrests the decay in the spirit of justice.

The good news of the Gospel, therefore, is not the law that we ought to love one another. The good news of the Gospel is that there is a resource of divine mercy which is able to overcome a contradiction within our own souls which we cannot ourselves overcome.

* * *

In its profoundest insights, then, the Christian faith sees the whole of human history as involved in guilt, and finds no release from guilt except in the grace of God. The Christian is freed by that grace to act in history; to give his devotion to the highest values he knows; to defend those citadels of civilization of which necessity and historic destiny have made him the defender; and he is persuaded by that grace to remember the ambiguity of even his best actions. If the providence of God does not enter the affairs of men to bring good out of evil, the evil in our good may easily destroy our most ambitious efforts and frustrate our highest hopes.

* * *

The fundamental task of "social Christianity" must be, however, not so much to advocate a particular nostrum for the solution of various economic and social evils, but to bring a full testimony of a Gospel of judgment and grace to bear upon all of human life. The problem of how to maintain freedom under the intense and complex forms of social cohesion in modern technical society and how to achieve justice when freedom is maintained cannot be solved by any neat principles. It must be approached pragmatically from case to case and point to point. We know that it is possible to buy security at too great a price of freedom; and to maintain freedom at too great a price of insecurity for the masses involved in the modern industrial society. The Christian faith as such has no solution for this problem. It ought, however, to be possible for a vital Christian faith to help people to see that both freedom and order are facets of the love commandment which we must approximate; and also that such approximations under conditions of sin and law are bound to be imperfect in all human history. The conflict between order and freedom is perfectly resolved only in the Kingdom of perfect love which cannot be completely realized in history.

Like the individual Christian, the Church as a community and institution must face the challenge of making its social teachings and actions relevant and responsible, while avoiding moralism and fanaticism. This is a peculiarly difficult task, considering how easily religion lends itself to the pretensions of possessing absolute truth and virtue.

Ideally, the Church, which defines what is truth or error, is not itself one of the forces contending in society for an advantage, but is a transcendent community above all contending forces. All of us who are Christians believe that the Church holds the "Oracles of God"–that is, that it is a community of grace, testifying to the final truth about life as given in the Christian revelation. But the fact is that this transcendent community is also an interest group, through the sins and interests of its members. Indeed, since the historic Church is always touched with human finiteness, is subject to sociological forces and pressures, and victim of the prejudices and illusions of particular ages, any tendency to obscure or deny this fact becomes the final and most terrible expression of human sinfulness. Yet of that sin no Church has been free.

When the sanctification of the Church is extended to the sanctification of political programs, movements, or systems, the baneful effects are compounded. One need not be a secularist to believe that politics in the name of God is of the devil. This should be obvious to right-minded religious people, for religious politics invariably gives an ultimate sanction to highly ambiguous political programs. Every political policy, however justified, must be regarded as ambiguous when it is related to the ultimate sanctity. Since the political order inevitably deals with power, a religious politics always means the identification of some position of power with God.

* * *

According to the Christian faith, life is and always will be fragmentary, frustrating, and incomplete. It has intimations of a perfection and completeness which are not attainable by human power. There are no simple congruities in life or history. The cult of happiness erroneously assumes them. It is possible to soften the incongruities of life endlessly by the scientific conquest of nature's caprices, and the social and political triumph over historic injustice. But all such strategies cannot finally overcome the fragmentary character of human existence. The final wisdom of life requires, not the annulment of incongruity, but the achievement of serenity within and above it.

Specifically, any hope for perfection of political life and order is illusory. Politics is always a contest of power. At its best it arrives at a tentative equilibrium of power. "The peace of the world," said Augustine, "is based on strife." There may be long periods of covert rather than overt struggle. But this is not the love and harmony of the Kingdom of God. Perhaps Jesus regarded the political aspect of messianism as such a terrible temptation because illusions about politics lead to the most baneful consequences. The contradictions of human existence which prevent power from ever being good enough to belong to the Kingdom and which equally prevent pure love from being powerful enough to establish itself in the world, must be finally overcome; but they can only be overcome by divine action.

Any illusion of a world of perfect love without these imperfect harmonies of justice must ultimately turn the dream of love into a nightmare of tyranny and injustice. But the tragic character of our moral choices, the contradiction between various equal values of our devotion, and the incompleteness in all our moral striving, prove that "if in this life only we had hoped in Christ, we are of all men most miserable."

Nothing that is worth doing can be fully achieved in our lifetime; therefore we must be saved by hope. Nothing which is true or beautiful or good makes complete sense in any immediate contest of history; therefore we must be saved by faith. Nothing we do, however virtuous, can be accomplished alone; therefore we are saved by love. No virtuous act is quite as virtuous from the standpoint of our friend or foe as it is from our standpoint. Therefore we must be saved by the final form of love which is forgiveness.

We cannot contemplate our political life decently without a proper and grateful understanding of the "grace" of God. For the grace of God is on the one hand the providential working in history by which God makes the wrath of man to praise him, and transmutes good out of evil. The other element in divine grace is the element of forgiveness. If we cannot believe that God has resources to negate and to wipe out the corruption of egoism that all our actions betray, if we do not know that we are "justified" not by our goodness but by the goodness of God, we remain in the awful predicament of either trying to find a vantage point in history from which we can act "purely," or persuading ourselves that we have found such a vantage point and declaring a "holy war" from it.

Of course, there can be no acceptance of grace without repentance. If we do not understand how sinful even good men and nations are, we will have no gratitude toward a merciful providence that makes us do good against our will and gives us a chance to serve mankind, even though we want to serve ourselves. But, also, there can be no repentance without faith; for in that case the realization of the awful realities of man's collective life drives us to despair.

So we are "saved by faith" and not "by works"; which is to say that our final peace is not the moral peace of having become what Christ defines as our true nature, but is the religious peace of knowing that a divine mercy accepts our loyalty to Christ despite our continued betrayal of Him.

One of the great resources of this faith for social achievement is the sense of humility which must result from the recognition of our common sinfulness. Christian brotherhood is the brotherhood of common need rather than of common achievement. Jews and Greeks are alike in this, that they are both in need of the mercy of God. To subject human righteousness to the righteousness of God is to realize the imperfection of all our perfections, the taint of interest in all our virtues, and the natural limitations of all our ideals. Men who are thus prompted to humility may differ in their ideals; but they will know themselves one in the fact that they must differ, that their differences are rooted in natural and historic circumstances and that these differences rise to sinful proportions beyond anything which nature knows.

They will not regard either their unities or differences in moral ideals as unimportant. They will know that men are called upon to make fateful decisions in human history and that these decisions sometimes set a son at variance with his father and a daughter with her mother. To subordinate the righteousness to which they are devoted under the righteousness of God does not mean to be less loyal to any cause to which conscience prompts them. Yet they will know that they are finite and sinful men, contending against others who are equally finite and equally sinful.

The only true peace within and among human communities is the peace of forgiveness which grows out of contrition for sin. It is not a peace of perfect accord of life with life, but a peace which is established beyond the frictions of life. And this is a peace beyond the understanding of the moralists, who never fully recognize how much the judgment of the righteous upon the evil doer is below the ultimate and divine judgment. It is the judgment of an unrighteous self upon his fellows. There are of course legitimate judgments of the relatively righteous upon the unrighteous. But even when the unrighteous are obviously so, there is no vantage point in history from which a simple judgment against them can be pronounced. Reconciliation with even the most evil foe requires forgiveness; and forgiveness is possible only to those who have some recognition of common guilt. The pain of contrition is the root of the peace of forgiveness.

Besides judgment, humility and forgiveness, the other great social resource of the faith is the confidence that God can work a redemptive purpose in and beyond the judgment and that His love operates in and beyond His justice. This can be proven true if it is believed, but it must first be believed. It does not of course offer any assurance of the preservation of this or any civilization. It is a confidence and hope which finally transcends the fate of all civilizations. Rightly interpreted, it can give us the serenity required to do our duty in an age in which alternate hopes and fears, fulfillments and frustrations threaten to rob us of the sanity required for the fulfillment of our duty.

Thus the much despised Christian "otherworldliness" becomes a resource for historic striving. We strive for the Kingdom of God in history, but we do not expect its full realization there. Historical realities ought not to tempt the Christian to despair because he ought to know that the final good does not appear in history. The Christian ought to know that we never have, in either individual or collective achievement, the perfect serenity of achieved ideals. Our peace is never a purely moral peace. Our final peace is the peace of forgiveness, of justificaiton by faith. The Kingdom of God always remains fragmentary and corrupted in history. Even the highest historic achievement points beyond itself to a more final consummation, even as every historic judgment points beyond itself to a more ultimate judgment. To know this is to have a final security beyond the securities of history, and a final hope beyond the achievements of history.

Such "otherworldliness" is not an escape from history. It gives us a fulcrum from which we can operate in history. It gies us a faith by which we can seek to fulfill our historic tasks without illusions and without despair.

Only a combination of repose and anxiety, of sesrenity and preparedness, can do justice to the whole of our life and the whole of our world. For our life is a brief existence, moving within a great stream of finiteness. Yet the stream moves within its bed; and the flux of existence is held together by the eternal purposes of God. We ourselves stand beyond the flux in memory and hope. But we do not stand beyond it so completely that we can touch the eternal in the present moment by our own strength. We touch it by faith. That faith is the source of our serenity, even as alertness for the promises and perils of tomorrow is a reminder of our continued finiteness and sin.

Martyr, prophet and statesman may each in his own way be servant o the Kingdom. Without the martyr we might live under the illusion that the kingdom of Caesar is the Kingdom of Christ in embryo and forget that there is a fundamental contradiction between the two kingdoms. Without the successful prophet, whose moral indictments effect actual changes in the world, we might forget that each moment of human history faces actual and realizable higher possibilities. Without the statesman, who uses power to correct the injustices of power, we might allow the vision of the Kingdom of Christ to become a luxury of those who can afford to acquiesce in present injustice because they do not suffer from it.

Chapter VIII Liberation Theology

GUSTAVO GUTIERREZ

Gustavo Gutierrez

INTRODUCTION

Gustavo Gutierrez (b. 1928) is a Latin American theologian and a leading representative of "Liberation Theology." Born in Lima, Peru, Gutierrez originally studied medicine; but after becoming politically active at the National University, he began studying philosophy and theology in preparation for the Roman Catholic priesthood. From 1951 to 1955 Gutierrez studied philosophy and psychology at the University of Louvain and from 1955 to 1959 he studied theology at the University of Lyon. He was ordained in 1959. Since then, Gutierrez has served as Professor of Theology at the Catholic University in Lima. His book, *A Theology of Liberation,* is considered the classic text in Liberation Theology and has been translated into many languages.

Liberation Theology attempts to combine the social anslysis of Marxism-Leninism with Christian Theology. Thus, it sees the politics of this world as reflective of class struggle, economic exploitation, imperialism, etc., and the role of the Church as aiding the poor and oppressed in their revolutionary battle with their oppressors. The end of this fight for social justice as defined by Marxism-Leninism is "Salvation in History," or, ultimately, the Kingdom of Heaven on Earth. So, the struggle for socialism is fighting for God. Its goal is the achievement of "true human existence" for all people. As Gutierrez writes:

> A broad and deep aspiration for liberation inflames the history of mankind in our day, liberation from all that limits or keeps man from self-fulfillment, liberation from all impediments to the exercise of his freedom.

For Gutierrez, this quest for human liberation and freedom from all impediments arises during the Enlightenment and continues in the French Revolution and the Russian Revolution. His goal is to see that it continues today in Latin America and Africa.

The source of the absence of human liberation in Third World countries is the uneven economic development caused by industrial imperialism. The advanced industrial countries (such as the U. S.) exploit the resources and people of Latin America and Africa, keeping them from achieving "dignity, liberty and personal fulfillment." This economic deprivation in the Third World affects the political, social, cultural and religious backwardness of that area.

In this Liberation Theology view, sin is not an individual or corporate separation from God or a violation of His laws; rather, sin is "social injustice" caused by the economic class system, which leads to inequality and the lack of human fulfillment.

The achievement of human liberation in the Third World requires a recognition of the economic basis of its oppression and the revolutionary overthrow of that imperialist system. Violence may be necessary to establish the "authentic peace" of socialism. The Church should assist this social revolution out of its concern for the poor and its charge to follow Christ as liberator of mankind from all limits to "self-fulfillment."

Most of Gutierrez's advice is to the Roman Catholic Church of Latin America. He suggests some major alterations in the traditional Catholic view of Church-State relations. First, the Church should abandon its stance as representative of the transcendent City of God and become attuned to worldly political matters. Second, it should engage not simply "politics" or "government," but the radical politics of the revolutionary masses. Marx, after all, regards the State as the violent apparatus of the ruling economic class; so, insofar as the Church engages *that* state, it is supporting an oppressive system. The Church ought to directly engage in politics, but only to support those progressive, revolutionary groups, as defined by Marxism-Leninism. By doing so, the Church helps build the Kingdom of God on earth through socialism.

Gutierrez is critical of the Roman Catholic Church in Latin America, which he claims has historically supported the *status quo* of oppressive regimes and capitalist imperialism. To combat this tendency of the Roman Catholic Church in Latin America, Gutierrez encourages the Catholic clergy to adopt a new approach to politics and religion. First, they should permit the laity to directly engage in politics, without relying on the intermediary of the Church hierarchy. Second, revolutionary priests should then join that laity in social revolution, moving outside the restrictive jurisdiction of their Bishoprics. Third, revolutionary Bishops should join their revolutionary priests, despite admonitions from their superiors and the Pope, and follow the revolutionary people in establishing socialism and contributing thereby to the coming of the Kingdom of Heaven on earth. Christ calls us to love others and Gutierrez insists that we love the poor by leading them in socialist revolution and we love oppressors "by fighting them."

While Gustavo Gutierrez's conception of politics is unique among Christian theologians, relying, as it does, on Marxist categories, his conception of how the Church should engage in worldly politics is almost radically Protestant, in its dismantling of the institutionalized Church hierarchy and in uring priests to engage in worldly politics for worldly (economic) ends. While it may be stretching the metaphor, one might say that Gutierrez is the most "Lutheran" of Catholic theologians in his attitude towards the Roman hierarchy and practical politics.

The following selections are from Gustavo Gutierrez's classic text of Liberation Theology, *A Theology of Liberation* (Maryknoll, NY: Orbis Books, 1973).

Introduction

This book is an attempt at reflection, based on the Gospel and the experiences of men and women committed to the process of liberation in the oppressed and exploited land of Latin America. It is a theological reflection born of the experience of shared efforts to abolish the current unjust situation and to build a different society, freer and more human. Many in Latin America have started along the path of a commitment to liberation, and among them is a growing number of Christians; whatever the validity of these pages, it is due to their experiences and reflections. Our greatest desire is not to betray their experiences and efforts to elucidate the meaning of their solidarity with the oppressed.

Our purpose is not to elaborate an ideology to justify postures already taken, nor to undertake a feverish search for security in the face of the radical challenges which confront the faith, nor to fashion a theology from which political action is "deduced." It is rather to let ourselves be judged by the Word of the Lord, to think through our faith, to strengthen our love, and to give reason for our hope from within a commitment which seeks to become more radical, total, and efficacious. It is to reconsider the great themes of the Christian life within this radically changed perspective and with regard to the new questions posed by this commitment. This is the goal of the so-called *theology of liberation.*

Many significant efforts along these lines are being made in Latin America. Insofar as we know about them, they have been kept in mind and have contributed to this study. We wish to avoid, however, the kind of reflection which–legitimately concerned with preventing the mechanical transfer of an approach foreign to our historical and social coordinates–neglects the contribution of the universal Christian community. It seems better, moreover, to acknowledge explicitly this contribution than to introduce surreptitiously and uncritically certain ideas elaborated in another context which can only be fruitful among us if they undergo a healthy and frank scrutiny.

A reflection on the theological meaning of the process of the liberation of man throughout history demands methodologically that we define our terms. The first part of this book is devoted to that purpose. This will enable us to indicate why we pay special attention in this work to the critical function of theology with respect to the presence and activity of man in history. The most important instance of this presence in our times, especially in underdeveloped and oppressed countries, is the struggle to construct a just and fraternal society, where people can live with dignity and be the agents of their own destiny. It is our opinion that the term *development* does not well express these profound aspirations. *Liberation,* on the other hand, seems to express them better. Moreover, in another way the notion of liberation is more exact and all-embracing: it emphasizes that man transforms himself by conquering his liberty throughout his existence and his history. The Bible presents liberation–salvation–in Christ as the total gift, which, by taking on the levels we indicate, gives the whole process of liberation its deepest meaning and its complete and unforeseeable fulfillment. Liberation can thus be approached as a single salvific process. This viewpoint, therefore, permits us to consider *the unity, without confusion,* of man's various dimensions, that is, his relationships with other men and with the Lord, which theology has been attempting to establish for some time; this approach will provide the framework for our reflection.

It is fitting, secondly, to show that the problem which the theology of liberation poses is simultaneously traditional and new. This twofold characteristic will be more evident if we analyze the different ways in which theology has historically responded to this problem. This will lead us to conclude that because the traditional approaches have been exhausted, new areas of theological reflection are being sought. Our examination should help us remove the obstacles from our path and move ahead more quickly. The second part of the work deals with this matter.

The preceding analysis leads us to reconsider the "practice" of the Church in today's world. The situation in Latin America, the only continent among the exploited and oppressed peoples where Christians are in the majority, is especially interesting. An attempt to describe and interpret the forms under which the Latin American Church is present in the process of liberation–especially among the most committed Christian groups–will allow us to establish the questions for an authentic theological reflection. These will be the first efforts along these lines. The third part of this treatise is devoted to this attempt.

The previous remarks make it clear that the question regarding the theological meaning of liberation is, in truth, a question *about the very meaning of Christianity and about the mission of the Church.* There was a time when the Church responded to any problem by calmly appealing to its doctrinal and vital resources. Today the seriousness and scope of the process which we call liberation is such that Christian faith and the Church are being radically challenged. They are being asked to show what significance they have for a human task which has reached adulthood. The greater part of our study is concerned with this aspect. We approach the subject within the framework of the unity and, at the same time, the complexity of the process of liberation centered in the salvific work of Christ. We are aware, however, that we can only sketch these considerations, or more precisely, outline the new questions–without claiming to give conclusive answers.

THEOLOGY AS CRITICAL REFLECTION ON PRAXIS

The function of theology as critical reflection on praxis has gradually become more clearly defined in recent years, but it has its roots in the first centuries of the Church's life. The Augustinian theology of history which we find in *The City of God,* for example, is based on a true analysis of the signs of the times and the demands with which they challenge the Christian community.

Historical Praxis

For various reasons the existential and active aspects of the Christian life have recently been stressed in a different way than in the immediate past.

In the first place, *charity* has been fruitfully rediscovered as the center of the Christian life. This has led to a more Biblical view of the faith as an act of trust, a going out of one's self, a commitment to God and neighbor, a relationship with others. It is in this sense that St. Paul tells us that faith works through charity: love is the nourishment and the fullness of faith, the gift of one's self to the Other, and invariably to others. This is the foundation of the *praxis* of the Christian, of his active presence in history. According to the Bible, faith is the total response of man to God, who saves through love. In this light, the understanding of the faith appears as the understanding not of the simple affirmation–almost memorization–of truths, but of a commitment, an overall attitude, a particular posture toward life.

In a parallel development, Christian *spirituality* has seen a significant evolution. In the early centuries of the Church there emerged the primacy, almost exclusiveness, of a certain kind of contemplative life, hermitical, monastic, characterized by withdrawal from the world, and presented as the model way to sanctity. About the twelfth century the possibility of sharing contemplation by means of preaching and other forms of apostolic activity began to be considered. This point of view was exemplified in the mixed life (contemplative and active) of the mendicant orders and was expressed in the formula: *contemplata aliis tradere* ("to transmit to others the fruits of contemplation"). Viewed historically this stage can be considered as a transition to Ignatian spirituality, which sought a difficult but fruitful synthesis between contemplation and action: *in actione contemplativus* ("contemplative in action"). This process, strengthened in recent years by the search for a spirituality of the laity, culminates today in the studies on the religious value of the profane and in the spirituality of the activity of the Christian in the world.

Moreover, today there is a greater sensitivity to the *anthropological aspects* of revelation. The Word about God is at the same time a promise to the world. In revealing God to us, the Gospel message reveals us to ourselves in our situation before the Lord and with other men. The God of Christian revelation is a God made man, hence the famous comment of Karl Barth regarding Christian anthropocentrism: "Man is the measure of all things, since God became man." All this has caused the revaluation of the presence and the activity of man in the world, especially in relation to other men. On this subject Congar writes: "Seen as a whole, the direction of theological thinking has been characterized by a transference away from attention to the being *per se* of supernatural realities, and toward attention to their relationship with man, with the world, and with the problems and the affirmations of all those who for us represent the *Others."* There is no *horizontalism* in this approach. It is simply a question of the rediscovery of the indissoluble unity of man and God.

On the other hand, *the very life of the Church* appears ever more clearly as a *locus theologicus.* Regarding the participation of Christians in the important social movements of their time, Chenu wrote insightfully more than thirty years ago: "They are active *loci theologici* for the doctrines of grace, the Incarnation, and the redemption, as expressly promulgated and described in detail by the papal encyclicals. They are poor theologians who, wrapped up in their manuscripts and scholastic disputations, are not open to these amazing events, not only in the pious fervor of their hearts but formally in their science; there is a theological datum and an extremely fruitful one, in the *presence* of the Spirit. The so-called "new theology" attempted to adopt this posture some decades ago. The fact that the life of the Church is a source for all theological analysis has been recalled to mind often since then. The Word of God gathers and is incarnated in the community of faith, which gives itself to the service of all men.

Vatican Council II has strongly reaffirmed the idea of a Church of service and not of power. This is a Church which is not centered upon itself and which does not "find itself" except when it "loses itself," when it lives "the joys and the hopes, the griefs and the anxieties of men of this age" *(Gaudium et spes,* no. 1). All of these trends provide a new focus for seeing the presence and activity of the Church in the world as a starting point for theological reflection.

What since John XXIII and Vatican Council II began to be called a theology of the *signs of the times* can be characterized along the same lines, although this takes a step beyond narrow ecclesial limits. It must not be forgotten that the signs of the times are not only a call to intellectual analysis. They are above all a call to pastoral activity, to commitment, and to service. Studying the signs of the times includes both dimensions. Therefore, *Gaudium et spes,* no. 44, points out that discerning the signs of the times is the responsibility of every Christian, especially pastors and theologians, to hear, distinguish, and interpret the many voices of our age, and to judge them in the light of the divine Word. In this way, revealed truths can always be more deeply penetrated, better understood, and set forth to greater advantage." Attributing this role to every member of the People of God and singling out the pastors–charged with guiding the activity of the Church–highlights the call to commitment which the signs of the times imply. Necessarily connected with this consideration, the function of theologians will be to afford greater clarity regarding this commitment by means of intellectual analysis. (It is interesting to note that the inclusion of theologians in the above-mentioned text met opposition during the conciliar debates.)

Another factor, this time of a *philosophical* nature, reinforces the importance of human action as the point of departure for all reflection. The philosophical issues of our times are characterized by new relationships of man with nature, born of advances in science and technology. These new bonds affect the awareness man has of himself and of his active relationships with others.

Maurice Blondel, moving away from an empty and fruitless spirituality and attempting to make philosophical speculation more concrete and alive, presented it as a critical reflection on action. This reflection attempts to understand the internal logic of an action through which man seeks fulfillment by constantly transcending himself. Blondel thus contributed to the elaboration of a new *apologetics* and became one of the most important thinkers of contemporary theology, including the most recent trends.

To these factors can be added the influence of *Marxist thought,* focusing on praxis and geared to the transformation of the world. The Marxist influence began to be felt in the middle of the nineteenth century, but in recent times its cultural impact has become greater. Many agree with Sartre that "Marxism, as the formal framework of all contemporary philosophical thought, cannot be superseded." Be that as it may, contemporary theology does in fact find itself in direct and fruitful confrontation with Marxism, and it is to a large extent due to Marxism's influence that theological thought, searching for its own sources, has begun to reflect on the meaning of the transformation of this world and the action of man in history. Further, this confrontation helps theology to perceive what its efforts at understanding the faith receive from the historical praxis of man in history as well as what its own reflection might mean for the transformation of the world.

Critical Reflection

All the factors we have considered have been responsible for a more accurate understanding that communion with the Lord inescapably means a Christian life centered around a concrete and creative commitment of service to others. They have likewise led to the rediscovery or explicit formulation of the function of theology as critical reflection. It would be well at this point to define further our terms.

Theology must be man's critical reflection on himself, on his own basic principles. Only with this approach will theology be a serious discourse, aware of itself, in full possession of its conceptual elements. But we are not referring exclusively to this epistemological aspect when we talk about theology as critical reflection. We also refer to a clear and critical attitude regarding economic and socio-cultural issues in the life and reflection of the Christian community. To disregard these is to deceive both oneself and others. But above all, we intend this term to express the theory of a definite practice. Theological reflection would then necessarily be a criticism of society and the Church insofar as they are called and addressed by the Word of God; it would be a critical theory, worked out in the light of the Word accepted in faith and inspired by a practical purpose–and therefore indissolubly linked to historical praxis.

By preaching the Gospel message, by its sacraments, and by the charity of its members, the Church proclaims and shelters the gift of the Kingdom of God in the heart of human history. The Christian community professes a "faith which works through charity." It is–at least ought to be–real charity, action, and commitment to the service of men. Theology is reflection, a critical attitude. Theology *follows;* it is the second step. What Hegel used to say about philosophy can likewise be applied to theology: it rises only at sundown. The pastoral activity of the Church does not flow as a conclusion from theological premises. Theology does not produce pastoral activity; rather it reflects upon it. Theology must be able to find in pastoral activity the presence of the Spirit inspiring the action of the Christian community. A privileged *locus theologicus* for understanding the faith will be the life, preaching, and historical commitment of the Church.

To reflect upon the presence and action of the Christian in the world means, moreover, to go beyond the visible boundaries of the Church. This is of prime importance. It implies openness to the world, gathering the questions it poses, being attentive to its historical transformations. In the words of Congar, "If the Church wishes to deal with the real questions of the modern world and to attempt to respond to them,. . .it must open as it were a new chapter of theologico-pastoral epistemology. Instead of using only revelation and tradition as starting points, as classical theology has generally done, it must start with facts and questions derived from the world and from history." It is precisely this opening to the totality of human history that allows theology to fulfill its critical function vis-a-vis ecclesial praxis without narrowness.

This critical task is indispensable. Reflection in the light of faith must constantly accompany the pastoral action of the Church. By keeping historical events in their proper perspective, theology helps safeguard society and the Church from regarding as permanent what is only temporary. Critical reflection thus always plays the inverse role of an ideology which rationalizes and justifies a given social and ecclesial order. On the other hand, theology, by pointing to the sources of revelation, helps to orient pastoral activity; it puts it in a wider context and so helps it to avoid activism and immediatism. Theology as critical reflection thus fulfills a liberating function for man and the Christian community, preserving them from fetishism and idolatry, as well as from a pernicious and belittling narcissism. Understood in this way, theology has a necessary and permanent role in the liberation from every form of religious alienation–which is often fostered by the ecclesiastical institution itself when it impedes an authentic approach to the Word of the Lord.

As critical reflection on society and the Church, theology is an understanding which both grows and, in a certain sense, changes. If the commitment of the Christian community in fact takes different forms throughout history, the understanding which accompanies the vicissitudes of this commitment will be constantly renewed and will take untrodden paths. A theology which has as its points of reference only "truths" will have been established once and for all–and not the Truth which is also the Way–can be only static and, in the long run, sterile. In this sense the often-quoted and misinterpreted words of Bouillard take on new validity: "A theology which is not up-to-date is a false theology."

Finally, theology thus understood, that is to say as linked to praxis, fulfills a prophetic function insofar as it interprets historical events with the intention of revealing and proclaiming their profound meaning. According to Cullmannn, this is the meaning of the prophetic role: "The prophet does not limit himself as does the fortune-teller to isolated revelations, but his prophecy becomes preaching, proclamation. He explains to the people the true meaning of all events; he informs them of the plan and will of God at the particular moment." But if theology is based on this observation of historical events and contributes to the discovery of their meaning, it is with the purpose of making the Christians' commitment within them more radical and clear. Only with the exercise of the prophetic function understood in this way, will the theologian be–to borrow an expression from Antonio Gramsci–a new kind of "organic intellectual." He will be someone personally and vitally engaged in historical realities with specific times and places. He will be engaged where nations, social classes, people struggle to free themselves from domination and oppression by other nations, classes, and people. In the last analysis, the true interpretation of the meaning revealed by theology is achieved only in historical praxis. "The hermeneutics of the Kingdom of God," observed Schillebeeckx, "consists especially in making the world a better place. Only in this way will I be able to discover what the Kingdom of God means." We have here a political hermeneutics of the Gospel.

CONCLUSION

Theology as a critical reflection on Christian praxis in the light of the Word does not replace the other functions of theology, such as wisdom and rational knowledge; rather it presupposes and needs them. But this is not all. We are not concerned here with a mere juxtaposition. The critical function of theology necessarily leads to redefinition of these other two tasks. Henceforth, wisdom and rational knowledge will more explicitly have ecclesial praxis as their point of departure and their context. It is in reference to this praxis that an understanding of spiritual growth based on Scripture should be developed, and it is through this same praxis that faith encounters the problems posed by human reason. Given the theme of the present work, we will be especially aware of this critical function of theology with the ramifications suggested above. This approach will lead us to pay special attention to the life of the Church and to commitments which Christians, impelled by the Spirit and in communion with other people, undertake in history. We will give special consideration to participation in the process of liberation, an outstanding phenomenon of our times, which takes on special meaning in the so-called Third World countries.

It is for all these reasons that the theology of liberation offers us not so much a new theme for reflection as a *new way* to do theology. Theology as critical reflection on historical praxis is a liberating theology, a theology of the liberating transformation of the history of mankind and also therefore that part of mankind–gathered into *ecclesia*–which openly confesses Christ. This is a theology which does not stop with reflecting on the world, but rather tries to be part of the process through which the world is transformed. It is a theology which is open–in the protest against trampled human dignity, in the struggle against the plunder of the vast majority of people, in liberating love, and in the building of a new, just, and fraternal society–to the gift of the Kingdom of God.

LIBERATION AND DEVELOPMENT

The world today is experiencing a profound and rapid socio-cultural transformation. But the changes do not occur at a uniform pace, and the discrepancies in the change process have differentiated the various countries and regions of our planet.

Man, the Master of his Own Destiny

To characterize the situation of the poor countries as dominated and oppressed leads one to speak of economic, social, and political liberation. But we are dealing here with a much more integral and profound understanding of human existence and its historical future.

A broad and deep aspiration for liberation inflames the history of mankind in our day, liberation from all that limits or keeps man from self-fulfillment, liberation from all impediments to the exercise of his freedom. Proof of this is the awareness of new and subtle forms off oppression in the heart of advanced industrial societies, which often offer themselves as models to the under-developed countries. In them subversion does not appear as a protest against poverty, but rather against wealth. The context in the rich countries, however, is quite different from that of the poor countries: we must beware of all kinds of limitations as well as new forms of imperialism–revolutionary this time–of the rich countries, which consider themselves central to the history of mankind. Such mimicry would only lead the revolutionary groups of the Third World to a new deception regarding their own reality. They would be led to fight against windmills.

But, having acknowledged this danger, it is important to remember also that the poor countries would err in not following these events closely since their future depends at least partially upon what happens on the domestic scene in the dominant countries. Their own efforts at liberation cannot be indifferent to that proclaimed by growing minorities in rich nations. There are, moreover, valuable lessons to be learned by the revolutionaries of the countries on the periphery, who could in turn use them as corrective measures in the difficult task of building a new society.

What is at stake in the South as well as in the North, in the West as well as the East, on the periphery and in the center is the possibility of enjoying a truly human existence, a free life, a dynamic liberty which is related to history as a conquest. We have today an ever-clearer vision of this dynamism and this conquest, but their roots stretch into the past.

The fifteenth and sixteenth centuries are important milestones in man's understanding of himself. His relationship with nature changed substantially with the emergence of experimental science and the techniques of manipulation derived from it. Relying on these achievements, man abandoned his former image of the world and himself. Gilson expresses this idea in a well-known phrase: "It is because of its physics that metaphysics grows old." Because of science man took a step forward and began to regard himself in a different way. This process indicates why the best philosophical tradition is not merely an armchair product; it is rather the reflective and thematic awareness of man's experience of his relationships with nature and with other men. And these relationships are interpreted and at the same time modified by advances in technological and scientific knowledge.

Descartes is one of the great names of the new physics which altered man's relationship to nature. He laid the cornerstone of a philosophical reflection which stressed the primary of thought and of "clear and distinct ideas," and so highlighted the creative aspects of human subjectivity. Kant's "Copernican Revolution" strengthened and systematized this point of view. For him our concept ought not to conform to the objects, but rather "the objects, or, in which is the same thing, that experience, which alone as given objects they are *cognized,* must conform to my conceptions." The reason is that "we only cognize in things *a priori* that which we ourselves place in them." Kant was aware that his leads to a "new method" of thought, to a knowledge which is critical of its foundations and thus abandons its naivete and enters an adult stage.

Hegel followed this approach, introducing with vitality and urgency the theme of history. To a great extent his philosophy is a reflection on the French Revolution. This historical event had vast repercussions, for its proclaimed the right of every man to participate in the direction of the society to which he belongs. For Hegel man is aware of himself "only by being acknowledged or 'recognized'" by another consciousness. But this being recognized by another presupposes an initial conflict, "a life-and-death struggle," because it is "solely by risking life that freedom is obtained."

Through the lord-bondsman dialectic (resulting from this original confrontation), the historical process will then appear as the genesis of consciousness and therefore of the gradual liberation of man. Through the dialectical process man constructs himself and attains a real awareness of his own being; he liberates himself in the acquisition of genuine freedom which through work transforms the world and educates man. For Hegel "world history is the progression of the awareness of freedom." Moreover, the driving force of history is the difficult conquest of freedom, hardly perceptible in its initial stages. It is the passage from awareness of freedom to real freedom. "It is Freedom in itself that comprises within itself the infinite necessity of bringing itself to consciousness and hereby, since knowledge about itself is its very nature, to reality." Thus man gradually takes hold of the reins of his own destiny. He looks ahead and turns towards a society in which he will be free of all alienation and servitude. This focus will initiate a new dimension in philosophy: social criticism.

Marx deepened and renewed this line of thought in his unique way. But this required what has been called an "epistemological break" (a notion taken from Gaston Bachelard) with previous thought. The new attitude was expressed clearly in the famous *Theses on Feuerbach,* in which Marx presented concisely but penetratingly the essential elements of his approach. In them, especially in the First

Thesis, Marx situated himself equidistant between the old materialism and idealism; more precisely, he presented his position as the dialectical transcendence of both. Of the first he retained the affirmation of the objectivity of the external world; of the second he kept man's transforming capacity. For Marx, to know was something indissolubly linked to the transformation of the world through work. Basing his thought on these first institutions, he went on to construct a scientific understanding of historical reality. He analyzed capitalistic society, in which were found concrete instances of the exploitation of man by his fellows and of one social class by another. Pointing the way towards an era in history when man can live humanly, Marx created categories which allowed for the elaboration of a science of history.

The door was opened for science to help man take one more step on the road to critical thinking. It made him more aware of the socio-economic determinants of his ideological creations and therefore freer and more lucid in relation to them. But at the same time these new insights enabled man to have greater control and rational grasp of his historical initiatives. (This interpretation is valid unless of course one holds a dogmatic and mechanistic interpretation of history.) These initiatives ought to assure the change from the capitalistic mode of production to the socialistic mode, that is to say, to one oriented towards a society in which man can begin to live freely and humanly. He will have controlled nature, created the conditions for a socialized production of wealth, done away with private acquisition of excessive wealth, and established socialism.

But modern man's aspirations include not only liberation from *exterior* pressures which prevent his fulfillment as a member of a certain social class, country, or society. He seeks likewise an *interior* liberation, in an individual and intimate dimension; he seeks liberation not only on a social plane but also on a psychological. He seeks an interior freedom understood however not as an ideological evasion from social confrontation or as the internalization of a situation of dependency. Rather it must be in relation to the real world of the human psyche as understood since Freud.

A new frontier was in effect opened up when Freud highlighted the unconscious determinants of human behavior, with repression as the central element of man's psychic make-up. Repression is the result of the conflict between instinctive drives and the cultural and ethical demands of the social environment. For Freud, unconscious motivations exercise a tyrannical power and can produce aberrant behavior. This behavior is controllable only if the subject becomes aware of these motivations through an accurate reading of the new language of meanings created by the unconscious. Since Hegel we have seen *conflict* used as a germinal explanatory category and *awareness* as a step in the conquest of freedom. In Freud however they appear in a psychological process which ought also to lead to a fuller liberation of man.

The scope of liberation on the collective and historical level does not always and satisfactorily include psychological liberation. Psychological liberation includes dimensions which do not exist in or are not sufficiently integrated with collective, historical liberation. We are not speaking here, however, of facilely separating them or putting them in opposition with one another. "It seems to me," writes David Cooper, "that a cardinal failure of all past revolutions has been the dissociation of liberation on the mass social level, i.e. liberation of whole classes in economic and political terms, and liberation on the level of the individual and the concrete groups in which he is directly engaged. If we are to talk of revolution today our talk will be meaningless unless we effect some union between the macro-social and micro-social, and between 'inner reality' and 'outer reality.'" Moreover, alienation and exploitation as well as the very struggle for liberation from them have ramifications on the personal and psychological planes which it would be dangerous to overlook in the process of constructing a new society and a new man. These personal aspects–considered not as excessively privatized, but rather as encompassing all human dimensions–are also under consideration in the contemporary debate concerning greater participation of all in political activity. This is so even in a socialist society.

In this area, Marcuse's attempt, under the influence of Hegel and Marx, to use the psychoanalytical categories for social criticism is important. Basing his observations on a work which Freud himself did not hold in high regard, *Civilization and its Discontents,* Marcuse analyzes the *over-repressive* character of the affluent society and envisions the possibility of a non-repressive society, a possibility skeptically denied by Freud. Marcuse's analyses of advanced industrial society, capitalistic or socialistic, lead him to denounce the emergence of a one-dimensional and oppressive society. In order to achieve this non-repressive society, however, it will be ncessary to challenge the values espoused by the society which denies man the possibility of living freely. Marcuse labels this the Great Refusal: "the specter of a revolution which subordinates the development of the productive forces and higher standards of living to the requirements of creating solidarity for the human species, for abolishing poverty and misery beyond all national frontiers and spheres of interest, for the attainment of peace."

We are not suggesting, of course, that we should endorse without question every aspect of this development of ideas. There are ambiguities, critical observations to be made, and points to be clarified. Many ideas must be reconsidered in the light of a history that advances inexorably, simultaneously confirming and rejecting previous assertions. Ideas must be reconsidered too in light of praxis, which is the proving ground of all theory, and in light of socio-cultural realities very different from those from which the ideas emerged. But all this should not lead us to an attitude of distrustful reserve toward these ideas; rather it should suggest that the task to be undertaken is formidable. And the task is all the more urgent because these reflections are attempts to express a deeply-rooted sentiment in today's masses: the aspiration to liberation. This aspiration is still confusedly perceived, but there is an ever greater awareness of it. Furthermore, for many people in various ways this aspiration–in Vietnam or Brazil, New York or Prague–has become a norm for their behavior and a sufficient reason to lead lives of dedication. Their commitment is the back-bone which validates and gives historical viability to the development of the ideas outlined above.

To conceive of history as a process of the liberation of man is to consider freedom as a historical conquest; it is to understand that the step from an abstract to a real freedom is not taken without a struggle against all the forces that oppress man, a struggle full of pitfalls, detours, and temptations to run away. The goal is not only better living conditions, a radical change of structures, a social revolution; it is much more: the continuous creation, never ending, of a new way to be a man, a *permanent cultural revolution.*

In other words, what is at stake aabove all is a dynamic and historical conception of man, oriented definitively and creatively toward his future, acting in the present for the sake of tomorrow. Teilhard de Chardin has remarked that man has taken hold of the reins of evolution. History, contrary to essentialist and static thinking, is not the development of potentialities preexistent in man; it is rather the conquest of new, qualitatively different ways of being a man in order to achieve an ever more total and complete fulfillment of the individual in solidarity with all mankind.

* * *

The product of a profound historical movement, this aspiration to liberation is beginning to be accepted by the Christian community as a sign of the times, as a call to commitment and interpretation. The Biblical message, which presents the work of Christ as a liberation, provides the framework for this interpretation. Theology seems to have avoided for a long time reflecting on the conflictual character of human history, the confrontations among men, social classes, and countries. St. Paul continuously reminds us, however, of the paschal core of Christian existence and of all of human life: the passage from the old man to the new, from sin to grace, from slavery to freedom.

"For freedom Christ has set us free" (Gal. 5:1), St. Paul tells us. He refers here to liberation from sin insofar as it represents a selfish turning in upon oneself. To sin is to refuse to love one's neighbors and, therefore, the Lord himself. Sin–a breach of friendship with God and others–is according to the Bible the ultimate cause of poverty, injustice, and the oppression in which men live. In describing sin as the ultimate cause we do not in any way negate the structural reasons and the objective determinants leading to these situations. It does, however, emphasize the fact that things do not happen by chance and that behind an unjust structure there is a personal or collective will responsible–a willingness to reject God and neighbor. It suggests, likewise, that a social transformation, no matter how radical it may be, does not automatically achieve the suppression of all evils.

But St. Paul asserts not only that Christ liberated us; he also tells us that he did it in order that we might be free. Free for what? Free to love. "In the language of the Bible," writes Bonhoeffer, "freedom is not something man has for himself but something he has for others. . . .It is not a possession, a presence, an object,. . .but a relationship and nothing else. In truth, freedom is a relationship between two persons. Being free means 'being free for the other,' because the other has bound me to him. Only in relationship with the other am I free." The freedom to which we are called presupposes the going out of oneself, the breaking down of our selfishness and of all the structures that support our selfishness; the foundation of this freedom is openness to others. The fullness of liberation–a free gift from Christ–is communion with God and with other men.

* * *

Summarizing what has been said above, we can distinguish three reciprocally interpenetrating levels of meaning of the term *liberation,* or in other words, three approaches to the process of liberation.

In the first place, *liberation* expresses the aspirations of oppressed peoples and social classes, emphasizing the conflictual aspect of the economic, social, and political process which puts them at odds with wealthy nations and oppressive classes. In contrast, the word *development,* and above all the policies characterized as developmentalist [*desarrollista*], appear somewhat aseptic, giving a false picture of a tragic and conflictual reality. The issue of development does in fact find its true place in the more universal, profound, and radical perspective of liberation. It is only within this framework that *development* finds its true meaning and possibilities of accomplishing something worthwhile.

At a deeper level, *liberation* can be applied to an understanding of history. Man is seen as assuming conscious responsibility for his own destiny. This understanding provides a dynamic context and broadens the horizons of the desired social changes. In this perspective the unfolding of all of man's dimensions is demanded–a man who makes himself throughout his life and throughout history. The gradual conquest of true freedom leads to the creation of a new man and a qualitatively different society. This vision provides, therefore, a better understanding of what in fact is at stake in our times.

THE CHURCH IN THE PROCESS OF LIBERATION

The Latin American Church has lived and to a large extent continues to live as a ghetto church. The Latin American Christian community came into being during the Counter-Reformation and has always been characterized by its defensive attitude as regards the faith. This posture was reinforced in some cases by the hostility of the liberal and anticlerical movements of the nineteenth century and, more recently, by strong criticism from those struggling to transform the society to which the Church is so tightly linked.

This hostility led the Church to seek the support of the established order and economically powerful groups in order to face its adversaries and assure for itself what it believed to be an opportunity to preach the Gospel peacefully.

But for some time now, we have been witnessing a great effort by the Church to rise out of this ghetto power and mentality and to shake off the ambiguous protection provided by the beneficiaries of the unjust order which prevails on the continent. Individual Christians, small communities, and the Church as a whole are becoming more politically aware and are acquiring a greater knowledge of the current Latin American reality, especially in its root causes. The Christian community is beginning, in fact, to read *politically* the signs of the times in Latin America. Moreover, we have witnessed the taking of positions which could even be characterized as daring, especially compared with previous behavior. We have seen a commitment to liberation which has provoked resistance and mistrust.

All this has required a task of reflection on the questions posed by this new attitude; hence the new theological thinking now occurring in Latin America comes more from the Christian groups committed to the liberation of their people than from the traditional centers for the teaching of theology. The fruitfulness of reflection will depend on the quality of these commitments.

The process is complex and things are changing before our very eyes. Here we focus our attention on participation in the process of liberation and thus do not concern ourselves with other aspects of the life of the Church. It will be helpful to point out some of the highlights which characterize the new situation now being created.

THE COMMITMENT OF CHRISTIANS

The different sectors of the People of God are gradually committing themselves in different ways to the process of liberation. They are becoming aware that this liberation implies a break with the status quo, that it calls for a social revolution. In relation to the entire Latin American Christian community it must be acknowledged that the number of persons involved is small. But the numbers are growing and active and every day they are acquiring a larger hearing both inside and outside the Church.

Laymen

What we have referred to as the pastoral approach of "New Christendom" brought about, among large groups of Christians, a political commitment to the creation of a more just society. In the past, the lay apostolate movements, especially among youth, have given a considerable number of their better leaders to the political parties of socio-Christian inspiration. The "distinction of planes" stage allowed for purification of the motivation of these commitments as well as for the discovery of new perspectives for the action of Christians in the world, in collaboration with people of different points of view. Today, apostolic youth movements have radicalized their political options. It has been true for some time now that in most Latin American countries young militants do not share the orientation of moderate renewal groups.

The ever more revolutionary political options of Christian groups–especially students, workers, and peasants–have frequently been responsible for conflicts between the lay apostolic movements and the hierarchy. These options have likewise caused the movement members to question their place in the Church and have been responsible for the severe crises experienced by some of them.

Moreover, many have discovered in these movements evangelical demands for an ever more resolute commitment to the oppressed peoples of this exploited continent. But the inadequacy of the theologico-pastoral plans which until recently were considered viable by these movements, the perception of the close ties which unite the Church to the very social order which the movements wish to change, the urgent albeit ambiguous demands of political action, the impression of dealing with the "concrete" in the revolutionary struggle–all these factors have caused many gradually to substitute working for the Kingdom with working for the social revolution–or, more precisely perhaps, the lines between the two have become blurred.

In the concrete, all this has often meant a commitment to revolutionary political groups. The political situation in Latin America together with the subversion of the status quo advocated by these groups force them to become at least partially clandestine. Moreover, as awareness of existing legalized violence grows, the problem of counterviolence is no longer an abstract ethical concern. It now becomes very important on the level of political efficacy. Perhaps more accurately, it is on this latter level that the question of man himself is concretely considered. Under these conditions, the political activity of Christians takes on new dimensions which have caught by surprise not only the ecclesial structures but also the most advanced pedagogical methods of the lay apostolic movement. It is clear, for example, that the kind of apostolic movement represented by the Catholic Action groups among the French workers–that is, communities of Christians with different political options who meet for a *revision de vie* in the light of the faith–is, as such, not viable. Among other reasons, this is so because political radicalization tends to lead to united–and impassioned–positions and because the kind of activity which develops does not allow for entirely free expression of ideas. The model of the Workers' Catholic Action is valid in a more or less stable society where political commitments can be lived out publicly. This model presupposes and facilitates, moreover, a theoretical dialogue with Marxism in a way which holds little interest for Latin America. On this continent, the oppressed and those who seek to identify with them face ever more resolutely a common adversary, and therefore, the relationship between Marxists and Christians takes on characteristics different from those in other places.

On the other hand, meetings between Christians of different confessions but of the same political option are becoming more frequent. This gives rise to ecumenical groups, often marginal to their respective ecclesiastical authorities, in which Christians share their faith and struggle to create a more just society. The common struggle makes the *traditional* ecumenical programs seem obsolete (a "marriage between senior citizens" as someone has said) and impels them to look for new paths toward unity.

A profound renewal or renaissance of various lay apostolic movements is nevertheless apparent. After the initial impact of a radical *politicization* for which they were inadequately prepared theologically, pedagogically, and spiritually, everything seems to indicate that they are beginning to find new approaches. There are also arising new kinds of groups as well as close collaboration among existing movements. These go beyond any particular specialization, yet recognize the need for specialized pedagogies and are oriented toward a specific social milieu; the "cement" holding them together is their particular posture within the Church and within the Latin American political process. A clear option in favor of the oppressed and their liberation leads to basic changes in outlook; there emerges a new vision of the fruitfulness and originality of Christianity and the Christian community's role in this liberation. This is not a matter merely of a reaffirmation of a choice but also of concrete experiences of how to witness to the Gospel in Latin America today. But many questions remain unanswered. The new vitality that can be foreseen does not have before it a completely clear path.

Priests and Religious

A clearer perception of the tragic realities of the continent, the clear options which political polarization demand, the climate of more active participation in the life of the Church created by Vatican II, and the impulse provided by the Latin American Bishops' Conference at Medellin–all these factors have made priests and religious today one of the most dynamic and restless groups in the Latin American Church. Priests and religious in ever increasing proportions seek to participate more actively in the pastoral decisions of the Church. But, above all, they want the Church to break its ties with an unjust order, and they want it–with renewed fidelity to the Lord who calls it and to the Gospel which it preaches–to cast its lot with those who suffer from misery and deprivation.

In a considerable number of countries, we observe the creation of groups of priests–with characteristics not foreseen by canon law!–who have organized to channel and reinforce their growing concern. These groups are characterized by their determination to commit themselves to the process of liberation and by their desire for radical change both in the present internal structures of the Latin American Church as well as in the manner in which the Church is present and active on this continent of revolution.

These concerns, as well as other factors, have led in many cases to friction with local bishops and apostolic nuncios. We can say that unless deep changes take place this conflictual situation will spread and become more serious in the immediate future.

Moreover, there are many priests who consider it a duty to adopt clear and committed personal positions in the political arena. Some participate actively in politics, often in connection with revolutionary groups. As a matter of fact, this participation is not essentially something new. In many ways the clergy have played and still play a direct participation in political life (barely veiled in some cases under pretexts of a religious nature). The new dimension is that many priests clearly admit the need and obligation to make such a commitment and above all that their options in one way or another place them in a relationship of subversion regarding the existing social order.

There are other factors: for example, the effects of a certain weariness caused by the intensity of the resistance that must be overcome within the Church; and then there is the disenchantment caused by the apparent futility of work regarded as purely "religious," which has little contact with the reality and social demands of the continent. We are facing an "identify crisis." For some this means a reassessment of the current life-style of the clergy; and for others it means even a reevaluation of the meaning of the priesthood itself. On the other hand, the numbers are growing of those who have found a renewed meaning for their priesthood or religious life in the commitment to the oppressed and their struggle for liberation. For them, the Gospel, the Word of the Lord, the message of love, is a liberating force which attacks the roots of all injustice. This leads them to put in second place the questions now being debated–with different priorities in other parts of the world–regarding the priestly or religious life.

Frequently in Latin America today certain priests are considered "subversive." Many are under surveillance or are being sought by the police. Others are in prison, have been expelled from their country (Brazil, Bolivia, Colombia, and the Dominican Republic are signficant examples), or have been murdered by terrorist anti-communist groups. For the defenders of the status quo, "priestly subversion" is surprising. They are not used to it. The political activity of some leftists groups, we might say, is–within certain limits–assimilated and tolerated by the system and is even useful to it to justify some of its repressive measures; the dissidence of priests and religious, however, appears as particularly dangerous, especially if we consider the role which they have traditionally played.

Bishops

The new and serious problems which face the Latin American Church and which shape the conflictual and changing reality find many bishops ill-prepared for their function. There is among them, nevertheless, an awakening to the social dimension of the presence of the Church and a corresponding rediscovery of its prophetic mission.

The bishops of the most poverty-stricken and exploited areas are the ones who have denounced most energetically the injustices they witness. But in exposing the deep causes of these injustices, they have had to confront the great economic and political forces of their countries. They naturally leave themselves open to being accused of meddling in affairs outside their competence and even of being friendly to Marxist ideas. Often this accusation is made, and vigorously, in conservative sectors, both Catholic and non-Catholic. Some of these bishops have become almost political personalities in their respective countries. The consequence has been tightened police vigilance and in some cases death threats on the part of groups of the extreme right.

But it is not just a question of isolated personalities. It is often entire conferences of bishops who openly take a position in this arena. We should also mention the efforts of many bishops to make changes–of varying degrees of radicalness–in Church structures. The results are still much below what is desired and necessary. The first steps do appear to have been taken, but the danger of retreat has not been eliminated, and, above all, there is much yet to be done.

In the majority of cases, options at the episcopal level regarding social transformation have been expressed in written statements, but there have also been cases in which these declarations have been accompanied by very concrete actions: direct intervention in workers' strikes, participation in public demonstrations, etc.

The conclusion to be drawn from all the above is clear: salvation embraces all men and the whole man; the liberating action of Christ–made man in this history and not in a history marginal to the real life of man–is at the heart of the historical current of humanity; the struggle for a just society is in its own right very much a part of salvation history.

It is fitting, nevertheless, to reconsider the question, reviewing how it has been posed and examining other aspects of it. This will allow us, furthermore, to summarize the ideas presented in this chapter.

* * *

Theologically, therefore, we will consider temporal progress as a continuation of the work of creation and explore its connection with redemptive action. Redemption implies a direct relation to sin, and sin–the breach of friendship with God and others–is a human, social, and historical reality which originates in a socially and historically situated freedom.

"Creation," the cosmos, suffers from the consequences of sin. To cite Rom. 8 in this regard is interesting and does broaden our perspective, but this passage is not directly related to the question at hand. The immediate relationship between creation and redemption easily leads to a juxtaposition or to an artificial inclusion of the former into the latter, in which creation is granted autonomy and yet struggles to escape from the straitjacket it is thus put into. It will be necessary to look at the question from a greater distance, or in other terms, to penetrate it more deeply, in order to capture in a single view or to establish on a single principle the creation-redemption relationship. In the way the problem has previously been stated, there is a curious omission of the liberating and protagonistic role of man, the lord of creation and coparticipant in his own salvation. As we have already pointed out in this chapter, only the concept of the mediation of man's self-creation in history can lead us to an accurate and fruitful understanding of the relationship between creation and redemption. This line of interpretation is suggested by the outstanding fact of the Exodus; because of it, creation is regarded as the first salvific act and salvation as a new creation. Without the perspective of political liberation we cannot go beyond a relationship between two separate "orders," that of creation and that of redemption. The liberation approach subverts also the very "order" involved in the posing of the question.

The work of man, the transformation of nature, continues creation only if it is a human act, that is to say, if it is not alienated by unjust socio-economic structures. A whole theology of work, despite its evident insights, appears naive from a political point of view. Teilhard de Chardin is among those who contributed most to a search for a unity between faith and the "religion of the world," but he does so from a scientific point of view. He values the dominion over nature man has achieved and speaks of it as the penetration point of evolution, enabling man to control it. Politically his vision is, on the whole, neutral. This focus has had a definite impact, as could be expected, on the views of theologians of the developed world. The faith-science conflict and the application of science to the transformation of the world have sapped most of their energy. This is why concern for human society is translated into terms of development and progress. In other areas the problems are different. The concerns of the so-called Third World countries revolve around the social injustice-justice axis, or, in concrete terms, the oppression-liberation axis. Thus there is a great challenge to the faith of Christians in these countries. In contradistinction to a pessimistic approach to this world which is so frequent in traditional Christian groups and which encourages escapism, there is proposed in these other countries an optimistic vision which seeks to reconcile faith and the world and to facilitate commitment. But this optimism must be based on facts. Otherwise, this posture can be deceitful and treacherous and can even lead to a justification of the present order of things. In the underdeveloped countries one starts with a rejection of the existing situation, considered as fundamentally unjust and dehumanizing. Although this is a negative vision, it is nevertheless the only one which allows us to go to the root of the problems and to create without compromises a new social order, based on justice and brotherhood. This rejection does not produce an escapist attitude, but rather a will to revolution.

The concept of political liberation–with economic roots–recalls the conflictual aspects of the historical current of humanity. In this current there is not only an effort to know and dominate nature. There is also a situation–which both affects and is affected by this current–of misery and despoliation of the fruit of man's work, the result of the exploitation of man by man; there is a confrontation between social classes and, therefore, a struggle for liberation from oppressive structures which hinder man from living with dignity and assuming his own destiny. This struggle is the human activity whose ultimate goal must in the first place be enlightened by faith. Once this has been achieved, other facets will likewise be illuminated. The horizon of political liberation allows for a new approach to the problem, it throws new light on it, and it enables us to see aspects which had been but dimly perceived; it permits us also to get away from an alleged apolitical science and provides a different context for the crucial role of scientific knowledge in the historical praxis of man. Other religions think in terms of cosmos and nature; Christianity, rooted in Biblical sources, thinks in terms of history. And in this history, injustice and oppression, divisions and confrontations exist. But the hope of liberation is also present.

The approach we have been considering opens up for us–and this is of utmost important–unforeseen vistas on the problem of sin. An unjust situation does not happen by chance; it is not something branded by a fatal destiny: there is human responsibility behind it. The prophets said it clearly and energetically and we are rediscovering their words now. This is the reason why the Medellin Conference refers to the state of things in Latin America as a "sinful situation," as a "rejection of the Lord." This characterization, in all its breadth and depth, not only criticizes the individual abuses on the part of those who enjoy great power in this social order; it challenges all their practices, that is to say, it is a repudiation of the whole existing system–to which the Church itself belongs.

In this approach we are far, therefore, form that naive optimism which denies the role of sin in the historical development of humanity. This was the criticism, one will remember, of the Scheme of Ariccia and it is frequently made in connection with Teilhard de Chardin and all those theologies enthusiastic about human progress. But in the liberation approach sin is not considered as an individual, private, or merely interior reality–asserted just enough to necessitate a "spiritual" redemption which does not challenge the order in which we live. Sin is regarded as a social, historical fact, the absence of brotherhood and love in relationships among men, the breach of friendship with God and with other men, and, therefore, an interior, personal fracture. When it is considered in this way, the collective dimensions of sin are rediscovered. This is the Biblical notion that Jose Maria Gonzalez Ruiz calls the "hamartiosphere," the sphere of sin: "a kind of parameter or structure which objectively conditions the progress of human history itself." Moreover, sin does not appear as an afterthought, something which one has to mention so as not to stray from tradition or leave oneself open to attack. Nor is this a matter of escape into a fleshless spiritualism. Sin is evident in oppressive structures, in the exploitation of man by man, in the domination and slavery of peoples, races, and social classes. Sin appears, therefore, as the fundamental alienation, the root of a situation of injustice and exploitation. It cannot be encountered in itself, but only in concrete instances, in particular alienations. It is impossible to understand the concrete manifestations without understanding the underlying basis and vice versa. Sin demands a radical liberation, which in turn necessarily implies a political liberation. Only by participating in the historical process of liberation will it be possible to show the fundamental alienation present in every partial alienation.

This radical liberation is the gift which Christ offers us. By his death and resurrection he redeems man from sin and all its consequences, as has been well said in a text we quote again: "It is the same God who, in the fullness of time, sends his

Son in the flesh, so that He might come to liberate all men from *all* slavery to which sin has subjected them: hunger, misery, oppression, and ignorance, in a word, that injustice and hatred which their origin in human selfishness." This is why the Christian life is a passover, a transition from sin to grace, from death to life, from injustice to justice, from the subhuman to the human Christ introduces us by the gift of his Spirit into communion with God and with all men. More precisely, it is *because* he introduces us into this communion, into a continuous search for its fullness, that he conquers sin–which is the negation of love–and all its consequences.

Temporal progress–or, to avoid this aseptic term, the liberation of man–and the growth of the Kingdom both are directed toward complete communion of men with God and of men among themselves. They have the same goal, but they do not follow parallel roads, not even convergent ones. The growth of the Kingdom of a process which occurs historically *in* liberation, insofar as liberation means a greater fulfillment of man. Liberation is a precondition for the new society, but this is not all it is. While liberation is implemented in liberating historical events, it also denounces their limitations and ambiguities, proclaims their fulfillment, and impels them effectively towards total communion. This is not an identification. Without liberating historical events, there would be no growth of the Kingdom. But the process of liberation will not have conquered the very roots of oppression and the exploitation of man by man without the coming of the Kingdom, which is above all a gift. Moreover, we can say that the historical, political liberating event *is* the growth of the Kingdom and *is* a salvific event; but it is not *the* coming of the Kingdom, not *all* of salvation. It is the historical realization of the Kingdom and, therefore, it also proclaims its fullness. This is where the difference lies. It is a distinction made from a dynamic viewpoint, which has nothing to do with the one which holds for the existence of two juxtaposed "orders," closely connected or convergent, but deep down different from each other.

* * *

In their political commitments, people today are particularly sensitive to the fact that the vast majority of mankind is not able to satisfy its most elementary needs; often they seek to make the service of those who suffer from oppression or injustice the guiding principle of their lives. Moreover, even Christians evaluate "religious" things in terms of their meaning for man. This approach is not without ambiguities, but many prefer, in the words of Jose Maria Gonzalez Ruis, "to err on the side of man."

* * *

The Old Testament is clear regarding the close relationship which exists between God and the neighbor. This relationship is a distinguishing characteristic of the God of the Bible. To despise one's neighbor (Prov. 14:21), to exploit the humble and poor worker, and to delay the payment of wages are to offend God: "You shall not keep back the wages of a man who is poor and needy, whether a fellow-countryman or an alien living in your country in one of your settlements. Pay him his wages on the same day before sunset, for he is poor and his heart is set on them: he may appeal to the Lord against you, and you will be guilty of sin" (Deut. 24:14-15; cf. Exod. 22:21-23). This explains why "a man who sneers at the poor insults his maker" (Prov. 17:5).

Inversely, to know, that is to say, to love Yahweh is to do justice to the poor and oppressed. When he proclaimed the New Covenant, after asserting that Yahweh would inscribe his law in the hearts of men, Jeremiah said: "No longer need they teach one another to know the Lord; all of them, high and low alike, shall know me" (31:34). But Jeremiah advises us exactly on what knowing God entails: "Shame on the man who builds his house by unjust means, and completes its roof-chambers by fraud, making his countrymen work without payment, giving them no wage for their labor! Shame on the man who says, 'I will build a spacious house with airy roof-chambers, set windows in it, panel it with cedar, and paint it with vermilion'! If your cedar is more splendid, does that prove you are a king? Think of your father: he ate and drank, dealt justly and fairly; all went well with him. He dispensed justice to the cause of the lowly and poor; did this not show he knew me? says the Lord" (22:13-16). Where there is justice and righteousness, there is knowledge of Yahweh; when these are lacking, it is absent: "There is no good faith or mutual trust, no knowledge of God in the land, oaths are imposed and broken, they kill and rob; there is nothing but adultery and license, one deed of blood after another" (Hos. 4:1-2; cf. Isa. 1). To know Yahweh, which in Biblical language is equivalent to saying to love Yahweh, *is* to establish just relationships among men, it *is* to recognize the rights of the poor. The God of Biblical revelation is known through interhuman justice. When justice does not exist, God is not known; he is absent. "God is everywhere," says the priest to the sacristan in Jose Maria Arguedas's novel *Todas las sangres.* And the sacristan, who knows no metaphysics, but is well acquainted with injustice and oppression, replies with accurate Biblical intuition: "Was God in the heart of those who broke the body of the innocent teacher Bellido? Is God in the bodies of the engineers who are killing 'La Esmeralda'? In the official who took the corn fields away from their owners...?" Likewise, Medllin asserts: "Where this social peace does not exist there will we find social, political, economic, and cultural inequities, there will we find the rejection of the peace of the Lord, and a rejection of the Lord himself" ("Peace," no. 14).

On the other hand, if justice is done, if the alien, the orphan, and the widow are not oppressed,"Then I will let you live in this place, in the land which I gave long ago to your forefathers for all time" (Jer. 7:7). This presence of Yahweh is active; he it is who "deals out justice to the oppressed. The Lord feeds the hungry and sets the prisoner free. The Lord restores sight to the blind and straightens backs which are bent; the Lord loves the righteous and watches over the stranger; the Lord gives heart to the orphan and widow but turns the course of the wicked to their ruin." So "the Lord shall reign forever" (Ps. 146:7-10).

This encounter with God in concrete actions towards others, especially the poor, is so profound and enriching that by basing themselves on it the prophets can criticize–always validly–all purely external worship. This criticism is but another aspect of the concern for asserting the transcendence and universality of Yahweh. "Your countless sacrifices, what are they to me? says the Lord; I am sated with whole offerings of rams. . . .The offer of your gifts is useless, the reek of sacrifice is abhorrent to me. . . .Though you offer countless prayers, I will not listen. There is blood on your hands. . . .Cease to do evil and learn to do right, pursue justice and champion the oppressed; give the orphan his rights, plead the widow's cause" (Isa. 1:10-17). We love God by loving our neighbor: "Is not this what I require of you as a fast: to loose the fetters of injustice, to untie the knots of the yoke, to snap every yoke and set free those who have been crushed? Is it not sharing your food with the hungry, taking the homeless poor into your house, clothing the naked when you meet them and never evading a duty to your kinsfolk?" (Isa. 58:6-7). Only then will God be with us, only then will he hear our prayer and will we be pleasing to him (Isa. 58:9-11). God wants justice, not sacrifices. Emphasizing the bond between the knowledge of God and interhuman justice, Hosea tells us that Yahweh wishes knowledge and not holocausts: "O Ephraim, how shall I deal with you? How shall I deal with you, Judah? Your loyalty to me is like the morning mist, like dew that vanishes early. Therefore have I lashed you through the prophets and torn you to shreds with my words; loyalty is my desire, not sacrifice, not whole-offerings but the knowledge of God" (Hos. 6:4-6).

Although it is true that in the texts cited the neighbor is essentially a member of the Jewish community, the references to aliens, who together with widows and orphans form a classic trilogy, indicate an effort to transcend these limitations. Nevertheless, the bond between the neighbor and God is changed, deepened, and universalized by the Incarnation of the Word. The famous text so often quoted in recent years, Matt. 25:331-445, is a very good illustration of this twofold process.

* * *

Human brotherhood, which has as its ultimate basis our sonship before God, is built in history. Today history is characterized by conflict which seems to impede this building of brotherhood. There is one characteristic in particular which holds a central place: the division of humanity into oppressors and oppressed, into owners of the means of production and those dispossessed of the fruit of their work, into antagonistic social classes. But this is not all; the division brings with it confrontations, struggles, violence. How then are we to live evangelical charity in the midst of this situation? How an we reconcile the universality of charity with the option for a particular social class? Unity is one of the notes of the Church and yet the class struggle divides men; is the unity of the Church compatible with class struggle?

These questions are being posed to the Christian conscience with a growing insistence. On them depend very concretely the meaning of the presence of the Church in the world, a central theme of the Council. In the case of Latin America this means a presence in a world in revolutionary turmoil and in which violence takes on the most varied forms, from the most subtle to the most open.

The council broke open a new path on which there is no turning back: openness to the world. In the conciliar texts this world appears above all in its positive and irenic aspects, but gradually the Church became more clearly aware of the conflicts and confrontations involved in it. The Church began to realize that this service to the world, into which it had thrown itself so joyfully, confronted it with demands and challenges beyond what it had foreseen. The class struggle is one of the cardinal problems of the world today which challenge the life and reflection of the Christian community and which can no longer be avoided.

It is undeniable that the class struggle poses problems to the universality of Christian love and the unity of the Church. But any consideratin of this subject must start from two elemental points: the class struggle is a fact, and neutrality in this matter is impossible.

The class struggle is a part of our economic, social, political, cultural, and religious reality. Its evolution, its exact extent, its nuances, and its variations are the object of analysis of the social sciences and pertain to the field of scientific rationality.

Recognition of the existence of the class struggle does not depend on our religious or ethical options. There are those who have claimed that it is something artificial, foreign to the norms which guide our society, contrary to the spirit of "Western Christian civilization," and the work of agitators and malcontents. Perhaps in spite of those who think this way, there is one thing that is true in this viewpoint: oppression and exploitation, and therefore the experience of the class struggle, are endured and perceived first of all by those who have been marginated by that civilization and do not have their own voice in the Church. Although there is an awareness of the class struggle on the periphery, this does not mean that the struggle does not exist at the center of society: the dispossessed exist because of those who direct and govern this society. The class struggle is the product of demented minds only for those who do not know, or who do not wish to know, what is produced by the system. As the French bishops stated some years ago, "The class struggle is first of all a fact which no one can deny." And they continue, "At the level of those responsible for the class struggle, the first are those who voluntarily keep the working class in an unjust situation, who oppose their collective advancement, and combat their efforts to liberate themselves."

Those who speak of class struggle do not "advocate" it–as some would say–in the sense of creating it out of nothing by an act of (bad) will. What they do is to recognize a fact and contribute to an awareness of that fact. And there is nothing more certain than a fact. To ignore it is to deceive and to be deceived and moreover to deprive onself of the necessary means of truly and radically eliminating this condition–that is, by moving towards a classless society. Paradoxically, what the groups in power call "advocating" class struggle is really an expression of a will to abolish its causes, to abolish them, not cover them over, to eliminate the appropriation by a few of the wealth created by the work of the many and not to make lyrical calls to social harmony. It is a will to build a socialist society, more just, free, and human, and not a society of superficial and false reconciliation and equality. To "advocate" class struggle, therefore, is to reject a situation in which there are oppressed and oppressors. But it is a rejection without deceit or cowardliness; it is to recognize that the fact exists and that it profoundly divides men, in order to be able to attack it at its roots and thus create the conditions of an authentic human community. To build a just society today necessarily implies the active and conscious participation in the class struggle that is occurring before our eyes.

In the second place, we must see clearly that to deny the fact of class struggle is really to put oneself on the side of the dominant sectors. Neutrality is impossible. It is not a question of admitting or denying a fact which confronts us; rather it is a question of which side we are on. The so-called "interclassist doctrine," writes Girardi in a well-known article on this question, "is in face very classist: it reflects the point of view of the dominant class." When the Church rejects the class struggle, it is objectively operating as a part of the prevailing system. By denying the existence of social division, this system seeks to perpetuate this division on which are based the privileges of its beneficiaries. It is a classist option, deeitfully camouflaged by a purported equality before the law. The history of this refusal is long, and its causes many and complex. But the ever more acute awareness that the oppressed have of their situation and the increasing participation of Christians in the class struggle are raising new questions in the Church which are more authentic and real.

The class struggle is a fact and neutrality in this question is not possible. These two observations delimit the indicated problems, prevent us from getting lost in facile solutions, and provide a concrete context for our search. More exactly, the questions raised with regard to the universal character of love and the unity of the Church are real questions precisely because the class struggle confronts us as a fact and because it is impossible not to take part in it.

The Gospel announces the love of God for all people and calls us to love as he loves. But to accept class struggle means to decide for some people and against others. To live both realities without juxtapositions is a great challenge for the Christian committed to the totality of the process of liberation. This is a challenge that leads him to deepen his faith and to mature in his love for others.

The universality of Christian love is only an abstraction unless it becomes concrete history, process, conflict; it is arrived at only through particularity. To love all men does not mean avoiding confrontations; it does not mean preserving a fictitious harmony. Universal love is that which in solidarity with the oppressed seeks also to liberate the oppressors from their own power, from their ambition, and from their selfishness: "Love for those who live in a conditon of objective sin demands that we struggle to liberate them from it. The liberation of the poor and the liberation of the rich are achieved simultaneously." One loves the oppressors by liberating them from their inhuman condition as oppressors, by liberating them from themselves. But this cannot be achieved except by resolutely opting for the oppressed, that is, by combatting the oppressive class. It must be a real and effective combat, not hate. This is the challenge, as new as the Gospel: to love our enemies. This was never thought to be easy, but as long as it was only a question of showing a certain sweetness of character, it was preached without difficulty. The council was not followed, but it was heard without any uneasiness. In the context of class struggle today, to love one's enemies presupposes recognizing and accepting that one has class enemies and that it is necessary to combat them. It is not a question of having no enemies, bur rather of not excluding them from our love. But love does not mean that the oppressors are no longer enemies, nor does it eliminate the radicalness of the combat against them. "Love of enemies" does not ease tensions; rather it challenges the whole system and becomes a subversive formula.

Universal love comes down from the level of abstractions and becomes concrete and effective by becoming incarnate in the struggle for the liberation of the oppressed. It is a question of loving all people, not in some vague, general way, but rather in the exploited person, in the concrete person who is struggling to live humanly. Our love for him does not "abstract" him, it does not isolate him from the social class to which he belongs, so that we can have "pity" on him. On the contrary, our love is not authentic if it does not take the path of class solidarity and social struggle. To participate in class struggle not only is not opposed to universal love; this commitment is today the necessary and inescapable means of making this love concrete. For this participation is what leads to a classless society without owners and dispossessed, without oppressors and oppressed. In dialectical thinking, reconciliation is the overcoming of conflict. The communion of paschal joy passes through confrontation and the cross.

The fact of class struggle also challenges the unity of the Church and demands a redefinition of what we understand by this unity.

The Church is in a world divided into antagonistic social classes, on a universal scale as well as at the local level. Because it is present in our society, the Church cannot attempt to ignore a fact which confronts it. What is more, this fact exists within the Church itself. Indeed, Christians belong to opposing social classes, which means that the Christian community itself is split by this social division. It is not possible to speak of the unity of the Church without taking into account its concrete situation in the world.

To try piously to cover over this social division with a fictitious and formalistic unity is to avoid a difficult and conflictual reality and definitively to join the dominant class. It is to falsify the true character of the Christian community under the pretext of a religious attitude which tries to place itself beyond temporal contingencies. In these conditons, to speak, for example, of the priest as "the man of unity" is to attempt to make him into a part of the prevailing system. It is to attempt to make him a part of an unjust and oppressive system, based on the exploitation of the great majorities and needing a religious justification to preserve itself. This is especially true in places like Latin America, where the Church has a great influence among the exploited masses.

> "We must love everyone, but it is not possible to love everyone in the same way: we love the oppressed by liberating them; we love the oppressors by fighting them. We love the oppressed by liberating them from their misery, and the oppressors by liberating them from their sin" (Girardi, "Cristianismo, pastoral y lucha de clases," p. 98).

CHAPTER IX The Christian Right

JERRY FALWELL

Jerry Falwell

INTRODUCTION

Jerry Falwell (b. 1933) is a television evangelist ("The Old Time Gospel Hour"), founder of The Moral Majority, Inc., and a leading representative of the contemporary "Christian Right" in America. Originally an engineering student, Falwell became a "born again" Christian at age 18 after hearng a radio gospel program and enrolled at the Baptist Bible College of Springfield, Missouri. He subsequently founded the independent Thomas Road Baptist Church in Lynchburg, Virginia. Falwell rose to political prominence in the late 1970's when he organized the Washington-based Moral Majority, Inc., a conservative lobbying organization ostensibly devoted to "Pro-God," "Pro-Family," "Pro-Life," "Pro-Moral," and "Pro-strong defense" policies. Falwell strongly endorsed the candidacy and presi-dency of conservative Republican, Ronald Reagan. His preaching and writing style is notable for its patriotic tone–frequently citing "The Founding Fathers" and iden-tifying conservative politics with Godliness.

Jerry Falwell's ideas on Religion and Politics are distinctive for their adaptability to a free society and their unqualified support of capitalism. In America, where religious freedom is guaranteed by the Constitution, Falwell argues for the strict separation of Church and State (by which he means the non-establishment of the Church) but this does not imply for him separation of religion and politics. Religion generally (especially Falwell's own simple, fundamentalist Christianity) has a place in politics, as a moral influence. The substance of morality for Falwell is primarily concerned with prohibiting and punishing individual sin. Therefore, the role of religion in politics is the encouraging of laws prohibiting immoral conduct, such as homosexuality, abortion, pornography, etc. Falwell insists that "The Founding Fathers" (Madison, Jefferson, Washington, etc.) based American law in Scripture, especially the Ten Commandments. The political freedom that Americans enjoy requires the discipline of these religious principles. Contemporary problems in America result from a decline in those moral principles and therefore an abuse of that freedom. The remedy, therefore, is not government restrictions on freedom (especially economic freedom), but the restoration of the underlying moral principles.

Falwell claims to be leading America back to traditional morality by preaching "fire and brimstone" and calling for "national repentance." To be effective politically, Falwell insists that "moral Americans" must form a coalition

(The Moral Majority) to lobby the government. The Moral Majority brings tradi-tional morality back into politics by registering voters (i.e., fundamentalist Christians), providing information (on contemporary immorality and legislation concerning it) and mobilizing the public behind important issues. In sharp contrast with traditional Baptist attitudes (which discouraged church involvement in politics), Falwell argues that much of this political activity should occur inside the churches. He cites as an example, his own Thomas Road Baptist Church campaign against legalized gambling in Virginia. Nationally, the Moral Majority works to resist "Humanism" (putting human desires before God's law) by encouraging legislation permitting prayer in public schools and cutting back on liberal programs that indulge sin (abortion, homosexuality, pornography, etc.).

Capitalism is considered by Falwell to be the most Godly economic system because political and religious freedom rests upon economic freedom. Therefore, government regulation of business hurts freedom and violates the Bible.

> The pattern is fitting together that when men take their eyes off the principles in the Word of God, there is trouble in every area. God said in the first book in the Bible, Genesis, that we are to earn our bread by the sweat of our brow. . . .The principles established by Almighty God work in every area of our lives. . . .Americans have violated Scripture, and with it their freedoms.

So, the Christian approach to government is, for Falwell, legislation prohibiting sin and the lifting of restrictions on free-enterprise.

Jerry Falwell is distinctively "American" in the same sense that Gustavo Gutierrez is distinctively "Latin American" or "Third World." Falwell's conception of the State or government is primarily contemporary conservative American politics, just as his understanding of "The Church" is primarily his own independent fundamentalist Baptist church. Falwell endorses capitalism as "God's economic system" in the same way that Gutierrez regards socialism as the most Christian of social systems. Thus, both the Christian Left (Liberation Theology) and the Christian Right (the Moral Majority) interpret Scripture through their political and economic ideologies. This renders them both more prominent in con-temporary politics and probably less enduring than the great theologians who wrote in more universal terms about Church and State.

The following selections are representative of the contemporary Christian Right and are drawn from Jerry Falwell's *Listen, America!* (New York: Doubleday, 1980).

OUR REPUBLIC

After representatives at the Constitutional Convention had completed their work, this question was put to old Ben Franklin: "Well, Dr. Franklin, what have you given us?" Dr. Franklin replied to the lady who had asked the question, "You have a republic, madame, if you can keep it." James Russell Lowell, an American poet and statesman of the late nineteenth century, was asked, "How long do you think the American republic will endure?" Lowell replied, "So long as the ideas of its Founding Fathers continue to be dominant."

The framers of our Constitution knew the great sacrifices that bought our liberty. They had worked diligently to produce a Constitution that would guarantee to their posterity that their liberty would never again be usurped, abused, misused, or denied. One of the framers of the Constitution, James Madison, explained the nature of the American republic: "We have staked the whole future of American civilization, not upon the power of government, far from it. We have staked the future of all of our political institutions upon the capacity of mankind for self-government; upon the capacity of each and all of us to govern ourselves, to control ourselves, to sustain ourselves according to the Ten Commandments of God."

Today we find that America is more of a democracy than a republic. Sometimes there is mob rule. In some instances a vocal minority prevails. Our Founding Fathers would not accept the tyranny of a democracy because they recognized that the only sovereign over men and nations was Almighty God. A republic is a government of law. In a republic there are checks and balances, and the majority represents the individual.

More than forty years ago, Dr. Nicholas Murray Butler, who was then the president of Columbia University, wrote in his book *Why Should We Change Our Form of Government?* ". . .there is under way in the United States at the present time a definite and determined movement to change our representative republic into a socialistic democracy. . .if it is successful, it will bring an end to the form of government that was founded when our Constitution was made. . . ." Our Founding Fathers intended that individuals be the master, and the state the servant. Thomas Jefferson said, "Man is not made for the State, but the State for man."

In his first inaugural address, George Washington spoke of the "Republican model of government." Article 4, section 4 of the Constitution of these United States states, "The United States shall guarantee to every State in this Union a Republican Form of Government." It was important to the framers of the Constitution that the rights of all Americans be protected and that the authority of every branch of government be limited. It was important to protect the rights of individuals. The goal of the republic, as our Founding Fathers established it, was to prevent the consolidation of political power.

When M. Frederic Auguste Bartholdi, designer of the Statue of Liberty, sailed into New York Harbor, he said, "We will rear here, before the eyes of the millions of strangers seeking a home in the New World, a colossal Statue of Liberty; in her upstretched hand the torch enlightening the world; in her other hand the Book of Laws, to remind them that true liberty is only found in obedience to law. . . ." Our Founding Fathers had profound respect for the law and knew that true liberty is found only in obedience to law because they recognized the fallen nature of man as recorded in the Bible. They understood that they needed law as a guide.

Let us remember as we pledge allegiance to the flag of the United States of America that it is "to the republic" that we make this pledge. And let us do more than remember; let us live by the laws recorded in God's Word.

The Issue of Church and State

We have seen that the goal of the framers of our Constitution was to govern the United States of America under God's laws, as evidenced by the fact that the guidelines for, as Hamilton later called it, "Our Experiment in Liberty" are directly based on the Ten Commandments. Most of the Ten Commandments are still written into the statute law in the various states.

Our Founding Fathers based our system of government on the First Commandment. Man was created to serve God, not the state. Since man was created in God's image, government could be used to help secure man's God-endowed rights. The goal of institutionalized government since the founding of our nation has been to be a servant of mankind, never the master of man. Our Founding Fathers sought to do this by advocating that people govern themselves under God's laws. Thomas Jefferson said, "God grant that we should never have a government that we can feel."

Of major concern in the United States today is a problem regarding the issue of "church and state." There are presently before the Congress of the United States several bills dealing with this issue. The First Amendment to our Constitution states, "Congress shall make no law respecting an establishment of religion, or forbidding the free exercise thereof. . ." This was included in the Bill of Rights because in England the state church had been determined by the religion of the monarchy; the intention of our Founding Fathers was to protect the American people from an established government church, a church that would be controlled by the government and paid for by the taxpayers. Our Founding Fathers sought to avoid this favoritism by separating church and state in function. This does not mean they intended a government devoid of God or of the guidance found in Scripture.

U. S. Senator Jessee Helms has pointed out that the same day that the First Amendment was adopted by Congress, that same Congress said that Washington could proclaim a national day of prayer. To separate personal religious preference from a forced establishment of religion is far different from separating godliness from government. The establishment of a state religion such as that which was established in England, the Church of England, and severing the relationship between God and government are two entirely different matters. Our Founding Fathers most certainly did not intend the separation of God and government.

* * *

The satanic campaign to discredit the Bible continues to this day. It has continued down through every generation to this present hour. Why is it wrong to refuse to accept the Genesis account of creation? If man is not basically bad; if he is not inherently evil, having received from the fall the very nature of sin and having had death passed upon him and all men; if the depravity of man is not a fact from the very fall in the garden, then the death, the burial, and the resurrection of Jesus Christ were needless and worthless.

Man was created in the image of God, with a body, a soul, and a spirit. Man was created a free moral agent with the choice of either obeying God or sinning and disobeying God. If man did not sin and fall from his original state, there is no need to accept the Gospel message. This is the concept of modern-day humanism and naturalism that has permeated our country and led men and women to believe foolishly that they are good and can pick themselves up by their own bootstraps. I here propose that man by nature is not good. One has only to look at the chaotic condition of our nation and our world to confirm the fact that men without Christ have no lasting peace and security. Each and every man and woman alive today needs a new birth experience. Man must be born again; he must be regenerated and believe in the death, the burial, and the resurrection of Jesus Christ and accept the shed blood of the Savior as the atonement for his sin in order to be complete.

A thorough study of the Bible will show that it is indeed the inerrant Word of the living God. The Bible is absolutely infallible, without error in all matters pertaining to faith and practice, as well as in areas such as geography, science, history, etc.

The disintegration of our social order can be easily explained. Men and women are disobeying the clear instructions God gave in His Word. Because of this, we live in a world of people with confused priorities who are giving maximum time to that which is of minor importance. It is no wonder that we see materialism on every hand today. People are living and dying for money. We see drug addiction and alcoholism and people worshiping the idol of and the god of sex. These people are spending their time, their talent, and their energies lusting after things that only lead to a dead end. We live in a world of confused and depressed people because, having violated divine laws, they have dissipated and ruined their lives. They have found that the pleasures of sin are but for a season.

The law of sowing and reaping is as immutable as the law of gravity: ". . . whatsoever a man soweth, that shall he also reap." In the Old Testament it is also stated this way: "Be sure your sin will find you out." Today we are living in an amoral society where millions of people are discounting the realityof sin as taught in the Bible.

Sin is a transgression of God's law, and God's law is unalterable. To sin is to voluntarily disobey God and His divine laws. When man does what is right in his own eyes, he is really saying that it does not matter to him what God thinks about it. He is endorsing what God has condemned, whether God likes it or not. The Bible clearly points out in Proverbs 14:34, "Righteousness exalteth a nation: But sin is a reproach to any people." Righteousness uplifts a nation. Sin brings reproach upon a people. This is the reason we are in a nosedive as a nation.

* * *

Men and women today try to rationalize their sins by calling them shortcomings or errors. Many modern theologians evade the word "sin." It is time that we began calling sin by its right name and calling for what is America's only hope–a biblical and spiritual awakening in the lives of her people. The Bible declares, "For the wages of sin is death; but the gift of God is eternal life through Jesus Christ our Lord."

* * *

Men and women cannot ignore God, live as they please, and expect to be happy and blessed. This is, however, precisely what has happened. Men and women have placed their priorities on acquiring tangible possessions and achieving tangible goals. Man, rather than God, has been placed at the center of all things. Humanism in some form has taken the place of the Bible. Secular humanism has become the religion of America. Through education and the media, man is constantly being told that he is nothing more than a machine.

According to Webster's New Collegiate Dictionary, humanism is "a doctrine, attitude, or way of life centered on human interests or values; a philosohy that asserts the dignity and worth of man and his capacity for self-realization through reason and that often rejects supernaturalism." Humanism is man's attempt to create a heaven on earth, exempting God and His Law. Humanists propose that man is in charge of his own destiny. Humanism exalts man's reason and intelligence. It advocates situation ethics, freedom from any restraint, and defines sin as man's maladjustment to man. It even advocates the right to commit suicide and recognizes evolution as a source of man's existence. Humanism promotes the socialization of all humanity into a world commune.

Christianity is ruled out of humanism and is said to be an obstacle to human progress and a threat to its existence. Mao Tse-tung once said, "Our God is none other than the masses of the people. Ye shall be as Gods." The first versions of the *Humanist Manifesto I* and *Humanist Manifesti II* openly deny the existence of a Creator, urge abolition of national sovereignty in favor of world government, and embrace complete sexual freedom, abortion, homosexuality, and euthanasia.

Naturalism also has gained a stronghold. Naturalism looks on man as a kind of biological machine. To those who believe this philosophy of life, sexual immorality is just another bodily function, as is eating or drinking. The birth of a child is no different than the birth of an animal. Man lives a sort of meaningless existence in life, and it really doesn't matter what significance he thinks he has or what goals he is headed for. The only thing that really is important for man is to try to make himself happy in the immediate now. "If something feels good, do it." It is this philosophy that is destroying the basis and foundation of our nation today.

America's decadent state is evident. A highly respected "key figure" in society today is Harvard psychologist B. F. Skinner. Skinner's hypothesis is that every man and woman is merely a bundle of behaviors determined by an environment and nothing more. He believes that through evolution the environment selected the behaviors that survive in man's genes and that environmental conditioning shapes the lives of each and every individual. He does not believe that men and women possess "inalienable rights." In more than forty years of psychological research, Skinner has developed techniques for the modification of behavior by operant condition. Behaviorists all across American are completely committed to Skinner's view. They accept man as a machine and treat him that way. Many of these men are now controlling the educational process in America.

When mankind absolves his Christian base, he loses respect for human life. This is clearly shown in America's recent change of attitude toward abortion. As men and women fall under the satanic effects of humanism and naturalism, they begin to lose value for the most important thing in God's universe–human beings. Humanists do not value humankind; they value themselves.

In his comencement address at Harvard University in 1978, Alexandr Solzhenitsyn made these comments: "Society appears to have little defense against the abyss of human decadence, such as, for example, misuse of liberty for moral violence against young peple, motion pictures full of pornography, crime, and horror.

"Such a tilt of freedom in the direction of evil has come about gradually but it was evidently born primarily out of a humanistic and benevolent conceit according to which there is no evil inherent to human nature; . . .Strangely enough, though the best social conditions have been achieved in the West, there still is criminality. . .

.How has this unfavorable relation of forces come about? How did the West decline from its triumphal march to its present sickness? . . .The West kept advancing socially in accordance with its proclaimed intentions, with the help of brilliant technological progress. And all of a sudden it found itself in its present state of weakness.

"This means that the mistake must be at the root, at the very basis of human thinking in the past centuries. I refer to the prevailing Western view of the world which was first born during the Renaissance and found its political expression from the period of the Enlightenment. It became the basis for government and social science and could be defined as rationalistic humanism or humanistic autonomy: the proclaimed and enforced autonomy of man from any higher force above him. It could also be called anthropocentricity, with man seen as the enter of everything that exists. . .we turned our backs upon the Spirit and embraced all that is material with excessive and unwarranted zeal. This new way of thinking, which had imposed on us its guidance, did not admit the existence of intrinsic evil in man nor did it see any higher task than the attainment of happiness on earth. It based modern Western civilization on the dangerous trend to worship man and his material needs. Everything beyond physical well-being, an accumulation of material goods, all other human requirements and characteristics of a subtler and higher nature were left outside the area of attention of state and social systems, as if human life did not have any superior sense. That provided access for evil, of which in our days there is a free and constant flow. Merely freedom does not in the least solve all the problems of human life and it even adds a number of new ones."

The Bible declares that men and women who do not acknowledge God, although professing themselves to be wise, become fools. God desires to give America revival. But before there can be revival, there must first be a conviction of sin, and there cannot be a conviction of sin until there is awareness of sin. The hope for America is for her people to believe the Bible to be the Word of God and to begin to live by the laws of God.

* * *

When America was founded, the legitimate purpose of government was to protect the lives, the liberties, and the property of the citizens. It was not the purpose of government to redistribute resources or to enforce any particular results in the relationships and dealings of the citizenry among themselves. Simply stated, government was to protect the God-given rights of the people.

The framers of our Constitution instituted a system of representative government, with clear limits upon what government could and could not do. This was done to ensure individual freedom. A system of checks and balances was instituted to make sure that government would not have the power to deprive individual men and women of rights that the Constitution stated were "endowed by their Creator." Our Founding Fathers recognized that the individual was God's precious earthly creation, and therefore men and women were born equal before God.

Individuals should be free to build their own lives without interference from government. Our Declaration of Independence states that governments derive "their just Powers from the Consent of the Governed," and that "whenever any Form of Government becomes destructive of these Ends, it is the Right of the People to alter or to abolish it. . ." The premise that our Founding Fathers established that those who govern do so only with the consent of the governed is being severely attached. We find today that government is threatening our basic freedoms because it is becoming, in the words of many of our modern freedom fighters, a "monster."

* * *

Our government now takes more than 40 per cent of the nation's personal income. Our government must print money to finance annual deficits of more than fifty billion dollars. Our government's total accumulated long-term debt and obligations (more than five trillion dollars) are more than the total worth of our economy. A vast number of govern-ment bureaucrats in Washington and across the nation are running our government and destroying the freedom that our Founding Fathers established at the birth of our nation. Our system of government is in a precarious state because men and women of America have their priorities mixed up. U. S. Senator Jesse Helms has summed it up well when he says, "when you have men who no longer believe that God is in charge of human affairs, you have men attempting to take the place of God by means of the Superstate. The Divine Providence on which our forefathers relied has been supplanted by the Providence of the All-Powerful State. I believe that this is the source of deep weakness in America, because it is a trans-gression of the first and greatest of the Ten Commandments. Atheism and socialism–or liberalism, which tends in the same direction–are inseparable entities."

* * *

The United States of America was experiencing a deep time of trouble in the election year of 1932. The terrible Depression had left millions of people out of work, and readlines were common sights. People were desperate; they had lost trust in the prevailing economic system. Franklin Delano Roosevelt offered hope to the American people. He promised the American people many things, which gradually grew into his "New Deal." It is important to review this time because our top economists agree that it was this period that marked the beginning of a changing role of government.

Economist Milton Friedman points out: "One simple set of statistics suggests the manitude of the change. From the founding of the republic to 1929, spending by governments at all levels, federal, state, and local, never exceeded 12 per cent of the national income except in time of major war, and two thirds of that was state and local spending. Federal spending typically amounted to 3 per cent or less of the national income. Since 1933 government spending has never been less than 20 per cent of national income and is now over 40 per cent, and two thirds of that is spending by the federal government. True, much of the period since the end of World War II has been a period of cold and hot war. However, since 1946 nondefense spending alone has never been less than 16 per cent of the national income and is now roughly one third of the national income. Federal government spending alone is more than one quarter of the national income in total, and more than a fifth for nondefense purposes alone. By this measure the role of the federal government in the economy has multiplied roughly tenfold in the past half century." (*Free to Choose*, p. 92)

Belief in individual responsibility, laissez-faire, and a decentralized and limited government changed to belief in social responsibility and a centralized and powerful government. Those men who advised Roosevelt felt that there had to be a change in the economy, which involved an increase in government ownership and operation of the means of production. Friedman points out that Roosevelt's advisers were ready to view the Depression as a failure of capitalism. They saw as the remedy the intervention of central government. Friedman points out, "World War II interrupted the New Deal, while at the same time strengthening greatly its foundations. . . .The war's effect on public attitudes was the mere image of the Depression's. The Depression convinced the public that capitalism was defective; the war, that centralized government was efficient. Both conclusions were false. The Depression was produced by a failure of government, not of private enterprise." (*Free to Choose*, p. 94)

In this viewing of history, we can see that government began to expand greatly. It was at this time that governmental intervention in business mushroomed. Today we see bigger and bigger government in the form of our welfare programs and regulatory activities. We have in our country today hundreds of governmental welfare and income-transfer programs. Friedman points out, "The Department of Health, Education, and Welfare, established in 1953 to consolidate the scattered welfare programs, began with the budget of $2 billion, less than 5 per cent of expenditures on national defense. Twenty-five years later, in 1978, its budget was $160 billion, one and a half times as much as total spending on the Army, the Navy, and the Air Force. It had the third largest budget in the world, exceeded only by the entire budget of the U. S. Government and of the Soviet Union." (*Free to Choose*, p. 96)

. . . .Governmental intrusion, rather than helping the American people, has actually reduced the sense of responsibility and initiative in her citizens. It is the way of socialism and communism to reduce a man's incentive by taking away from him the fruits of his labors. The sad fact is that government is the major source of our economic instability in this country.

Our Founding Fathers knew that free enterprise was the best economic organization to maintain the free society they had created. . . .

Free enterprise is consistent with freedom. It naturally rises from a country that has liberty. America has enjoyed the highest standard of living in the world, since the founding of our nation, as a direct result of the free marketplace. We have only to look at history to find that no nation has survived long when its citizens were denied the free market and individual initiative. Government was never meant to dominate the economic affairs of its citizens; this is not the way of freedom. As we continue to move toward collectivism, individual freedoms are eroded.

Protection of each and every individual's right to acquire property is a necessity of freedom. To destroy or to control a man's right to own and use property is to diminish him as an individual, for property rights are human rights. Freedom to own property is a basic tenet of this society.

More and more today, we are seeing our government run by thousands of bureaucracies that destroy the productive institutions they supervise. It is all too obvious that Congress is becoming more and more antibusiness. The attack on business is ultimately an attack upon the principles of free enterprise. In his book former Secretary of the Treasury William Simon points out: "Government control of production results in artificial shortages which produce crises, and if not corrected, it will culminate in a drive to economic dictator-ship. The principle is inviolate. Our capacity for innovation must decay, our standard of living must drop, and our wealth and freedom–and the wealth and freedom of those nations which depend on us–must deteriorate until the principle is finally understood." (Simon, p. 85) Immigrants by the millions have come to the United States. They knew that in this country they could make a way for themselves and their families if they worked hard enough, and most were not afraid of hard work.

The pattern is fitting together that when men take their eyes off the principles in the Word of God, there is trouble in every area. God said in the first book in the Bible, Genesis, that we are to earn our bread by the sweat of our brow. He was giving us the principles of reward for work. The principles established by Almighty God work in every area of our lives. . . .

Let us now look at government spending and see where our tax dollars go. I have heard it said that it is unbelievable but true that taxpayers are paying for their own destruc-tion. With the government taking more than one third of every dollar of income generated in the United States, it follows that the erosion of freedom results as people have less and less choice as to what they are doing with their money. No power has been more abused by Congress than that of the free spending of each and every citizen's tax money.. The taxation of the American people is today an overwhelming burden.

According to the Tax Foundation, the typical taxpayer works from January 1 to April 30 for money he never sees. It is only right that citizens share in the responsibility of the functions of their government, but when government is not responsible, its citizens become overburdened. Our forefathers did much to emphasize the idea of a limited and frugal government. When he left office on September 19, 1796, President Washington said in his farewell address, "Avoid likewise the accumulation of debt, not only by shunning occasions of expense, but by vigorous exertion in time of peace to discharge the debts which unavoidable wars may have occasioned, not ungenerously throwing upon posterity the burden which we ourselves ought to bear."

In the first 124 years of our national existence, the federal government of the United States spent $16.5 bilion; in the next 40 years (1901-40), the government spent $149.5 billion. From 1941 to 1950, the federal government spent $535 billion. From 1951 to 1960, it spent $744 billion. From 1961 to 1970, it spent $1.4 trillion. And from 1971 to 1977, the federal government spent $2.1 trillion. The total expenditures of our federal government (actual and estimated) were $450.8 billion in 1978, $493.4 billion in 1979, and $531.6 bilion in 1980. That represents an increase of federal spending of 117.9 per cent in the last two years.

Government spending is out of control. Government spending is rising far faster than the economy can support it. There are today more than one thousand federal programs for the transferral of a producer's income to a non-producer's pocket. Our government is the nation's largest employer. Defense spending is the only category of federal spending that has been reduced drastically in the last several years.

* * *

Let us look at our welfare system. Our whole welfare system is built on a basic premise that is detrimental to our society. We cannot survive economically when the working population of America is faced with an ever-increasing burden of governmental spending to support a tremendously large nonworking segment of our society.

In the Bible, in the third chapter of 2 Thessalonians, we find the Apostle Paul writing to a congregation in the city of Thessalonica regarding the subject of work. This is not a labor or management discussion. It is a spiritual discussion. Paul says, "Now we command you, brethren, in the name of our Lord Jesus Christ, that ye withdraw yourselves from every brother that walketh disorderly, and not after the tradition which he received of us. For yourselves know how ye ought to follow us: we eat any man's bread for naught, but wrought with labor and travail night and day, that we might not be chargeable to any of you: Not because we have not power, but to make ourselves an example unto you to follow us. For even when we were with you, this we commanded you, that if any would not work, neither should he eat. For we hear that there are some which walk among you disorderly, working not at all, but are busybodies. Now them that are such we command and exhort by our Lord Jesus Christ, that with quietness they work and eat their own bread. But ye, brethren, be not weary in well-doing."

The work ethic is a biblical principle. I am not totally anti-welfare; those who need help, those who cannot care for themselves, the sick and the aged should be taken care of. God will bless our country for doing so. There have been times in our country's history when there were not enough jobs to go around, or when the jobs did not provide enough money to buy the food necessary to keep the family alive. There are times when we should help those people who are able to work, but who because of extenuating circumstances simply cannot. But I believe that, generally, there are now enough jobs to go around. Too many people who could work, do not. Have they forgotten what the word "work" means? Will they live off giveaway programs, supported by those people who work hard for a living, forever? We must not forget that our government does not give away anything that it does not take from someone else.

During the past decade the number of citizens living on welfare has increased 500 per cent. A January 1979 issue of *U. S. News & World Report* says that without government help, some forty-three million Americans–that is, 20 per cent of the population–would be classified as being poor. Many experts are puzzled that this figure has remained stagnant for the past twelve years despite rising wages and millions of new jobs being available.

Food stamps are only one of a random number of food-assistance programs, and some nineteen million Americans receive them once a month. The food-stamp program alone is a multibillion-dollar program. When the government cares for its people, why should its people care for themselves? Welfare programs tend to destroy one's initiatives, skill, work habits, and productivity.

It is time for our welfare program to be examined and much of it done away with. People will not starve to death, although their standard of living may not be sustained. We have two dogs at our home. They are big, beautiful Irish setters. The fellow who gave them to us is a dear friend who owns a supermarket. When he gave me the dogs, he told me what kind of meat they had to have and where I could buy it. The more he talked the more I realized that I could not afford to keep the dogs, but when he left, I went up to the store and bought a big bag of brown nuggets, dumped them into two pans, and put them outside for the dogs. Sure enough, at first they would not eat them, but four days later they did. They did not eat luxuriously, but they did eat.

* * *

In light of our present moral condition, we as a nation are quickly approaching the point of no return. There can be no doubt that the sin of America is severe. We are literally approaching the brink of national disaster. Many have exclaimed, "If God does not judge America soon, He will have to apologize to Sodom and Gomorrah." In almost every aspect of our society, we have flaunted our sinful behavior in the very face of God Himself. Our movies, television programs, magazines, and entertainment in general are morally bankrupt and spiritually corrupt. We have become one of the most blatantly sinful nations of all time. We dare not continue to excuse ourselves on the basis of God's past blessing in our national heritage. The time for a national repentance of God's people has now come to America.

The great English statesman, Winston Churchill, once said, "The moral climate of a nation will be in direct proportion to the amount of hellfire and damnation that is preached from its pulpits." As a preacher of the Gospel, I could not more heartily agree! Pastors and religious leaders do not enjoy pointing out the sins of people. I entered the ministry nearly thirty years ago because of a genuine love and concern for people. I wanted to see their lives changed, their problems solved, and their families put back together to the glory of God. As much as I labored to help people and to encourage them and to understand their hurts and problems, I soon realized that one of my vital responsibilities was to expose sin even in my own life as well as in theirs. The Bible clearly teaches that it is the preacher's responsibility to "warn every man" against the consequences of sinful living.

* * *

Wallowing in our materialism, self-centeredness, and pride, we decided that we really didn't need God after all. We began to tamper with His absolute standards, making them subject to our own opinions and decisions. We did not immediately discard all of God's laws; rather, we began to tolerate variations in them. That which God says is never right, we determined could sometimes be right, depending on the situation. Our courts, which had once legislated against immorality, began to grant freedom to every man to do that which was right in his own eyes. As people who no longer felt accountable to a holy God, we began to accept and even admire immoral behavior. Where once we were openly shocked at the outwardness of sin, we have now become gradually conditioned to accepting it.

Today we tolerate, laugh at, and even enjoy what twenty years ago would have deeply shocked us.

Having pushed God out of our conscience, we soon discovered that as a nation we could get away with almost anything. All we had to do was change the terminology. What God called a sin, we called a sickness. Man has always tended to find a euphemism to cover the reality of sin. What God called drunkenness, we called alcoholism. What God called perversion, we called an alternate life style. What God called immorality, we called the new morality. What God called pornography, we called adult entertainment. What God called murder, we call abortion.

Is God blind to the sin of our nation? Will He continue to allow us to live in rebellion to His moral standards while He looks upon our idols of silver and gold, on our pride of personal achievement, our monuments to ourselves? Can God bless that which He ought to curse?

The Bible clearly states: "Righteousness exalteth a nation; but sin is a reproach to any people." (Pr. 14:34) God will not be mocked, for whatever an individual or a nation sows, that shall he also reap. America is not big enough to shake her fist in the face of a holy God and get away with it. Sodom and Gomorrah fell under the judgment of God, so did Israel, Babylon, Greece, Rome, and countless other civilizations as well. Like Isreal of old, we are "oppressed, trampled in judgment, intent on pursuing idols." Our crumbling economy, our fractured family structures, and unrestrained immorality, as well as our international reproach are all signs of the fact that we are already headed on a collision course.

Is there no hope? Is our doom inevitable? Can the hand of God's judgment not be stayed? Many of us are convinced that it can. We believe that there is yet an opportunity for a reprieve in God's judgment of this great nation. But that hope rests in the sincerity of national repentance led by the people of God.

First, God's people must be humble. Humility, however, is the very opposite of pride, which so often besets us. Scripture says, "God resists the proud, but gives grace to the humble." (James 4:6) We must acknowledge that we are not deserving of God's favor. We must realize that we are totally inadequate to deal with the sins of our own lives, let alone those of our entire nation. We must acknowledge that we are utterly dependent upon God and His grace to deliver us. Our financial resources will not turn this nation back to God, and our elaborate church structures will not cause Him to change His mind and restrain His judgment. We must allow Him to strip us of all that we put our confidence in, so that we may trust in Him alone.

Second, we must pray. We must not just talk about praying, we must pray! We must lay aside our pious and structured prayers in order to beseech the God of heaven to have mercy on us. Let us echo the prayer of confession offered by Ezra the priest as he fell on his face before God and acknowledged, "O my God, I am ashamed and blush to lift up my face to thee, my God; for our iniquities are increased over our head, and our trespasses are grown up into the heavens."

Third, we must learn to seek the face of God. When King Jehoshaphat called the people of Judah together to seek the face of God, they acknowledged, "We have no might against this great company that cometh against us, neither know we what to do; but our eyes are upon thee." We must turn our eyes from ourselves and seek the face of Almighty God. We must be willing to give up ourselves as the measure of all things, and acknowledge that He alone is the measure of truth.

Fourth, God's people must turn from their wicked ways. It is one thing for us to be concerned about the sins of our nation, but before we are prepared to confess the sins of an unbelieving society, we must repent of our own sins. We have not fulfilled our function as the "salt of the earth." We have failed to speak out for God on serious moral issues. We have often endorsed what we should have opposed. We must repent for judging the wickedness of our nation while ignoring the sin in our own homes. More than ever before America needs fathers who are willing to be godly leaders and moral examples in their own homes. We need mothers who are determined to be models of virtuous living, and we need children who are committed to live in obedience to the moral leadership of their parents. May God forgive us who claim His name for tolerating things in our own lives that are not holy, pure, and undefiled. We need to turn from our sinful ways in our churches as well, for we have all too often substituted playing for praying; feasting for fasting; religion for righteousness; organizing for agonizing; and compatibility for confrontation. We need a return to the kind of churches that lead the vanguard of decency while upholding the moral conscience of our nation.

* * *

The time has come for America's Christians to confess the sins of our nation as well. While it is true that we are not a theocracy, as was ancient Israel, we nevertheless are a nation that was founded upon Christian principles, and we have enjoyed a unique relationship toward God because of that foundation. In order to confess sin, we must have a genuine conviction of sin based on an awareness of sin. We need to define and articulate the issues of sin and sinful living, which are destroying our nation today. The secularist will argue: What right do you have to define sin? If our definition rested only upon our personal opinion, he would have every right to reject our message. That is why it is essential that our concept of sin be based clearly upon Scripture itself. One reporter recently asked me if this would not lead to a kind of censorship or a kind of Christian Nazism. My reply was that we cannot allow an immoral minority of our population to intimidate us on moral issues. People who take a weak stand on morality inevitably have weak morals.

We need moral leadership today more than ever before. We need that kind of leadership in the media as well as in our schools and in our churches. Leadership must always be responsible to society. Our freedoms certainly guarantee the right to free speech, but they do not give us the right to use our speech irresponsibly to the harm of others. Just because we have free speech doesn't mean that a person has a right to make obscene phone calls or to yell "Fire!" in a crowded building when there is no fire. I believe that the family is the cornerstone of America, and whatever undermines the family is wrong. If our leaders are to care about this country at all we must care about its people and its families. It is time that we no longer be driven by economic considerations and political favors but instead were determined to stand for right whether it is convenient or not, popular or not.

While sins of America are certainly many, let us summarize the five major problems that have political consequences, political implications, that moral Americans need to be ready to face.

1. ABORTION–Nine men, by majority vote, said it was okay to kill unborn children. In 1973, two hundred million Americans and four hundred thousand pastors stood by and did little to stop it. Every year millions of babies are murdered in America, and most of us want to forget that it is happening. The Nazis murdered six million Jews, and certainly the Nazis fell under the hand of the judgment of God for these atrocities. So-called Christian America has murdered more unborn innocents than that. How do we think that we shall escape the judgment of God?

2. HOMOSEXUALITY–In spite of the fact that the Bible clearly designates this sin as an act of a "reprobate mind" for which God "gave them up" (Rm. 1:26-28), our government seems determined to legalize homosexuals as a legitimate "minority." The National Civil Rights Act of 1979 (popularly referred to as the Gay Rights Bill) would give homosexuals the same benefits as the 1964 Civil Rights Act, meaning they could not be discriminated against by any employing body because of "sexual preference." Even the ancient Greeks, among whom homosexuality was fairly prevalent, never legally condoned its practice. Plato himself called it "abnormal." If our nation legally recognizes homosexuality, we will put ourselves under the same hand of judgment as Sodom and Gomorrah.

3. PORNOGRAPHY–The four-billion-dollar-per-year pornographic industry is probably the most devastating moral influence of all upon our young people. Sex magazines deliberately increase the problem of immoral lust and thus provoke increased adultery, prostitution, and sexual child abuse. Jesus said that if a man looks upon a woman and lusts after her in his heart, he has committed adultery with her already! Pornography is certainly the No. 1 enemy against marital fidelity and therefore against the family itself. Recent psychological studies are showing without a doubt that divorce caused by adultery is having a devastating affect upon children. Pornography is not a victimless crime–the real victims are wives and

children!

4. HUMANISM–The contemporary philosophy that glorifies man as man, apart from God, is the ultimate outgrowth of evolutionary science and secular education. In his new book *The Battle for the Mind,* Dr. Tim LaHaye argues that the full admission of humanism as the religion of secular education came after prayer and Bible reading were excluded from our public schools. Ultimately, humanism rests upon the philosophy of existentialism, which emphasizes that one's present existence is the true meaning and purpose of life. Existentialism has become the religion of the public schools. Applied to psychology, it postulates a kind of moral neutrality that is detrimental to Christian ethics. In popular terminology it explains, "Do your own thing," and "If it feels good, do it!" It is an approach to life that has no room for God and makes man the measure of all things.

5. THE FRACTURED FAMILY–With a skyrocketing divorce rate, the American family may well be on the verge of extinction in the next twenty years. Even the recent White House Conference on Families has called for an emphasis on diverse family forums (common-law, communal, homosexual, and transsexual "marriages"). The Bible pattern of the family has been virtually discarded by modern American society. Our movies and magazines have glorified the physical and emotional experience of sex without love to the point that most Americans do not even consider love to be important at all anymore. Bent on self-gratification, we have reinterpreted our moral values in light of our immoral life styles. Since the family is the basic unit of society, and since the family is desperately in trouble today, we can conclude that our society itself is in danger of total collapse. We are not moving toward an alternate family life style; we are moving closer to the brink of destruction.

Bible-believing Christians and concerned moral Americans are determined to do something about the problems that we are facing as a nation. In our family we were recently sitting in the family room having a time of Bible study and devotions and discussing some of these crucial issues. One of my children asked, "Dad, will I ever grow up to be as old as you are in a free America?" Another one of my children asked, "Will I ever get to go to college?" and "Will I ever get married?" Speaking about the virtal issues is not just a question of dealing with our generation but with the generations to come. Our children and our grandchildren must forever be the recipients or the victims of our moral decisions today.

My responsibility as a parent-pastor is more than just concern. The issue of convenience is not even up for discussion. If the moral issues are really matters of conviction that are worth living for, then they are worth fighting for. In discussing these matters further with other pastors and concerned Christian leaders, I have become convinced of the need to have a coalition of God-fearing, moral Americans to represent our convictions to our government. I realize that there would be those pastors who misunderstand our intentions. I know that some object that we are compromising in our involvement with people of different doctrinal and theological beliefs. As a fundamental, independent, separatist Baptist, I am well aware of the crucial issues of personal and ecclesiastical separation that divide fundamentalists philosophically from evangelicals and liberals. I do not believe that it is ever right to compromise the truth in order to gain an opportunity to do right. In doctrinal and spiritual matters, there is no real harmony between light and darkness.

I am convinced of two very significant factors. First, our very moral existence as a nation is at stake. There are many moral Americans who do not share our theological beliefs but who do share our moral concerns. Second, we must face the fact that it will take the greatest possible number of concerned citizens to reverse the politicization of immorality in our society. Doctrinal difference is a distinctive feature of a democracy. Our freedoms have given us the privilege and the luxury of theological disagreement. I would not for a moment encourage anyone to water down his distinctive beliefs. But we must face realistically the fact that there are Christians in the world today who have lost the luxury of disagreement. When the entire issue of Christian survival is at stake, we must be willing to band together on at least the major moral issues of the day.

Moral Americans can make the difference in America if we are willing to exert the effort to make our feelings known and if we are willing to make the necessary sacrifices to get the job done. In October 1978, our church entered what seemed at the time to be a losing battle. Pre-election polls in September 1978 in the state of Virginia indicated that there was general apathy regarding pari-mutuel betting. Those in favor of pari-mutuel betting expected it to win approval easily. Convinced that gambling is typical of a nation losing its moral values and that it is a sin based upon a lust for things, we took a strong stand against it. While some of our politicians argue that gambling would increase revenue in the state, I knew that it would ultimately cost taxpayers in increased welfare costs or destroy families and increase police protection in prison costs. Gambling is supported by men who are dominated by greed, and who do not consider the havoc that gambling causes to the home.

Our church took a stand against pari-mutuel betting and rallied other good people in the state of Virginia against it also. On November 7, 1978, pari-mutuel betting was rejected y the voters in the state of Virginia. Virginia newspapers stated, "Both the winners and the losers credited an aggressive campaign by the religious leader as bringing about the betting proposal's demise." Those newspapers went on to quote my comment: "The vote is an indication of what the Christian people in Virginia have been able to do by simply uniting their efforts.

This is the first time that six thousand Virginia churches of all denominations have joined hands in a moral campaign, and this should be, as I see it, a forecast of future endeavors together."

To change America we must be involved, and this includes three areas of politial action:

1. REGISTRATION

A recent national poll indicated that eight million American evangelicals are not registered to vote. I am convinced that this is one of the major sins of the church today. Until concerned Christian citizens become registered voters there is very little that we can do to change the tide of political influence on the social issues in our nation. Those who object to Christians being involved in the political process are ultimately objecting to Christians being involved in the social process. The political process is really nothing more than a realization of the social process. For us to divorce ourselves from society would be to run into the kind of isolationism and monasticism that characterized the medieval hermits. Many Christians are not even aware of the importance of registering to vote. It is perfectly legal, for example, for a deputy registrar to come right to your local church at a designated time and register the entire congregation. I am convinced that those of us who are pastors have an obligation to urge our people to register to vote. I am more concerned that people exercise their freedom to vote than I am concerned for whom they vote.

2. INFORMATION

Many moral Americans are unaware of the real issues affecting them today. Many people do not know the voting record of their congressman and have no idea how he is representing them on political issues that have moral implications. This is one of the major reasons why we have established the Moral Majority organization. We want to keep the public informed on the vital moral issues. The Moral Majority, Inc., is a nonprofit organization, with headquarters in Washington, D. C. Our goal is to exert a significant influence on the spiritual and moral direction of our nation by: (a) mobilizing the grassroots of moral Americans in one clear and effective voice; (b) informing the moral majority what is going on behind their backs in Washington and in state legislatures across the country; (c) lobbying intensely in Congress to defeat left-wing, social-welfare bills that will further erode our precious freedom; (d) pushing for positive legislation such as that to establish the Family Protection Agency, which will ensure a strong, enduring America; and (e) helping the moral majority in local communities to fight pornography, homosexuality, the advocacy of immorality in school textbooks, and other issues facing each and every one of us.

Christians must keep America great by being willing to go into the halls of

Congress, by getting laws passed that will protect the freedom and liberty of her citizens. The Moral Majority, Inc., was formed to acquaint Americans everywhere with the tragic decline in our nation's morals and to provide leadership in establishing an effective coalition of morally active citizens who are (a) prolife, (b) profamily, (c) promoral, and (d) pro-American. If the vast majority of Americans (84 per cent, according to George Gallup) still believe the Ten Commandments are valid today, why are we permitting a few leading amoral humanists and naturalists to take over the most influential positions in this nation?

Tim LaHaye has formed a code of minimum moral standards dictated by the Bible; his code would be used to evaluate the stand of candidates on moral issues. These minimum standards are:

a. Do you agree that this country was founded on a belief in God and the moral principles of the Bible? Do you concur that this country has been departing from those principles and needs to return to them?
b. Would you favor stricter laws relating to the sale of pornography?
c. Do you favor stronger laws against the use and sale of hard drugs?
d. Are you in favor of legalizing marijuana?
e. Would you favor legalizing prostitution?
f. Do you approve of abortion on demand when the life of the mother is not in danger?
g. Do you favor laws that would increase homosexual rights?
h. Would you vote to prevent known homosexuals to teach in schools?
i. Do you favor capital punishment for capital offenses?
j. Do you favor the right of parents to send their children to private schools?
k. Do you favor voluntary prayer in the public schools?
l. Do you favor removal of the tax-exempt status of churches?
m. Do you favor removal of the tax-exempt status of church-related schools?
n. Do you believe that government should remove children from their parents' home except in cases of physical abuse?
o. Do you favor sex education, contraceptives, or abortions for minors without parental consent?
p. Except in wartime or dire emergency, would you vote for government spending that exceeds revenue?

q. Do you favor a reduction in taxes to allow families more spendable income?
r. Do you favor a reduction in government?
s. Do you favor passage of the Equal Rights Amendment?
t. Do you favor busing schoolchildren out of their neighborhood to achieve racial integration?
u. Do you favor more federal involvement in education?

The answers to these questions would be evaluated in the light of scriptural principles.

* * *

Right living must be re-established as an American way of life. We as American citizens must recommit ourselves to the faith of our fathers and to the premises and moral foundations upon which this country was established. Now is the time to begin calling America back to God, back to the Bible, back to morality! We must be willing to live by the moral convictions that we claim to believe. There is no way that we will ever be willing to die for something for which we are not willing to live. The authority of Bible morality must once again be recognized as the legitimate guiding principle of our nation. Our love for our fellow man must ever be grounded in the truth and never be allowed to blind us from the truth that is the basis of our love for our fellow man.

As a pastor and as a parent I am calling my fellow American citizens to unite in a moral crusade for righteousness in our generation. It is time to call America back to her moral roots. It is time to call America back to God. We need a revival of righteous living based on a proper confession of sin and repentance of heart if we are to remain the land of the free and the home of the brave! I am convinced that God is calling millions of Americans in the so-often silent majority to join in the moral-majority crusade to turn America around in our lifetime. Won't you begin now to pray with us for revival in America? Let us unite our hearts and lives together for the cause of a new America. . .a moral America in which righteousness will exalt this nation. Only as we do this can we exempt ourselves from one day having to look our children in the eyes and answer this searching question: "Mom and Dad, where were you the day freedom died in America?"

The choice is now ours.

PART II

American Documents on Church and State

1. The Mayflower Compact
INTRODUCTION

The Mayflower Compact (1620) is considered the first "social contract" in America. It was signed by all adult males on board the ship Mayflower prior to their landing at Plymouth and formed civil polity that governed the Colony until 1691, when it joined Massachusetts. This short document is interesting for its stated purpose of the new settlement ("for the glory of God, And Advancement of the Christian Faith and Honor of our King and Country. . . .") and its implications for future Puritan political thought, as revealed in the next selection.

* * *

THE MAYFLOWER COMPACT

In the name of God, amen. We whose names are underwritten, the loyal subjects of our dread sovereign lord, King James, by the grace of God, of Great Britain, France and Ireland, King, Defender of the Faith, etc.

Having undertaken, for the glory of God, and advancement of the Christian faith and honor of our King and Country, a voyage to plant the first colony in the northern parts of Virginia, do by these presents solemnly and mutually in the presence of God, and one of another, covenant and combine ourselves together into a civil body politic, for our better ordering and preservation and furtherance of the ends aforesaid: and by virtue hereof to enact, constitute and frame such just and equal laws, ordinances, acts, constitutions and offices, from time to time, as shall be thought most meet and convenient for the general good of the Colony: unto which we promise all due submission and obedience.

In witness where we have hereunder subscribed our names at Cape Cod the *11th of November, in the year of the reign of our Sovereign Lord, King James of England, France and Ireland the eighteenth, and of Scotland the fifty-fourth. Ano. Dom. 1620

John Carver	Richard Warren	John Turner	Edmon Margeson
William Bradford	John Howland	Francis Eaton	Peter Brown
Edward Winslow	Stephen Hopkins	James Chilton	Richard Britteridge
William Brewster	Edward Tilly	John Crackston	George Soule
Isaac Allerton	John Tilly	John Billington	Richard Clarke
Myles Standish	Francis Cooke	Moses Fletcher	Richard Gardiner
John Alden	Thomas Rogers	John Goodman	John Allerton
Samuel Fuller	Thomas Tinker	Degory Priest	Thomas English
Christopher Martin	John Rigdale	Thomas Williams	Edward Doty
William Mullins	Edward Fuller	Gilbert Winslow	Edward Leister
William White			

* Old Calendar

2. John Winthrop's "Little Speech"*
INTRODUCTION

John Winthrop (1588-1649) was an English Puritan who became Governor of the Massachusetts Bay Colony in 1630. The Puritans, as English Calvinists, saw a distinct role for religion in politics and this is reflected in John Winthrop's writings. After Calvin, Winthrop saw magistrates as God's servants and human law as properly grounded in Scripture. His distinction between "natural liberty" (or simple freedom to follow individual desires) and civil or "moral liberty" (the free choice to follow God's laws) demonstrates the religious element in Puritan politics. Civil or moral liberty is properly enjoined by the State and obedience to just authority is part of the Christian's obedience to God. Government, therefore, is not simply concerned with securing individual's freedom, but advancing that moral liberty enjoined by Christ and compatible with Godly and civil authority.

* * *

...The great questions that have troubled the country, are about the authority of the magistrates and the liberty of the people. It is yourselves who have called us to this office, and being called by you, we have our authority from God, in way of an ordinance, such as hath the image of God eminently stamped upon it, the contempt and violation whereof hath been vindicated with examples of divine vengeance. I entreat you to consider, that when you choose magistrates, you take them from among yourselves, men subject to like passions as you are. Therefore when you see infirmities in us, you should reflect upon your own and that would make you bear the more with us, and not be severe censurers of the failings of your magistrates, when you have continual experience of the like infirmities in yourselves and others. We account him a good servant, who breaks not his covenant. The covenant between you and us is the oath you have taken of us, which is to this purpose, that we shall govern you and judge your causes by the rules of God's laws and our own, according to our best skill. When you agree with a workman to build you a ship or house, etc., he undertakes as well for his skill as for his faithfulness, for it is his profession, and you pay him for both. But when you call one to be a magistrate, he doth not process nor undertake to have sufficient skill for that office, nor can you furnish him with gifts, etc., therefore you must run the hazard of his skill and ability. But if he fail in faithfulness, which by his oath he is bound unto, that he must answer for. If it fall out that the case be clear to common apprehension, and the rule clear also, if he transgress here, the error is not in the skill, but in the evil of the will: it must be required of him. But if the case be doubtful, or the rule doubtful, to men of such understanding and parts as your magistrates are, if your magistrates should err here, yourselves must bear it.

For the other point concerning liberty, I observe a great mistake in the country about that. There is a twofold liberty, natural (I mean as our nature is now corrupt) and civil or federal. The first is common to man with beasts and other creatures. By this, man, as he stands in relation to man simply, hath liberty to do what he lists; it is a liberty to evil as well as to good. This liberty is incompatible and inconsistent with authority, and cannot endure the least restraint of the most just authority. The exercise and maintaining of this liberty makes men grow more evil, and in time to be worse than brute beasts; omnes sumus licentia deteriores. This is that great enemy of truth and peace, that wild beast, which all the ordinances of God are bent against, to restrain and subdue it. The other kind of liberty I call civil or federal, it may also be termed moral, in reference to the covenant between God and man, in the moral law, and the politic covenants and constitutions, amongst men themselves. This liberty is the proper end and object of authority, and cannot subsist without it; and it is a liberty to that only which is good, just, and honest. This liberty you are to stand for, with the hazard (not only of your goods, but) of your lives, if need be. Whatsoever crosseth this, is not authority, but a distemper thereof. This liberty is maintained and exercised in a way of subjection to authority; it is of the same kind of liberty wherewith Christ hath made us free. The woman's own choice makes such a man her husband; yet being so chosen, he is her lord, and she is to be subject to him, yet in a way of liberty, not of bondage; and a true wife accounts her subjection her honor and freedom, and would not think her condition safe and free, but in her subjection to her husband's authority. Such is the liberty of the church under the authority of Christ, her king and husband; his yoke is so easy and sweet to her as a bride's ornaments; and if through forwardness or wantonness, etc., she shake it off, at any time, she is at no rest in her spirit, until she take it up again; and whether her lord smiles upon her, and embraceth her in his arms, or whether he frowns, or rebukes, or smites her, she apprehends the sweetness of his love in all, and is refreshed, supported, and instructed by every such dispensation of his authority over her. On the other side, ye know who they are that complain of this yoke and say, let us break their hands, etc., we will not have this man to rule over us. Even so, brethren, it will be between you and your magistrates. If you stand for your natural corrupt liberties, and will do what is good in your own eyes, you will not endure the least weight of authority, but will murmur, and oppose, and be always striving to shake off that yoke; but if you will be satisfied to enjoy such civil and lawful liberties, such as Christ allows you, then you will quietly and cheerfully submit unto that authority which is set over you, in all the administrations of it, for your good. Wherein, if we fail at any time, we hope we shall be willing (by God's assistance) to hearken to good advice from any of you, or in any other way of God; so shall your liberties be preserved, in upholding the honor and power of authority amongst you.

3. Jefferson's Statute for Religious Freedom
INTRODUCTION

Thomas Jefferson's Bill for Establishing Religious Freedom (1779) was written in response to the effects of the Established Anglican Church in Virginia. The Established Church required all citizens, Anglicans and non-Anglicans alike, to support the Church financially (under civil penalty) and restricted the legal and political rights of non-Anglicans. By the time of Jefferson's Bill, this Established Church had become untenable, as the majority of Virginians were no longer Anglican. While Eastern (Tidewater) Virginia remained predominantly Church of England, the western portions of the Commonwealth (where the greatest population growth was occurring) were infused with Scottish Presbyterians, German Lutherans, Baptists and Methodists. This religious diversity rendered religious freedom and toleration the most practical approach to Church-State relations in Virginia, and soon throughout the United States, as guaranteed by the First Amendment of the U. S. Constitution.

Jefferson's argument for religious freedom and the separation of Church and State is that belief is a matter of individual reason and conscience and insusceptible to coercion by either temporal or ecclesiastical authority. Himself a disaffected Anglican (over his rationalist inability to comprehend the Trinity), Jefferson still considered himself a Christian and regarded Christian Ethics essential to a just polity. He simply believed that the best way to further religion was not through legal sanction, but through religious liberty.

* * *

A Bill for Establishing Religious Freedom [1779]
Well aware that the opinions and belief of men depend not on their own will, but follow involuntarily the evidence proposed to their minds; that Almighty God hath created the mind free, and manifested his supreme will that free it shall remain by making it altogether insusceptible of restraint; that all attempts to influence it by temporal punishments, or burthens, or by civil incapacitations, tend only to beget habits of hypocrisy and meanness, and are a departure from the plan of the holy author of our religion, who being lord both of body and mind, yet chose not to propagate it by coercions on either, as was in his Almighty power to do, *but to extend it by its influence on reason alone;* that the impious presumption of legislators and rulers, civil as well as ecclesiastical, who, being themselves but fallible and uninspired men, have assumed dominion over the faith of others, setting up their own opinions and modes of thinking as the only true and infallible, and as such endeavoring to impose them on others, hath established and maintained false religions over the greatest part of the world and through all time: That to compel a

man to furnish contributions of money for the propagation of opinions which he disbelieves *and abhors*, is sinful and tyrannical; that even the forcing him to support this or that teacher of his own religious persuasion, is depriving him of the comfortable liberty of giving his contributions to the particular pastor whose morals he would make his pattern, and whose powers he feels most persuasive to righteousness; and is withdrawing from the ministry those temporary rewards, which proceeding from an approbation of their personal conduct, are an additional incitement to earnest and unremitting labours for the instruction of mankind; that our civil rights have no dependance on our religious opinions, any more than our opinions in physics or geometry; that therefore the proscribing any citizen as unworthy the public confidence by laying upon him an incapacity of being called to offices of trust and emolument, unless he profess or renounce this or that religious opinion, is depriving him injuriously of those privileges and advantages to which, in common with his fellow citizens, he has a natural right; that it tends also to corrupt the principles of that *very* religion it is meant to encourage, by bribing, with a monopoly of worldly honours and emoluments, those who will externally profess and conform to it; that though indeed these are criminal who do not withstand such temptation, yet neither are those innocent who lay the bait in their way; *that the opinions of men are not the object of civil government, nor under its jurisdiction;* that to suffer the civil magistrate to intrude his powers into the field of opinion and to restrain the profession or propagation of principles on supposition of their ill tendency is a dangerous falacy, which at once destroys all religious liberty, because he being of course judge of that tendency will make his opinions the rule of judgment, and approve or condemn the sentiments of others only as they shall square with or differ from his own; that it is time enough for the rightful purposes of civil government for its officers to interfere when principles break out into overt acts against peace and good order; and finally, that truth is great and will prevail if left to herself; that she is the proper and sufficient antagonist to error, and has nothing to fear from the conflict unless by human interposition disarmed of her natural weapons, free argument and debate; errors ceasing to be dangerous when it is permitted freely to contradict them.

4. The United States Constitution: The First Amendment

Religious freedom in America is secured by the portion of the First Amendment of the United States Constitution which reads:

> Congress shall make no law respecting an establishment of religion, or prohibiting the free exercise thereof. . . .

This amendment actually contains two clauses: the "establishment" cualse, which forbids the State to support a particular church and the "free exercise" clause, which forbids the State to discourage religious belief and practice. The difficulty arises when the State tries to abide by one of the clauses and is accused of violating the other. For example, when the U. S. Supreme Court declares School Prayer unconstitutional, because it violates the "establishment" clause (through the use of public facilities for religious practices) it is accused of limiting citizens' "free exercise" of religion (through conducting prayers when and where they please). And when the State allows certain religious groups (such as the Amish or the Jehovah's Witnesses) special dispensations with regard to civil law (such as exempting their children from mandatory public schooling or saluting the flag), it is accused of violating the "establishment" clause (by "supporting" certain religious groups over others). Consequently, the history of Constitutional Law relating to Church-State issues is complex, and often, seemingly contradictory. This complexity, however, does not derive from the U. S. Supreme Court's varying interpretation of the First Amendment as much as the inherent complexity in the concept of religious freedom itself, as reflected in the two clauses dealing with religion.

5. United States Supreme Court Rulings
INTRODUCTION

The following selections include some of the major Supreme Court decisions relating to Church and State in America. Reynolds v. United States (1878) is the first example of the State limiting freedom of religious practice which violates civil law (in this case the Mormon practice of polygamy) and its distinction between religious "belief" and religious "practice" and the State's supremacy in matters of the latter is strikingly Lutheran in tone. However, in West Virginia Board of Education v. Barnette (1943) the Supreme Court upheld the right of Jehovah's Witnesses to refuse to salute the flag in school because of religious beliefs.

Many of the leading cases concerning freedom of religion have centered around the public schools, since public education is the principal context in which the State affects citizens in America. Both the "establishment" clause and the "free exercise" clause are found in these cases relating to religion in the public schools. In Pierce v. Society of Sisters (1925) the Supreme Court struck down an Oregon law requiring all children to attend the state's public school (thereby violating the "free exercise" clause by prohibiting private, parochial schools). And in Cochran v. Louisiana State Board of Education (1930) and Everson v. Board of Education (1947) the Court allowed the State to "support" religion through the lending of public textbooks to private religious schools and the reimbursement of travel expenses to parochial schools.

The issue of religious*education* in the public schools remains ambiguous in American Constitutional Law. In Illinois ex rel. McCollum v. Board of Education (1948), the Supreme Court held that religious instruction during the school day inside the public school building, even when voluntary and ecumenical, was unconstitutional, as violative of the "establishment" clause. This case involved a program in the Champaign, Illinois, school system supported by Jewish, Catholic and certain Protestant denominations which provided free religious instruction for 30 minutes each week to children whose parents gave them permission to attend. But in Zorach v. Clauson (1952) the Court allowed a "release-time" program which permitted school children to leave the school building to attend religious classes and devotion during school hours. The Supreme Court's distinction, therefore, seems to be in whether or not the public school building is used for religious instruction, declaring those programs conducted within the public school buildings to be unconstitutional as violative of the "establishment" clause. The recent Equal Access Bill passed by Congress allowing students to hold religious meetings inside the public schools before and after regular school hours may affect this issue of religious education in the future. Another major issue relating to religious freedom in the public schools has been "School Prayer." The U. S. Supreme Court has consistently declared prayers in public schools to be unconstitutional, as violative of both the "establishment" and the "free exercise" clauses of the U. S. Constitution. In <u>Engel</u> <u>v.</u> <u>Vitale</u> (1962) the Court declared unconstitutional the New York State's Regents' prayer, and in <u>Abingdon</u> <u>School</u> <u>District</u> <u>v.</u> <u>Schempp</u> (1963) the Court declared Bible reading and recitation of the Lord's Prayer in public schools unconstitutional.

WEST VIRGINIA STATE BOARD OF EDUCATION v. BARNETTE
319 U.S. 624; 62 Sup. Ct. 1178; 87 L. Ed. 1628 (1943)

Mr. Justice Jackson delivered the opinion of the Court:

...The freedom asserted by these appellees does not bring them into collision with rights asserted by any other individual. It is such conflicts which most frequently require intervention of the State to determine where the rights of one end and those of another begin. But the refusal of these persons to participate in the ceremony does not interfere with or deny rights of others to do so. Nor is there any question in this case that their behavior is peaceable and orderly. The sole conflict is between authority and rights of the individual. The State asserts power to condition access to public education on making a prescribed sign and profession and at the same time to coerce attendance by punishing both parent and child. The latter stand on a right of self-determination in matters that touch individual opinion and personal attitude.

* * *

If official power exists to coerce acceptance of any patriotic creed, what it shall contain cannot be decided by courts, but must be largely discretionary with the ordaining authority, whose power to prescribe would no doubt include power to amend. Hence validity of the asserted power to force an American citizen publicly to profess any statement of belief or to engage in any ceremony of assent to one, presents questions of power that must be considered independently of any idea we may have as to the utility of the ceremony in question.

Nor does the issue as we see it turn on one's possession of particular religious views or the sincerity with which they are held. While religion supplies appellees' motive for enduring the discomforts of making the issue in this case, many citizens who do not share these religious views hold such a compulsory rite to infringe constitutional liberty of the individual. It is not necessary to inquire whether nonconformist beliefs will exempt from the duty to salute unless we first find power to make the salute a legal duty....

EVERSON vs. BOARD OF EDUCATION
330 U.S. 1; 67 Sup. Ct. 504; 91 L. Ed. 711 (1947)

Mr. Justice Black delivered the opinion of the Court:

...The New Jersey statute is challenged as a "law respecting an establishment of religion." The First Amendment, as made applicable to the states by the Fourteenth...commands that a state "shall make no law respecting an establishment of religion, or prohibiting the free exercise thereof."...These words of the First

Amendment reflected in the minds of early Americans a vivid mental picture of conditions and practices which they fervently wished to stamp out in order to preserve liberty for themselves and for their posterity. . . .

The "establishment of religion" clause of the First Amendment means at least this: Neither a state nor the Federal Government can set up a church. Neither can pass laws which aid one religion, aid all religions, or prefer one religion over another. Neither can force nor influence a person to go to or to remain away from church against his will or force him to profess a belief or disbelief in any religion. No person can be punished for entertaining or professing religious beliefs or disbeliefs, for church attendance or non-attendance. No tax in any amount, large or small, can be levied to support any religious activities or institutions, whatever they may be called, or whatever form they may adopt to teach or practice religion. Neither a state nor the Federal Government can, openly or secretly, participate in the affairs of any religious organizations or groups and *vice versa*. In the words of Jefferson, the clause against establishment of religion by law was intended to erect "a wall of separation between church and State. . . ."

Measured by these standards, we cannot say that the First Amendment prohibits New Jersey from spending tax-raised funds to pay the bus fares of parochial-school pupils as a part of a general program under which it pays the fares of pupils attending public and other schools. It is undoubtedly true that children are helped to get to church schools. . . .

Its legislation, as applied, does not more than provide a general program to help parents get their children, regardless of their religion, safely and expeditiously to and from accredited schools.

The First Amendment has erected a wall between church and state. That wall must be kept high and impregnable. We could not approve the slightest breach. New Jersey has not breached it here.

ILLINOIS ex. rel. McCOLLUM v. BOARD OF EDUCATION
333 U.S. 203; Sup. Ct. 461; 91 L. Ed. 648 (1948)

Mr. Justice Black delivered the opinion of the Court:

This case relates to the power of a state to utilize its tax-supported public school system in aid of religious instruction in so far as that power may be restricted by the First and Fourteenth Amendments to the Federal Constitution. . . .

Appellant's petition for mandamus alleged that religious teachers, employed by private religious groups, were permitted to come weekly into the school buildings during the regular hours set apart for secular teaching, and then and there for a period of thirty minutes substitute their religious teaching for the secular education provided under the compulsory education law. . . .

Here not only are the State's tax-supported public school buildings used for the dissemination of religious doctrines. The State also affords secretarian groups an invaluable aid in that it helps to provide pupils for their religious classes through the use of the State's compulsory public school machinery. This is not separation of Church and State. . . .

ZORACH v. CLAUSON
343 U.S. 306; 72 Sup. Ct. 679; 96 L. Ed. 954 (1952)

Mr. Justice Douglas delivered the opinion of the Court:

New York City has a program which permits its public schools to release students during the school day so that they may leave the school buildings and school grounds and go to religious centers for religious instruction or devotional exercises. A student is released on written request of his parents. Those not released stay in the classrooms. The churches make weekly reports to the schools, sending a list of children who have been released from public school but who have not reported for religious instruction.

This "released-time" program involves neither religious instruction in public-school classrooms nor the expenditure of public funds. All costs, including the application blanks, are paid by the religious organizations. The case is therefore unlike *McCollum v. Board of Education*. . . .In that case the classrooms were turned over to religious instructors. We accordingly held that the program violated the First Amendment which (by reason of the Fourteenth Amendment) prohibits the states from establishing religion or prohibiting its free exercise. . . .

We would have to press the concept of separation of Church and State to these extremes to condemn the present law on constitutional grounds. . . .

ENGEL v. VITALE
370 U.S. 421; 82 Sup. Ct. 1261; 8 L. Ed. 2d 601 (1962)

Mr. Justice Black delivered the opinion of the Court:

. . .We think that by using its public school system to encourage recitation of the Regents' prayer, the State of New York has adopted a practice wholly inconsistent with the Establishment Clause. There can, of course, be no doubt that New York's program of daily classroom invocation of God's blessings as prescribed in the Regents' prayer is a religious activity. It is solemn avowal of divine faith and supplication for the blessings of the Almighty. The nature of such a prayer has always been religious, none of the respondents has denied this. . . .

It is a matter of history that this very practice of establishing governmentally composed prayers for religious services was one of the reasons which caused many of our early colonists to leave England and seek religious freedom in America. The Book of Common Prayer, which was created under governmental direction and which was approved by Acts of Parliament in 1548 and 1549, set out in minute detail the accepted form and content of prayer and other religious ceremonies to be used in the established, tax-supported Church of England. . . .

ABINGTON SCHOOL DISTRICT v. SCHEMPP
MURRAY vs. CURLETT
347 U.S. 203; 83 Sup. Ct. 1560; 10 L. Ed. 2d 844 (1963)

Mr. Justice Clark delivered the opinion of the Court:

Once again we are called upon to consider the scope of the provision of the First Amendment to the United States Constitution which declares that "Congress shall make no law respecting an establishment of religion or prohibiting the free exercise thereof. . . ." These companion cases present the issues in the context of state action requiring that schools begin each day with readings from the Bible. While raising the basic questions under slightly different factual situations, the cases permit of joint treatment. In light of the history of the First Amendment and of our cases interpreting and applying its requirements, we hold that the practices at issue and the laws requiring them are unconstitutional under the Establishment Clause, as applied to the states through the Fourteenth Amendment. . . .

It is insisted that unless these religious exercises are permitted a "religion of secularism" is established in the schools. We agree of course that the State may not establish a "religion of secularism" in the sense of affirmatively opposing or showing hostility to religion, thus "preferring those who believe in no religion over those who do believe." . . .We do not agree, however, that this decision in any sense has that effect. In addition, it might well be said that one's education is not complete without a study of comparative religion or the history of religion and its relationship to the advancement of civilization. It certainly may be said that the Bible is worthy is study for its literary and historic qualities. Nothing we have said here indicates that such study of the Bible or of religion, when presented objectively as part of a secular program of education, may not be effected consistent with the First Amendment. But the exercises here do not fall into those categories. They are religious exercises, required by the States in violation of the command of the First

Amendment that the Government maintain strict neutrality, neither aiding nor opposing religion.

DATE DUE

	2000		
OCT 2	1 2002		
Feb. 4,	2003		

HIGHSMITH 45-220